JAPAN'S MANAGED GLOBALIZATION

JAPAN'S MANAGED GLOBALIZATION

Adapting to the
Twenty-first Century

Ulrike Schaede
William Grimes
Editors

AN EAST GATE BOOK

M.E. Sharpe
Armonk, New York
London, England

An East Gate Book

Serialized in *The Japanese Economy*, Volume 28, Nos. 4, 5, and 6

Library of Congress Cataloging-in-Publication Data

Japan's managed globalization : adapting to the twenty-first century / edited by Ulrike
Schaede and William Grimes
    p. cm.
Includes bibliographical references and index.
ISBN 0-7656-0951-7 (hc. : alk. paper) ISBN 0-7656-0952-5 (pbk. : alk. paper)
  1. Japan—Economic conditions—1989– 2. Japan—Economic policy—1989–
3. Globalization—Economic aspects—Japan I. Schaede, Ulrike, 1962– II. Grimes,
William W.

HC462.95.J363 2002
337.52—dc21

                                         2002021713

Printed in the United States of America

The paper used in this publication meets the minimum requirements of
American National Standard for Information Sciences
Permanence of Paper for Printed Library Materials,
ANSI Z 39.48-1984.

BM (c) 10   9   8   7   6   5   4   3   2   1
BM (p) 10   9   8   7   6   5   4   3   2   1

Contents

Part I: Introduction

**Part II: International Political Economy and
Permeable Insulation**

Part III: Domestic Political Economy and Permeable Insulation

Part IV: Conclusion

List of Tables and Figures

Tables

Figures

List of Abbreviations

AFL-CIO	American Federation of Labor - Congress of Industrial Organizations
AMF	Asian Monetary Fund
APEC	Asia Pacific Economic Cooperation
ASEAN	Association of Southeast Asian Nations
ASEAN+3	ASEAN plus Japan, China, and South Korea
BOJ	Bank of Japan
BRIE	Berkeley Roundtable on the International Economy
DSB	Dispute Settlement Body
DSU	Dispute Settlement Understanding
EPA	Economic Planning Agency
EU	European Union
FB	Financing Bill
FDI	foreign direct investment
FILP	Fiscal Investment and Loan Program
G-7	Group of Seven
GATS	General Agreement on Trade in Services
GATT	General Agreement on Tariffs and Trade
GDP	Gross Domestic Product
IC	integrated circuit
IL	interchangeable lenses
IMF	International Monetary Fund
IT	information technology
JBIC	Japan Bank for International Cooperation
JDB	Japan Development Bank
JEXIM	Japan Export-Import Bank
JFS	Japan Finance Corporation for Small Businesses
JFTC	Japan Fair Trade Commission
JGB	Japanese Government Bond
JODC	Japan Overseas Development Corporation
JTA	Japan Tariff Association

LDP	Liberal Democratic Party
LSI	large-scale integration
METI	Ministry of Economy, Trade, and Industry
MITI	Ministry of International Trade and Industry
MNC	multinational corporation
MOF	Ministry of Finance
MOFA	Ministry of Foreign Affairs
MOJ	Ministry of Justice
MPT	Ministry of Posts and Telecommunications
NIEs	newly industrializing economies
NTT	Nippon Telegraph and Telephone
ODA	official development assistance
OECF	Overseas Economic Cooperation Fund
OEM	original equipment manufacturer
PX	post exchange
R&D	research and development
SLR	single-lens reflex
SME	small- and medium-size enterprises
TB	Treasury Bill
TRIMs	Agreement on Trade-Related Investment Measures
TRIPs	Agreement on Trade-Related Aspects of Intellectual-Property Rights
USTR	United States Trade Representative
VLSI	very large-scale integration
WTO	World Trade Organization

Preface

Globalization and multilateralization of the world political economy have created new pressures for all industrialized democracies to adapt, change, and reform their policies and economic structures. However, none seems more challenged by these pressures than Japan, a country that has resisted global rules for its domestic markets for many years. The country's postwar focus on strategic industrial policy, infant industry protection, and export promotion has created many obstacles to becoming a truly integral player in a globalized economy. So, is Japan changing, and how? To what extent will the combined pressures of decade-long recession, "hollowing-out" of production, deregulation, and strengthened international trade rules turn Japan into a different marketplace?

This book argues that rather than assuming a passive, compliant stance, Japan is trying to manage the effects of globalization with policies that are proactive and occasionally aggressive, and that result in "permeable insulation." "Insulation" is the outcome of a set of policies that have at their core an attempt at continued protection of domestic interests—for example, by allowing restrictive practices in the distribution system that fall outside the scope of international agreements. However, in contrast to previous instances of industrial policy, this new insulation is "permeable" in that it allows those sectors in need of more freedom in corporate strategy to break free from the fetters of domestic protection.

Permeable insulation is Japan's attempt to manage the forces of globalization by affecting both the speed and the reach with which global rules and markets affect domestic players. It is Japan's attempt to structure a process that is potentially upsetting and disruptive. It is the outcome of a mix of active and passive measures by both government and firms taken in response to world challenges in the twenty-first century.

This book began serendipitously as a panel at the New England Political Science Association annual meeting in May 2000 organized by Mireya Solís, and also including William Grimes, Patricia Nelson, Saadia Pekkanen, and Ulrike Schaede. While the topics included some of the hoariest and most picked-over debates in the field of Japanese political economy—trade, aid, exchange rates, and cartel behavior—we were excited to find that each of us had taken a new, interesting tack at these themes. The papers emphasized innovative attempts by Japanese policy makers and firms to pursue their interests in a deeply changed policy environment.

Over several head-clearing lattes in Harvard Square, the co-editors went on to identify a unified framework for understanding Japan's complex, managed response to globalization, which we termed "permeable insulation." The project that followed has been a truly multinational, multidisciplinary one, straddling the insights of political science, business, law, and economics. Still, this book is emphatically not eclectic, as it centers very tightly around the unified focus of permeable insulation. As in any collaborative work, the editors had to make some choices, particularly in terms of chapter selection. Permeable insulation is a widespread phenomenon in twenty-first century Japan, and we could easily think of many more areas in which permeable insulation and structural adjustment are transforming established policies and relationships. In the end, we decided to pick topic areas where the terms of the debate seemed to have been most static over the years, to see whether and how important changes were bubbling up.

In putting it all together, we have incurred many debts of gratitude. The project received a major boost from the generous financial assistance by the Japan Foundation Center for Global Partnership for a March, 2001, conference entitled "Japan Changes: The New Political Economy of Structural Adjustment and Globalization" at IR/PS (Graduate School of International Relations and Pacific Studies) at the University of California, San Diego. The conference included revised versions of the earlier papers, as well as new contributions by Christina Ahmadjian and Mark Elder. The authors were fortunate to benefit from the insights and suggestions of an outstanding cast of discussants: Richard Feinberg, Stephan Haggard, Takeo Hoshi, Lawrence Krause, Ellis Krauss, Koichi Kurokawa, David McKendrick, Barry Naughton, James Shinn, and Yoshiro Tsutsui. Ellis Krauss also kindly served as a first, and tremendously helpful, critic of our introductory chapter. Joseph A. Grimes provided useful comments on Chapters 1, 2, 3, and 10. We are also grateful to Patricia Loo at M.E. Sharpe for her support and enthusiasm for this book, and for her efficiency at moving it through the publication process.

The editors and authors collectively thank the many Japanese policy makers and company officials who have been so generous in providing information and opinions regarding the issues addressed in this book. Most prefer anonymity, but some individuals are cited in the chapters that follow. The standard academic disclaimer applies, as the authors alone are responsible for any remaining errors.

Finally, the co-editors especially thank the contributors to this book for their cooperation and diligence. We had been forewarned by many colleagues about the headaches of editing—what a relief to find that this project was different! Particularly, in addition to being reliable authors, Saadia Pekkanen and Chris Ahmadjian provided valuable comments on Chapters 1, 2, and 10. As we spent many weekends and evenings stooped over our computers writing, revising, and editing several times over, we often neglected home affairs in favor of incoming e-mails. We thank Charles and Melinda for their positive encouragement and good-humored patience.

U.S. and W.W.G.
La Jolla and Boston
October 2001

Throughout the book, personal names appear in Western order, with the given name followed by the surname. Macrons (ō, ū) indicate long vowels in Japanese terms, except for Americanized phrases and well-known cities (Tokyo).

Part I

Introduction

1

Introduction

The Emergence of Permeable Insulation

Ulrike Schaede and William W. Grimes

Circumstances have changed dramatically between the early 1990s, when the world hailed Japan as one of its economic superpowers, and the early twenty-first century, as the country entered its second decade of economic stagnation. Domestically, Japan's industries have experienced major structural change, the relocation of production abroad, deregulation, and experimental macroeconomic policy such as zero-level interest rates. Internationally, the rise of the yen after 1985 and the increasing competitiveness of industrializing economies in Asia have reduced opportunities for firms producing inside Japan. At the same time, trade liberalization and financial market integration have increased pressure for governments throughout the developed world to comply with international rules in such diverse areas as competition policy, financial regulation, subsidization of private investment, and the adoption of multilateral trade dispute settlement. External and internal pressures have thus combined to force Japan to change in potentially fundamental ways. Interestingly, however, many Japan observers disagree about just how much, and into what, Japan is changing.

How Japan is changing is so difficult to evaluate because Japan's reactions to these pressures for change have unfolded in ways few would have predicted. At one level, Japan has reacted to the internal and external challenges by removing regulations, restructuring industries, revising associated policies, and playing a more prominent role

3

in multilateral organizations. But despite change in some unexpected areas, many pockets of old practices remain in the very areas where true change seems to be most called for. Many seasoned observers of Japan are therefore at a loss as to how existing models and past experience provide a roadmap to predict change in Japan. Overstating the case only slightly, one can say that by the late 1990s Japan analysts were largely divided into two schools of "change forecast." One group has argued that Japan is not actually changing at the core, but is basically continuing its attempts at industrial and other policies that preserve the Japanese system (e.g., Yamamura 1997, Dore 2000, Carlisle and Tilton 1998). Analysts from the opposite camp have argued that for Japan to regain its competitive strength, it will finally have to open up and completely reform; some even claim that this complete overhaul has already begun, and is turning Japan into a fundamentally new entity (e.g., Nakatani 1999, Katz 1998, Edwards 1999).

In contrast to these two scenarios, we submit that Japan is in fact changing significantly, but in unforeseen ways and often with surprising consequences, leading to possible misinterpretation by those who adhere to one of the two polar views. Some of Japan's new policy choices are unprecedented, whereas others look much like previous measures and reactions. If we want to understand the new Japan fully, we need to evaluate both new and familiar policies in light of a fundamentally altered domestic and global situation. And even in instances where the actual policy measures look familiar, their intended and unintended consequences may well be different, given the changing global environment.

We argue that Japan's responses to the economic and global political challenges of the twenty-first century are best understood as "permeable insulation"—a dual-track approach that allows for sectoral policy differentiation, and therefore calls for a case-by-case evaluation of policy intent and policy outcome. Permeable insulation is Japan's attempt to manage the process of globalization by differentiating its speed and reach by political issue-area and economic sector.

Changing Japan

The main reason why Japan observers continue to be divided in their interpretations is that at the turn of the century, the past is a less than perfect predictor of Japan's future strategies. This difference derives from the fact that throughout the postwar period of rapid growth, Japan fundamentally reacted to shocks, whether external or internal, from a position of strength. Even though Japan's policy makers may not have seen it that way at the time, during the 1960s and even following the oil shock recession in the 1970s, Japan's economy operated under signs of enormous upward potential. In terms of international competition, Japan could continue to purchase advanced technologies abroad, as "catch-up" was not yet fully accomplished and the international environment allowed ongoing infant industry protection and export promotion. Industrial policy was especially effective in the face of global excess capacity in basic materials such as steel in the late 1970s and early 1980s, allowing Japanese firms to survive worldwide slumps and capitalize on the ensuing disarray in global markets caused by recessions in other countries. Specific structures of economic organization, such as *keiretsu* corporate alliances and enterprise-based unions, provided insulation without rigidity and contributed to Japanese firms' ability to avoid the kind of paralysis seen in many Western countries beginning in the 1970s.[1]

Domestically, too, the Japanese state worked from a position of strength. Even well into the 1980s, the state had many tools at its disposal to reconfigure economic structure in a relatively orderly way—both through direct means, such as the ability to arrange recession cartels and create incentives to increase energy efficiency following the 1973 oil crisis, and more indirectly, such as through tax policies that encouraged research and development. Moreover, solid government finances in the early 1970s allowed the Japanese state considerable latitude to encourage adjustment in some industries, and to maintain protection in others through the heavy use of deficit-financed compensation during global stagflation later that decade.[2]

However, by the early twenty-first century, Japan's position had changed dramatically, due to a domestic push for change in some important sectors of the economy, the concurrent external pressure for economic globalization, and the multilateralization of world politics. The changing domestic and global environment in the 1990s and the early twenty-first century mean that Japan can no longer operate from a position of comparative strength; the country now has to face adversity from a position of comparative weakness. With technological catch-up accomplished in the manufacturing sectors, Japan is struggling to adopt new models of industrial policy and business organization in an attempt to induce more rigorous efforts at innovation. Trade disputes with the United States and the European Union put limits on overt government policies aimed at blocking imports and promoting exports. Multilateral organizations such as the World Trade Organization (WTO) further limit Japan's latitude to protect specific industries at the expense of free trade flows. The slow but continuous process of deregulating and revising foreign trade laws and specific industry laws since the 1980s has progressively undermined the state's powers of administrative guidance.[3] While the state's guidance of business strategies has never been one-directional or absolute, it is now more than ever dependent on industry cooperation. Finally, the combination of electoral politics and the ongoing economic crisis of the 1990s and early twenty-first century has caused Japanese fiscal policy to focus almost completely on helping the economically weakest (often also the politically strongest) sectors through distributive, rather than strategic, economic policies (Grimes 2001). The transformation of large parts of industrial policy into compensation has also reduced potential for economic growth—and thus growth in both government revenues and corporate profits. In combination, these factors have fundamentally altered policy intent and policy measures in Japan.

Given this underlying shift in relative power, the Japanese state has had to modify its policy approach to allow new openness in some instances while providing continued protection in others. To be sure, other countries faced similar challenges as they approached the turn of the century. However, among industrialized nations, Japan is arguably the one that has pushed the political agenda of industrial policies hardest—regardless of whether or not these were successful. The reliance on industrial policy throughout the postwar period has created or strengthened institutions and processes that, in combination, have resulted in a distinctive political economic path that continues to guide and constrain Japan's future choices. The very existence of interventionist tools and precedents makes it difficult for policy makers to leave matters to the market, even where they prefer to do so. As a result of this legacy of industrial promotion and protection policies, Japan faces particular challenges in dealing with the changing domestic and global situation at the beginning of the twenty-first century.

Permeable Insulation

The shift in relative strength of the Japanese state, combined with this legacy in political processes and institutions, makes it difficult to apply past experience and assumptions in evaluating current Japanese policies. Even where policy measures look quite familiar, their causes and consequences are often unexpectedly different. We propose that the analysis of Japan's new policy measures, and their intended and unintended outcomes, is greatly advanced by the new perspective of "permeable insulation." While permeable insulation includes parts of the 1980s trade concept of the "new protectionism," which was mainly implemented through nontariff barriers, it extends well beyond trade policies. As an analytical category, permeable insulation calls for more precision in that it introduces differentiation, both by sector and issue area, into the study of Japanese policies.

"Insulation" occurs in the sense that, in many areas, government and corporate policies continue to have at their core an attempt to shield companies from full competition and the rigor of market forces. Insulation is seen in the continued efforts by the Japanese government to design policies that support domestic firms in international competition and also shield domestic sectors from that same competition. It can also be seen in industry-led efforts to ensure survival by informally regulating domestic competition. These efforts fit comfortably into the traditions of managed competition that have characterized Japanese industrial policy for so long.

Importantly, this insulation is "permeable" in that it is not absolute, but rather allows for differentiated application by industry, institutions, or issue areas. Permeability has two main consequences. First, not all parts of government pull in the same direction, leading to trade-offs and loopholes for industries to get around rules they reject. The "embedded mercantilism," which Pempel argues has constituted a dominant policy paradigm in Japan's political economy, is being replaced with a less comprehensive policy approach, even if the underlying principle of protection or promotion may remain unchanged. Thus, Japanese foreign economic policy is becoming ever more "unbundled," or much less coherent (Pempel 1987, 1998). Second, industrial policies have become less inclusive or binding. For instance, under the former industrial policy regime, if one industry (perhaps steel) asked for continued protection while another (perhaps automobiles) preferred to operate independently, the pro-active industry would have been held back by protectionist policies. In contrast, in the new environment, the policy outcomes or protectionist walls are more permeable for industries not interested in this protection. In fact, policies of insulation are themselves permeable to the new dynamics of international markets. An example of this paradox can be seen in the campaign for internationalization of the yen—a policy that, as Grimes (Chapter 3) shows, was aimed at insulating Japan's markets from external volatility, but where success would ironically depend on acceptance by international markets.

Thus, the new insulation is permeable because reductions in state power vis-à-vis the private sector since the 1990s have combined with stricter world trade rules and diminished solidarity among private institutions such as *keiretsu*. "Insulation" in post-developmental Japan is increasingly flexible, as it is used either to stave off change or to make its pace more manageable, depending upon the sector. In the twenty-first century, more than ever before, Japanese firms are making strategic decisions about how to embrace the global economy in the context of more diversified and less predictable government policies.

"Permeable insulation" means that Japan's response to the global and domestic challenges of the 1990s is neither one of retreat and denial, nor one of full acceptance of global standards and practices. Instead, the basic thrust is one of pragmatic utilization of new rules and circumstances to continue industry policies of promotion or protection in a new, post-developmental, paradigm. Moreover, the approach sees Japan, for the first time in memory, as an active player in actually shaping the international environment through political and legal means, rather than simply reacting to real or perceived shocks. This new approach of shifting its insulation strategies to global or regional frameworks is one of the most important facets of Japan's response to the global economic and political pressures of the twenty-first century.

Politics and Permeable Insulation

The new permeable insulation does not rely on a unitary state.[4] Rather, even more than before, it is based on clientelistic subgovernments, or what Calder (1988) has called "circles of compensation" among firms in a given sector, and the bureaucrats and politicians who support them. What is more, the new vulnerability of ruling coalitions and of individual Diet members, caused by the long-dominant Liberal Democratic Party's (LDPs) initial breakup in 1993, has created more interest in the substance of policies among politicians (see Chapter 2).[5] Moreover, politicians' endeavors to play a more prominent role were helped by the obvious policy failures of the post-bubble 1990s, which politicians were quick to attribute exclusively to the bureaucrats. The increased diversity of a larger number of political players represented by more activist politicians also resulted in more diverse results. While the increasing role of politicians, as agents of constituent interests or ideological preferences, served as a catalyst to change in some areas (such as corporate governance reform or the campaign to promote the yen as an international currency), it may also have hindered such change in others (such as policies related to the distribution system). Moreover, the shift in power from bureaucrats to politicians has also increased the tendency to support certain sectors for reasons of pork-barrel politics, rather than industrial growth strategy. Economically troubled sectors that can mobilize votes and political funds now find it easier to receive support, often at the expense of politically weaker, though potentially more viable, sectors.

Despite the increasing role assumed by politicians, bureaucrats still fight to maintain or expand their jurisdiction. In any country, the inherent rigidity of laws and governmental processes means that the bureaucrats' incentives and regulations change only incrementally, even though reforms may accumulate into significant transformation over time. Path-dependence limits policy choices, as future actions are dependent on decisions and commitments made in the past. Thus, even in the face of changing needs, conscious efforts to transform behavior—of politicians, bureaucrats, companies, and consumers—tend to coexist with surprising continuity in existing practices. System inertia and deliberate efforts to uphold established routines translate into resistance to change even in the face of apparently unavoidable pressures for structural adjustment. Japan is no exception to this general rule—and in the early twenty-first century, the outcome has been permeable insulation.

Evidence and Examples

Pressure for permeable insulation can be observed both externally and domestically. Externally, trade and financial deregulation have disabled most official levers of control previously employed by industry-promoting agencies such as the former Ministry of International Trade and Industry (MITI; now the Ministry of Economy, Trade, and Industry [METI]). Moreover, a fundamentally bilateral approach to solving trade disputes with the United States has largely been replaced with multilateral agreements administered by the World Trade Organization. Financial controls on cross-border transactions, too, have been visibly reformed. And so it seems that compliance with the rules of global trade has been achieved. Yet, whereas officially Japan has indeed proceeded with deregulation, lifted market entry rules, and ended overt subsidies and other preferential policies that may distort free trade, many of these measures have been accompanied by a variety of complementary, compensatory, or substitute policies that must not be overlooked. These additional policies mean that while there may be compliance on paper, we find *de facto* resistance and continuing policy insulation in many areas.

The chapters in this book show how Japan's permeable insulation paradigm functions in practice across a variety of key policy issue-areas. The very range and scope of different industries and policy issues underscore that permeable insulation is indeed a generic practice, and thus an important phenomenon that constitutes a specific, identifiable approach to regulating economic activity. The book first addresses Japan's use of permeable insulation in international affairs, and then focuses in on domestic issues.

At the international level, Japan must address most directly the challenge of managing globalization. Here we see both the state and firms trying to shift the global competitive playing field through policies of permeable insulation. In trade and currency issues, the Japanese government has consciously sought to exploit global rules in order to insulate its domestic economy from globalization-induced volatility. Meanwhile, the actions of both firms and the state in moving increasing amounts of manufacturing abroad show a clear attempt to shape the Japanese economy's structural transformation so as to minimize the costs of adjustment in Japan.

William W. Grimes (Chapter 3) describes attempts to make the yen a key currency in Asia as a step toward increasing the economic integration of East and Southeast Asia and, more importantly, as a means of insulating the Japanese economy from financial and currency shocks. Paradoxically, to achieve this insulation by making the yen more attractive as an international currency, Japan has to open its financial markets. Yet, financial market liberalization coexists uneasily with more interventionist measures meant to manipulate directly the international supply and demand for yen. To promote insulation through permeability in the most globalized of sectors has been a bold move, which highlights the difficulties of managing globalization.

Saadia M. Pekkanen (Chapter 4) observes a skillful application of WTO rules to further Japan's foreign policy purposes, as well as its sectoral domestic interests. Aggressive legalism has served Japan's interests in opening markets abroad; at the same time, Japan has been very successful at finding industrial policy measures that go beyond, and thus remain outside, the range of international agreements and conflict resolution mechanisms. This has allowed the continuation of protectionist policies without directly violating international rules—indeed, Japan has claimed that it has been stricter than some of its trading partners in adhering to official international rules, even as many of its product markets remained effectively insulated.

Focusing in on the government role in the relocation of production outside Japan, Mireya Solís (Chapter 5) presents evidence of subsidies for outbound foreign direct investment (FDI) during the postwar era that dwarf the efforts of any other country. These subsidies have been directed to manufacturing industries, including in industries that were likely to compete with production inside Japan. This is surprising, given that Japan has long been among the world's pre-eminent practitioners of export promotion and import protection. Solís shows that FDI subsidies were used with the dual purposes of promoting the competitiveness of Japanese firms by insulating them from the effects of a consistently high yen after the mid-1980s, and also relocating small firms in declining sectors outside Japan to alleviate pressures on Japan's industrial structure.

Patricia Nelson (Chapter 6) looks at the efforts of Japanese firms to maintain competitiveness by relocating production outside the country. Some have argued that relocation of production threatens the Japanese economy with becoming "hollowed out"—that the government's inability or unwillingness to stop the relocation of production to Southeast Asia by Japan's flagship industries might undermine the country's export base. Nelson analyzes patterns in the opto-electronic industry to show how Japanese firms have responded to the pressures of globalization and cost competition in a sector that has been internationally dominated by Japanese firms for decades.

These four case studies of permeable insulation in the external arena give evidence of unprecedented, though quiet, attempts by Japan to shape the international environment to its own changed needs, rather than simply responding to existing global reality. Ironically, these efforts to change its external environment paralleled the weakening of

Japan's economy and an increase in competition from other Asian countries. Despite the pro-active nature of the policies, the goals were often defensive. For example, Japan's more pro-active WTO policies reflected at least partly its continued vulnerability to bilateral U.S. pressures; by multilateralizing trade disputes, policy makers hoped to draw on the strength of international commitments and pressure from the United States and Europe. The main rationale for yen international-ization was, similarly, insulation. Meanwhile, Japan's FDI assistance programs were aimed at improving structural adjustment within Japan, while supporting Japanese firms in their struggle to attain or maintain competitive advantage.

Permeable insulation is equally visible in domestic economic poli-cies and industry organization, where distinctive patterns of ministerial guidance of industry, competition (antitrust) policy, and interfirm and labor-management relations persist. While politicians and industry have both gained more influence at the expense of the bureaucracy, and legislation has gained importance relative to administrative guid-ance, Japan's political economy is still by no means an open and trans-parent political marketplace. Organizational features such as corporate governance, *keiretsu* relations, and employment structures, while un-der revision, are evolving—but into a new system that resembles exist-ing global practices in some parts while maintaining traditional Japanese practices in others.

The second section of this book contains three in-depth case stud-ies that highlight these processes. Mark Elder (Chapter 7) shows how METI has shifted its policies of industry promotion in response to new realities. While traditional industry promotion policies are no longer attractive to successful firms, and have been widely derided as useless for new economy sectors, Elder argues that METI has indeed managed to develop an array of market-conforming policies that are sensitive to the challenges of economic globalization. While it is too early to judge their effectiveness, these policies clearly indicate METI's active participation in the shift toward permeable insulation.

Ulrike Schaede (Chapter 8) argues that, due to an increase in the rela-tive importance of private sector self-regulation, deregulation has not led to open markets across all industries. As deregulation has progressed and ministries have lost many of their former control mechanisms over in-dustry, trade associations have filled the regulatory void and increased their self-regulation—that is, autonomous, private sector formulation and enforcement of industry rules. In relying on self-regulation, industries have a choice between self-promotion (opening markets to competition) and self-protection (closing markets through restrictive rules that substitute for previous government rules). The outcome is a classic case of permeable insulation: Industries that prefer continued protection face little government interference with their use of anticompetitive measures to insulate their markets, while more competitive industries can eliminate protective barriers if they wish.

The concept of industry self-regulation points to the possibility of privatized permeable insulation—in other words, leaving policy choices on industry structure to the private sector. This is particularly effective in areas where sectoral interests are so greatly divergent that a single, uniform national solution would be infeasible. Christina L. Ahmadjian (Chapter 9) argues that the corporate governance debate of the early twenty-first century is a case in point. Several years of discussion of how to reform corporate governance—that is, the processes by which chief executives of large, publicly traded firms are held accountable to and by their shareholders—led to only limited legal revisions to enhance transparency and uniformity. Instead, the outcomes have largely been agreements to disagree, leaving each company to structure its governance system as it sees fit for its own strategic purposes. Despite familiar-sounding terminology, in most Japanese companies proposals for change more closely reflect enduring Japanese systemic and legal characteristics than they resemble U.S. practices.

In both external and domestic policy issue-areas, we find that efforts at market opening are often less complete than they appear at first, or are accompanied by additional measures that shift the effects and outcomes of policies in directions that favor well-connected firms or sectors. What looks like a progressive policy, if viewed in isolation, often combines with other policies and practices to reinforce the policy objectives of permeable insulation.

As we note in the concluding chapter, permeable insulation may well be an effective way for Japan to cope with globalization and domestic reorganization. Globalization creates pressures for large-scale structural adjustment in the economy, but such adjustment is always painful, both economically and politically. Permeable insulation is

Japan's particular attempt both to adapt to globalization and still to maintain some of the bases of the domestic political and social order. Managed globalization may mean that Japan's integration into the global economy will be slowed—but that may well be the intended consequence of permeable insulation.

Notes

1. *Keiretsu* are corporate groups in which firms maintain preferential trade relationships buttressed by cross-shareholdings. *Keiretsu* member firms offer each other preferential treatment in commercial and financial transactions through a main bank and trading company, may exchange personnel and information, and in times of crisis are expected to help each other out (Gerlach 1992; Aoki 1988; Hoshi and Kashyap 2001). Japanese labor-management relations are also based on long-term, exclusive relationships. Labor unions are typically enterprise-based. Related to the practice of lifetime employment within major firms, there is a strong expectation that firms and unions will cooperate, because their long-term goals overlap: Ensuring the survival of the firm in crisis is more important than fighting a temporary wage cut (Kume 1998; Ito 1992). Dore (1986) has argued that such long-term relationships within the Japanese political economy were important in allowing for flexible responses to crises, even though they may have appeared to constrain firms' choices.

2. Many authors have argued the importance of industrial policy for Japan's postwar economic development, although debate continues on how successful these policies really were, and who designed them (Johnson 1982; Komiya, et al. 1988; Okimoto 1989; Schaede 2000; Woo-Cumings 1998). Industrial policy sought to promote heavy industry in the 1950s and 1960s, and later high-technology industries, through a variety of measures, including tax incentives, preferential access to finance research consortia, and access to foreign exchange and other resources. Recession cartels were temporary cartels authorized by the government to maintain prices in a given sector in the face of a short-term downturn in demand; these were important policy tools because industrial policies encouraged high levels of investment that made firms vulnerable to slowdowns in demand (Yamamura 1982). Energy policy was particularly interesting, given Japan's extremely high levels of reliance on foreign energy sources (Samuels 1986). As the Japanese economy matured, adjustment policies for declining industries became an increasingly important task relative to infant industry promotion (Lincoln 1988; Calder 1988).

3. Administrative guidance is one of the fundamental tools for the implementation of industrial policy (see, for example, Johnson 1982; Upham 1987). It consists of ministries making recommendations or offering judgments that are informal and do not carry the weight of law. Despite the lack of legal enforceability, such recommendations are effective because they entail implicit rewards for cooperation and the potential for administrative punishments for noncompliance (such as the refusal of business licenses in an unrelated field) (Shindō 1992; Haley 1991). The reduction of licensing requirements and of ministries' discretionary funds have reduced the effectiveness of administrative guidance (Schaede 2000).

4. Based on Johnson's (1982) initial analysis of Ministry of Trade International Industry (MITI) and his concept of a "developmental state," many subsequent observers have overdrawn the strong state picture and assumed a unitary government with politicians and bureaucrats all driven by one goal. Johnson did not claim this in his 1982 book, and it would have been a misrepresentation, as Japanese politicians have always been concerned about their particular constituencies, whose interests were often at odds with other interests or the bureaucrats' agenda. Yet, the uninterrupted rule by the Liberal Democratic Party (LDP) from 1955 to 1993, the continuity in bureaucratic promotion processes, and the overarching goal of economic growth across all economic sectors created the appearance of unity and continuity in policy goals between the 1950s and the early 1990s. By 2001, this situation had changed in that differences across affected interests were more clearly discernible, and arguments on policy options were more often held publicly.

5. The LDP, conservative in spite of its name, has dominated Japanese politics since it was formed in 1955. In 1993, an internal conflict led to the exit of a significant fraction of its members in the Diet (parliament), and a seven-party coalition ruled the country for about ten months before the LDP was able to return to power in a coalition with two smaller parties. In the years since then, the LDP has remained dominant, albeit within coalition governments. On LDP dominance and the events of 1993, see Satō and Matsuzaki (1986), Curtis (1988, 1999), Calder (1988), Kohno (1996), and Pempel (1998).

References

Aoki, Masahiko. 1988. *Information, Incentives, and Bargaining in the Japanese Economy*. Cambridge: Cambridge University Press.

Calder, Kent. 1988. *Crisis and Compensation: Public Policy and Political Stability in Japan, 1946–1986*. Princeton: Princeton University Press.

Carlile, Lonnie E., and Mark Tilton, eds. 1998. *Is Japan Really Changing Its Ways? Regulatory Reform and the Japanese Economy*. Washington: Brookings Institution.

Curtis, Gerald. 1988. *The Japanese Way of Politics*. New York: Columbia University Press.

———. 1999. *The Logic of Japanese Politics: Leaders, Institutions, and the Limits of Change*. New York: Columbia University Press.

Dore, Ronald. 1986. *Flexible Rigidities: Industrial Policy and Structural Adjustment in the Japanese Economy, 1970–1980*. London: Athlone Press.

———. 2000. *Stock Market Capitalism: Welfare Capitalism: Japan and Germany Versus the Anglo-Saxons*. Oxford: Oxford University Press.

Edwards, Ben. 1999. "No More Tears: After a Lost Decade, Japanese Business Is Beginning to Embrace Radical Change." *The Economist* (November 25).

Gerlach, Michael. 1992. *Alliance Capitalism*. Berkeley: University of California Press.

Ito, Takatoshi. 1992. *The Japanese Economy*. Cambridge: MIT Press.

Grimes, William W. 2001. *Unmaking the Japanese Miracle: Monetary Politics, 1985–2000*. Ithaca: Cornell University Press.

Haley, John. 1991. *Authority Without Power: Law and the Japanese Paradox*. New York: Oxford University Press.

Hoshi, Takeo, and Anil Kashyap. 2001. *Corporate Financing and Corporate Governance in Japan: The Road to the Future*. Cambridge: MIT Press.
Johnson, Chalmers. 1982. *MITI and the Japanese Miracle*. Stanford: Stanford University Press.
Katz, Richard. 1998. *Japan: The System That Soured*. Armonk, NY: M.E. Sharpe.
Kohno, Masaru. 1997. *Japan's Postwar Party Politics*. Princeton: Princeton University Press.
Komiya, Ryutaro, Masahiro Okuno, and Kotaro Suzumura, eds. 1988. *Industrial Policy of Japan*. San Diego: Academic Press.
Kume, Ikuo. 1998. *Disparaged Success: Labor Politics in Postwar Japan*. Ithaca: Cornell University Press.
Lincoln, Edward. 1988. *Japan: Facing Economic Maturity*. Washington: Brookings Institution.
Nakatani, Iwao. 1998. "Reforming the Catch-Up Economy." In Frank Gibney, ed., *Unlocking the Bureaucrats' Kingdom: Deregulation and the Japanese Economy*, 30–40. Washington: Brookings Institution.
Okimoto, Daniel. 1989. *Between MITI and the Market: Japanese Industrial Policy for High Technology*. Stanford: Stanford University Press.
Pempel, T.J. 1987. "The Unbundling of 'Japan, Inc.': The Changing Dynamics of Japanese Policy Formation." In Kenneth Pyle, ed., *The Trade Crisis: How Will Japan Respond?*, 117–52. Seattle: Society for Japanese Studies.
———. 1998. *Regime Shift: Comparative Dynamics of the Japanese Political Economy*. Ithaca: Cornell University Press.
Samuels, Richard. 1987. *The Business of the Japanese State: Energy Markets in Comparative and Historical Perspective*. Ithaca: Cornell University Press.
Satō, Seizaburō, and Tetsuhisa Matsuzaki. 1986. *Jimintō seiken* (LDP Rule). Tokyo: Chūo kōronsha.
Schaede, Ulrike. 2000. *Cooperative Capitalism: Self-Regulation, Trade Associations, and the Antimonopoly Law in Japan*. Oxford: Oxford University Press.
Shindō, Muneyuki. 1992. *Gyōsei shidō: Kanchō to gyōkai no aida* (Administrative Guidance: Between Agencies and Industries). Tokyo: Iwanami shinsho.
Upham, Frank K. 1987. *Law and Social Change in Postwar Japan*. Cambridge: Harvard University Press.
Woo-Cumings, Meredith, ed. 1999. *The Developmental State*. Ithaca: Cornell University Press.
Yamamura, Kozo. 1982. "Success That Soured: Administrative Guidance and Cartels in Japan." In Kozo Yamamura, ed., *Policy and Trade Issues of the Japanese Economy: American and Japanese Perspectives*, 77–112. Seattle: University of Washington Press.
———. 1997. "The Japanese Political Economy After the 'Bubble': Plus ça change?" *Journal of Japanese Studies* 23, no. 2: 291–331.

—— 2 ——

Japanese Policy Making in a World of Constraints

William W. Grimes and Ulrike Schaede

As Japan moved into the twenty-first century, it found its position and options within the world economy and domestically fundamentally changed. In contrast to most of the postwar era, which had been a period of growing opportunities, the 1990s and early twenty-first century were characterized by growing constraints. Legal, political, and economic changes both within and outside Japan had narrowed the possibilities for policy makers and corporations seeking to protect firms and sectors from the challenges of an ever more competitive marketplace.

While the early 1990s offer a convenient dividing line between rising opportunities and rising constraints, in fact most of the trends that became visible then had already come into play much earlier. For example, cost pressures began to affect the economic calculus for the most advanced Japanese firms as early as in the 1960s (see chapter 6). Problems of declining industries accelerated over the course of the 1970s, 1980s, and 1990s. The roots of Japan's worsening fiscal situation in the late 1990s dated back to the rapid growth of deficits in the 1970s. Deregulation in finance began in the early 1980s (although it lagged behind more aggressive efforts in the United States and United Kingdom), and the push for administrative reform and privatization can be traced back to the Second Provisional Council on Administrative Reform (Rinchō) in 1980. Flux in the world of electoral politics came to the surface in the break-up of the long-time dominant Liberal Democratic Party

(LDP) in 1993, but the forces that underlay the change had been building for at least a decade or two (Pempel 1998; Murakami 1982). Similarly, while the World Trade Organization (WTO) was established in 1995, the importance of legalism in international trade disputes had been on the rise since the mid-1980s (see Chapter 4).

As the Japanese state moved from a position of strength to one of weakness over the course of the 1990s, economic policy making became more and more challenging. This shift occurred at a time when economic globalization and the multilateralization of world politics made domestic policy increasingly interdependent with forces outside Japan. Economic stagnation in the 1990s greatly reduced the public acceptance of traditional, informal, and deal-based policy tools that solely benefited firms in trouble. As a result, a whole set of economic policy tools became either ineffective, prohibitively expensive, or too difficult to use, raising a profoundly difficult challenge for Japanese policy makers used to firmly established procedures in regulating and promoting the sectors under their jurisdiction.

Thus, at the turn of the century the economic situation called for policy innovation, just as the state had lost considerable leverage over economic and societal actors. In the face of such constraints, "permeable insulation" emerged as the *de facto* consensus solution for Japanese policy makers and firms. As subsequent chapters in this book demonstrate, attempts at permeable insulation were often hit-and-miss, and in some instances permeable insulation was an unintended, but welcome result. Regardless of how it came about, permeable insulation meant that policies provided continued protection for those sectors demanding it, while also allowing more competitive industries to break out. Whether or not this policy approach will ultimately prove beneficial for Japan remains to be seen; but in any event, the policies of permeable insulation imply continued attempts by Japan's government to protect certain parts of the economy. In this sense, permeable insulation reinforces the bifurcation of Japanese industries into world-competitive exporting sectors and domestically focused, less efficient ones. Permeable insulation also means that Japan is adapting to new world rules of globalization while maintaining pockets of its old mercantilist approaches at home.

This chapter considers the economic and political issues that affected the Japanese government's ability to respond to the challenges of economic globalization, and thus led to permeable insulation. Some of these constraints, such as rising deficits, deflation, and an aging society, resulted in practical difficulties in funding initiatives, while others, such as deregulation, reduced the ability of the state to influence private actors. At the same time, political flux and the changing relationship between politicians and bureaucrats affected the actual processes of policy making, bringing new voices to the table and potentially reducing the strategic focus of economic policy. While the substance and origins of these issues varied considerably, they had the combined effect of calling for new approaches and closing off options previously available and feasible for policy makers.

Global Challenges

The economic pressures brought on by globalization and the mounting domestic call for less state intervention created inexorable pressure for a different approach to economic policy and structural transformation in Japan. The rise of competition, particularly from other East Asian countries, as well as the globalization of production networks in industries such as automobiles and information technology hardware, created pressures for changing a broad spectrum of business practices.

Meanwhile, increased multilateralism in the world political economy pushed Japan toward more acceptance of legalism and trade openness. This new international regulation reached well beyond just trade in goods, and both the scope and the enforceability of such regulation had expanded considerably since the latter 1980s to include capital-adequacy rules for banks engaging in international lending (the so-called Basel Accord), trade in services (the General Agreement on Trade and Services), and protection of intellectual property rights (the Agreement on Trade-Related Aspects of Intellectual-Property Rights), among others.

In particular, the establishment of the WTO subjected trade disputes to a much higher degree of legal argumentation and legal finality. As Pekkanen (Chapter 4) observes, while Japanese trade officials were quick to learn how to use this legalism to support domestic trade interests, the increased focus on legal processes nevertheless introduced constraints for Japan's policy makers in trying to protect domestic firms and sectors. Thus, while in some cases Japan tried to employ the new multilateralism as a "shield" to protect domestic interests, globalization nevertheless limited the ways in which policy makers and corporations could affect insulation.

In terms of markets, the main transmission mechanism of globalization is price, or the cost of production. The long-term process of economic development naturally shifts cost advantage from labor-intensive to capital-intensive and then to knowledge-intensive economic activities, and Japan's rapid rise only accelerated this process. While exit from some inefficient sectors was accomplished successfully starting as early as the 1970s (e.g., in aluminum smelting), industry decline also triggered loud calls for protection. Policies of protection thus shifted away from a focus on infant industry support toward maintaining profit levels in some of Japan's most inefficient industries, such as food processing and textiles (Katz 1998). Productivity in many of these protected sectors has stagnated, creating ever greater gaps with producers outside Japan.

The long-term process of shifting production costs accelerated considerably in the latter half of the 1980s, due to the rapid rise in the value of the yen that began in 1985. When it became clear that the doubling of the nominal value of the yen would be long-term, Japanese firms realized they were at a structural cost disadvantage relative to their international competitors. This accelerated the pace of outward foreign direct investment (FDI), including considerable investment in manufacturing facilities in low-wage, high-skills economies in East and Southeast Asia (see Chapter 6). Meanwhile, competitors in Korea, Taiwan, and elsewhere in Asia enjoyed improved productivity coupled with an overall devaluation of their currencies against the strengthening yen. Because this new competition came mostly from lower value-added, less knowledge-intensive production, the squeeze was particularly strong on Japan's lower-tech manufacturing and assembly. The trend of relocating this type of production into East Asia continued through the 1990s and into the twenty-first century.

Meanwhile, the strength of U.S. and European firms in information and biotechnology created severe competitive pressures in high-tech manufacturing and services. While some Japanese firms were important players in research and development of new materials (such as in superconductivity), the shift to the new economy did not play into Japan's established strengths in high-quality mass production of consumer durables. Industrial policies that had been so supportive of the manufacturing industries were evidently much less helpful in fostering cutting-edge frontier industries (Vogel and Zysman 2002). Thus, at the beginning of the twenty-first century, Japan faced the dual challenges of a "hollowing-out" of production and the need for innovative business models based on new technologies. One industry where this challenge was successfully tackled was telecommunications, where Japan quickly assumed a leading position in cellular phone technology. In spite of individual success stories, however, Japanese manufacturers as a whole were struggling.

Political Constraints

Japan's responses to the challenges of global competition were naturally based on domestic politics. Concurrent with the challenges of multilateralism and globalization, however, fundamental domestic changes affected the political processes from within. The malaise of the Japanese economy and the fiscal problems of the government greatly reduced the state's ability to deal effectively with ailing sectors through public works and other support programs. In addition to the quantitative limits, the established processes of Japan's domestic politics also experienced a qualitative shift. For many years, observers of the Japanese political scene quite readily accepted Chalmers Johnson's notion that the politicians "reigned" while the bureaucrats "ruled" (Johnson 1990, p. 80). Even scholars heralding the rise in influence of LDP Diet members in the 1980s (especially the so-called *zoku*, or policy tribes) based their analyses on the assumption that the strength of individual politicians was a function of their access to the bureaucracy (Inoguchi and Iwai 1987; Satō and Matsuzaki 1986).[1] Critiques of policy failures starting in the early 1990s built on this apparent truth, and reformist politicians as well called for a reassertion of political control over bureaucracies that were no longer responsive to the national interest (Katō 1997; Nikkei 1994; Ozawa 1994).

Advocates of the view that bureaucracy-led industrial policy was a key factor in Japan's rapid postwar economic growth have often pointed to pragmatic flexibility as one of its most positive attributes. A small cadre of bureaucrats with excellent technical skills and access to pertinent information was able to make decisions quickly and effectively, without the endless negotiations and adjudication of a variety of interests that characterize legislative activity. While this way of looking at bureaucratic decision making has come under considerable attack from those who argue that bureaucracies are either utterly self-interested, hidebound, or simply agents of politicians, evidence suggests that Japanese bureaucrats have generally enjoyed a considerable degree of freedom from heavy oversight, especially when compared with their counterparts in other industrialized democracies (Kim, et al. 1995). Yet, at the beginning of the twenty-first century, the fundamentals of this system were increasingly challenged.

Parties in Flux

Probably the single most startling political change of the last half-century was the end of 38 years of LDP one-party dominance in 1993.[2] While the immediate policy implications were only short-lived, with the LDP regaining power within a year, it marked a new era of political flux and affected in important ways not only the relations between politicians and bureaucrats, but also the role of politicians in policy making more generally.

Despite a bewildering array of party formations, splits, and mergers that made a full account of post-1993 Japanese politics read like a Russian novel, one clear trend emerged: the realignment of Japanese electoral politics to the center-right of the political spectrum. While the LDP was going through divisions and mergers, the Left seemed to be wasting away. By 2001, the Social Democratic Party of Japan was almost a vestigial party and the Japan Communist Party, while good at receiving protest votes, was virtually a nonentity in single-member districts.[3] By the Upper House election of 2001, none of the parties that were viable players in Japanese politics—including pre-eminently the LDP, the Democratic Party, Kōmeitō, and the Liberal Party—could be clearly identified as "progressive."

As of 2001, it was unclear whether the new Democratic Party would prove to be as short-lived as some of its predecessors; but regardless of its fate, Japanese politics seemed to revolve around a much smaller slice of the ideological spectrum. In earlier years, the main opposition parties were composed mostly of politicians whom hardly anyone thought fit to govern. By the late 1990s debates over actual policies, rather than just political posturing, had become a focal concern for Diet members, and concrete policy measures had become the center of political debate. The new ideological interchangeability of many members of the LDP with opposition party politicians suddenly made defection across party lines easy and created leverage for politicians with strong policy positions to push those issues, rather than confining their energy to LDP party power struggles. Moreover, the shift toward the center also brought on a much more vigorous and informed policy debate than previously, since differences between parties rested on more subtle distinctions than before.

By the turn of the century, the increased fight for votes ironically often created confusion and even gridlock. Moreover, uncertainty over the efficacy of existing party strategies was growing. For example, in the summer 2000 Lower House election, the LDP's decision to cater to traditional farming and public works constituencies led to the loss of many urban seats, threatening to turn the LDP into a rural party—an unpalatable long-term option in heavily urbanized Japan. The intra-party reaction to that loss eventually led to the accession of Jun'ichirō Koizumi, a self-proclaimed anti–pork barrel reformer, as the party's leader in an unprecedented internal election in the spring of 2001. On the back of Koizumi's extraordinary personal popularity and an allegedly radically different reform agenda, the LDP scored an important victory in the 2001 Upper House election. Even so, the remaining strength of traditional constituencies within the LDP created considerable doubt that the new strategy would be sustainable, and observers were divided as to whether Japanese politics was really changing, or just allowing more permeability and flexibility into a fundamentally closed core system.

Patterns of Political Support

Japanese electoral politics has often been described as "compensation" based (Calder 1988; Woodall 1996). In this view, subgovernments composed of knowledgeable *zoku* politicians, bureaucrats, and firms in a given sector have cooperated to ensure prosperity for the sector, votes for the politicians, and ease of regulation and access to post-retirement jobs for the bureaucrats. When policies became necessary that might harm other firms, those firms would be compensated through public policy—whether through specific, beneficial deregulation or reregulation, or through public funds in the form of tax breaks, public works projects, or government procurement.

Such equalization of benefits and costs worked quite well in a growing economic situation such as Japan experienced through the 1980s. However, the logic of compensation critically relied on one of two processes: the offering of public funds on a large scale, or extensive licensing requirements based on a discretionary approval process. Either of these could be offered selectively to firms or sectors considered to be deserving of compensation. This system required that the government had something to distribute that economic agents wanted, and that there were sufficient resources to satisfy all interests concerned.

Changes in the 1990s and early twenty-first century brought to the fore the contradictions of compensation as a basic principle of political decision making. First, the immense costs of compensating large numbers of ailing firms and sectors in an overall stagnant economy, with little return in terms of job creation, only served to exacerbate the budget deficit. And despite their political utility, the long-term effect of these policies was to help create pockets of economic inefficiency that contributed to slower economic growth (Katz 1998; Takenaka 1999). Over time, compensation also created political costs in the form of fissures within the LDP. At the turn of the century, the leadership of old-style compensation-oriented politicians, such as Shizuka Kamei and Yoshirō Mori, was challenged by "reformers" such as Taku Yamasaki, Jun'ichirō Koizumi, and Kōichi Katō (collectively known as YKK). The massive setback for the LDP among urban voters in the June 2000 Lower House election demonstrated that the limits of compensation politics as an electoral strategy had been reached. While compensation was likely to remain one tool of governing, the fiscal situation made it impossible for it to be the main principle of governance, and forced the government to choose among constituencies.

Politicians and Bureaucrats

Whatever differences there may have been among individual LDP politicians and across the various LDP factions, one thing was clearly apparent across all ranks of politicians in 2001: the desire to present themselves as reformers not beholden to bureaucrats. Rightly or wrongly, the series of policy failures of the 1990s were attributed to the bureaucrats and undermined the public trust in Japan's elite administrators. Political entrepreneurs were quick to take advantage of this sentiment to gain stature by defying bureaucratic power. An outstanding early example of this strategy was former Minister of Health and Welfare Naoto Kan's revelation of a cover-up regarding HIV-tainted blood by his ministry in 1996. Likewise, Foreign Minister Makiko Tanaka's highly publicized rows with her subordinates in 2001 and 2002 were populist—and popular—assaults on the alleged sins of an entrenched bureaucracy. More consequentially, heated criticism of policy mistakes of the Ministry of Finance (MOF) by politicians across the entire spectrum led to the removal of the MOF's financial oversight functions to a new agency in 1998. Moreover, in the course of the 1990s, politicians also assumed more important roles in the process of compiling general budgets and fiscal stimulus plans (Grimes 2001; Mabuchi 1997). In contrast to earlier attempts at assuming leadership, at the turn of the century politicians did indeed become more deeply involved in policy making and implementation. In addition to asserting more authority over bureaucrats, politicians sought to change the structure of their interactions with the bureaucracy; this process culminated in a complete ministerial reorganization in 2001, combined with an effort to expand the politicians' roles in the administration.

Government-Business Relationships

Just as bureaucrats became increasingly vulnerable to scrutiny by politicians, they were also losing power vis-à-vis private business and society due to a reduction of policy tools, more rules on transparency, and a longer-term trend of growing corporate independence from government guidance.

Perhaps the single most distinctive feature of Japanese regulation has been its informal nature. So-called administrative guidance was often effective because bureaucrats possessed a variety of rewards and punishments to change companies' costs of cooperation. In particular, the ability to approve or deny access to resources such as tax breaks, subsidized loans, and entry into restricted business sectors, combined with the fact that bureaucratic decisions were effectively not subject to outside review, meant that bureaucrats could influence companies' actions even where they apparently lacked legal standing to do so (Upham 1987, Shindō 1992). Yet, the scope and importance of such rewards and punishments progressively declined, especially from the 1980s onward. Formal entry barriers, such as legal trade restrictions and tariffs, were eliminated or reduced in many sectors, and direct government financial support was generally of less importance except in specific sectors (e.g., construction, agriculture) and for small firms (Schaede 2000a; see also Chapter 5).

Moreover, the bureaucrats' tools of administrative guidance became more open to public scrutiny with the Administrative Procedures Law of 1993. This new law required bureaucrats to issue a written explanation of a permit approval or denial, thereby opening up the possibility of legal recourse on such decisions. To be sure, to protect their turf bureaucrats tirelessly designed ways around these rules, such as turning a permit requirement into a notification requirement that, while possibly less effective, remained outside the new review process. Regulated firms that strove for the good will of their cognizant ministry often still felt obligated to follow the ministry's advice. Importantly, however, the new law made it easier for firms that opposed government interference to challenge or resist that guidance.

More broadly, there was evidence for a rise in the rule of law. As a number of authors have argued, a considerable amount of regulation in Japan has not traditionally been strictly based on law, but has rather been based on regulators' extended interpretations of law (Shindō 1992; Haley 1987, 1991; Upham 1987). Haley (1991) even argued that this was a strategic move by the bureaucrats to evade Diet members' and courts' scrutiny of their actions. With the reduction in nontransparent punishment available to regulators, however, firms could more forcefully threaten to challenge administrative action, thus further reducing the flexibility with which officials could respond to changed economic circumstances.

Adding to the bureaucrats' dilemma in how to uphold their roles in Japan's political economy was the revelation, through a series of scandals, that Japan's elite bureaucracy was not as impartial as had been claimed. In particular, officials of the MOF were found to have been entertained by the very banks they were supposed to supervise, inspect, and regulate (Mabuchi 1997; Nikkei 1994). In addition to the spin-off of the banking supervision functions to the newly created Financial Supervisory Agency (later renamed the Financial Services Agency) in 1998, these scandals triggered calls for more rule-based regulation and fewer informal contacts between the ministries and their regulated firms. Reformers singled out the functions of the MOF-*tan* (a special employee position in a bank in charge of regular contacts with the ministry; see also Chapter 8) and the system of post-retirement employment of government officials by the private sector (*amakudari*) as main mechanisms of informal regulation, and called for their reform or even removal.[4] Yet, in spite of loud media calls for a reform of the *amakudari* system, there was evidence that the core features of the system were to remain in place. Some retiring officials kept a low profile for a few years to avoid criticism, but 2001 data on the number of retired officials and their destinations showed little change over previous years. Over time, the system may well become less rigid and institutionalized, but its benefits in terms of expertise, information flows, and regulatory insulation were sufficiently large to make a complete abolition unlikely.

Government and Society

Issues of legalism also speak to the relationship between state and society. One aspect of this relationship was the problem of nontransparency caused by informal regulation. In the 1990s, the issue of transparency was forced onto the bureaucracy through both incremental process reforms and the effects of the already mentioned Administrative Procedures Law. A potentially more important breakthrough in the legal relationship between the government and citizens was the 1999 passage of the Information Disclosure Law, implemented in April 2001. As of 2001, the actual effects of this new law were unclear, but local examples in Japan suggested that it would considerably increase the transparency of state behavior (MacLachlan 2000). At the same time, however, the law contained a number of loopholes and escape clauses that allowed the government to protect information where that was deemed to be in the public interest. Thus, while the new law allowed for more permeable access to information, it also maintained bureaucrats' power to avoid full disclosure of information.

More broadly, the role of noneconomic interest groups in Japanese policy making remained marginal. In particular, there was still little pressure from consumer groups to change the political economy in any fundamental way (Vogel 1999). In the absence of such pressure, policy was likely to continue to be made by subgovernments, albeit within the constraints of high deficits and international rules and global competition, thus only perpetuating the dynamics of permeable insulation.

Economic Constraints

The 1990s saw a culmination of the various economic and structural challenges faced by Japan's government and firms. As of 2002, Japan's economy had been stagnant for a decade, and this had affected all economic actors. Outgrowths of the recession included a large-scale government deficit, deflation in spite of extremely low interest rates, an urgent need for financial system reform, a credit crunch, rising unemployment, and corporate bankruptcies, especially (but not exclusively) among small firms. Directly or indirectly, these phenomena combined into a powerful challenge to some of the distinctive pillars of Japan's economic system, such as *keiretsu* organization, the main bank system, lifetime employment, and corporate governance.

Government Finance

Starting in 1992, Japan began to experience the second great wave of fiscal deterioration since the immediate postwar years, following that of the post oil shock years in the 1970s. After maintaining essentially balanced budgets for over 20 years, Japan's central government budget deficit had risen to nearly 35 percent of expenditures (6 percent of the gross national product [GNP]) from 1973 to 1979. Following great efforts to reduce deficits and increase revenues by partially privatizing government-owned corporations, by 1991 deficits had been brought below 10 percent of annual expenditures, and debt relative to the gross domestic product (GDP) was declining slowly (Suzuki 2000). Yet, in spite of these successes, total outstanding government debt in 1991 stood at nearly 40 percent of GDP.[5]

In the 1990s, the fiscal situation deteriorated sharply, reflecting the stagnation first of asset prices (e.g., stocks and real estate), and then of economic growth. By far the most important factor in rapidly rising deficits was declining tax revenue. Some of the decline was policy-induced, including income tax cuts in 1994 and 1998. But mostly it was the result of dwindling economic activity: Corporate tax revenues plummeted with reductions in firm profits and increases in bankruptcies; income tax revenues fell due to a decrease in both job creation and overtime pay; and capital gains tax revenues evaporated with the decline in asset prices (Posen 1998; Grimes 2001).[6]

Annual central government deficits peaked in fiscal year 1998 at 10.4 percent of GDP, while total outstanding general government debt in 2001 was approximately 140 percent of GDP and growing (MOF 2001b). In comparison, the U.S. budget deficit peaked in 1992 at under 6 percent of GDP, and total debt outstanding peaked at 76 percent of GDP in 1993 (Council of Economic Advisers 2001). To make matters worse, prospects for rapid improvement in the Japanese economy remained dim. The long-term forecast for government spending was alarming, given the rapid aging of the Japanese population in the face of low (and declining) birth rates and high life expectancy. Many analysts questioned the adequacy of Japan's national pension and health insurance systems and, with a decline in the number of workers per retired citizen, government finances would only become increasingly difficult to handle (Smithers and Asher 1998). With no relief in sight, the general public—and with it the policy makers—became ever more aware of the long-term dangers associated with these high deficits.[7] Clearly, as Japan entered the twenty-first century, large-scale new spending programs or tax reductions to reinvigorate certain industries became less likely. High deficits thus began to crack the core pillar of compensation-based policies: Whereas previously, politicians had been able to "pay off" injured interest groups simply by launching government-financed programs, the new fiscal constraints placed severe limits on this approach.

Fiscal and Investment Loan Program

The story of Japan's government finances and of the decline of compensation as an important policy tool remains incomplete without an analysis of what is often referred to as Japan's "second budget," the Fiscal Investment and Loan Program (FILP).[8] The FILP is a government lending program set up to mobilize trust funds and certain non-tax revenues for special financing purposes (Johnson 1978). For example, in the 1950s, the government-owned Japan Development Bank used FILP funds to offer subsidized loans to support long-term investment by Japan's capital-intensive industries, such as steel, shipbuilding, and chemicals. Over time, FILP was financed increasingly through Japan's postal saving system: Households deposited part of their savings in the time deposits and life insurance offered through the postal system, and a large portion of these deposits (along with national pension contributions) were channeled through the program to "FILP agencies." These included special-purpose banks like the Japan Development Bank and public corporations in charge of infrastructure projects and special public works, such as the Japan Highway Public Corporation.

In the course of the postwar period, a number of developments coincided to make the FILP ever more important. First, the high propensity to save among Japanese households made the postal savings system the world's largest financial institution, and in turn made the FILP a fiscal policy tool of extraordinary dimensions. As of April 2000, outstanding funds available to the FILP account totaled ¥433 trillion, or roughly $3.5 trillion. Not all these "trust funds" were cycled through FILP agencies; much of the total was invested in government bonds and elsewhere. Yet, the FILP lending program was still very large: planned FY2000 disbursements through FILP were ¥52.9 trillion (about $423 billion), roughly equivalent to 60 percent of the general account budget (MOF 2000a).

However, by the turn of the century, what had once been an efficient way to finance public works programs had turned into a pork-barrel system for providing post-retirement employment for bureaucrats, and a highly inefficient way to provide compensation policies to the construction sector. Prime Minister Koizumi therefore made the reorganization of the entire FILP program and a privatization of the FILP-financed agencies a core feature of his political platform in 2001.

As of 2001, it was too early to foresee just how this reform would work out. One likely scenario was for the solution to be very much in the context of permeable insulation: The system would be reformed to weed out rigidities and institutionalized allotments of funds, but some of the core features that had traditionally afforded the Japanese government discretionary funds for specific domestic policy purposes were likely to be maintained. Regardless of the specific outcomes, however, the FILP reforms were clearly going to affect many of the mechanisms with which Japan's government had previously disbursed deals and compensation. Thus, FILP reform further undermined state power at a time when the general budget deficit had already curtailed the government's reach in public works.

Banking and Finance

Government spending and loans were increasingly important to struggling firms in the late 1990s and the early twenty-first century because private sector financing was drying up for many firms that needed capital, either to improve competitiveness or just to survive. Poor lending decisions by commercial banks throughout the 1980s and 1990s had tied up many funds in unproductive investments, some of which continued purely on the basis of loan rollovers. While Japan's multinationals had less trouble gaining access to funding at home or abroad, small and medium-size firms that provided the bulk of employment in Japan were at a severe disadvantage, even if they proposed and operated viable businesses.

The problems of the financial system stemmed from early over-regulation, regulatory failures, and uneven deregulation across banking groups in the 1990s. For much of the postwar period, Japan's financial system was characterized by three outstanding features. First, it was highly segmented—specific categories of financial institutions (e.g., city banks, long-term credit banks, savings banks) had narrowly defined, specialized tasks and business areas. Second, until the early 1980s, all major interest rates were regulated by law. Thus, there was little price competition among banks, which earned a stable and predictable spread between deposit rates and lending rates. Third, strict government regulation of bond and stock markets meant that most corporate finance occurred through bank loans. The restricted nature of competition in finance gave regulators important tools with which to pursue informal regulation through administrative guidance: They used formal control over licenses and permits to encourage financial institutions to change their behavior in a variety of ways. Informal regulation also extended to bank inspections and decisions on whether and how to bail out failing companies (Schaede 2000b; Hoshi and Kashyap 2001; Horiuchi 1998).

In the late 1980s, Japan experienced a run-up in asset prices (i.e., the values of equity and real estate) known as the "bubble" economy. With many investors apparently believing that Japanese asset prices would never go down, financial speculation was rampant—and often based on bank lending that was collateralized with other overpriced assets. With the burst of the bubble in 1990–92, the face value of many of these bank loans far exceeded the market value of the collateral, leading in turn to widespread defaults and withheld payments. The result was a banking crisis that lasted through the 1990s and into the twenty-first century.

In addition to the forces of the bubble, financial liberalization gradually changed the traditional features of Japan's banking system. Interest rates had been fully liberalized by the early 1990s, and bond and stock markets were opened up step by step. The 1994 Financial Reform Act and a 1998 revision of related laws finally abolished the previous segmentation of the banking system. A revision of the Antimonopoly Law in 1997 made possible the creation of financial holding companies that combined commercial and investment banking, as well as insurance and other financial services by one company. Beginning in 2001, this caused a merger frenzy that changed the landscape of Japan's banking industry. Reforms were further pushed by the 1998–2001 "Big Bang" program of financial liberalization.

Yet, three problems continued to pose severe challenges for Japan's financial system: the continuing existence of anachronistic small banks (such as credit unions), the persistence of informal regulation, and the accumulation of large stocks of nonperforming loans (NPLs) in the banking system. In the period of strict interest rate regulation through the 1980s, small banks could profitably fill market niches (e.g., small rural markets). Deregulation introduced price competition to the banking system, just as large banks were extending their business fields (e.g., commercial banks moving into loans to small firms and households). Small banks lost their niches, and responded by enticing customers with higher interest rates—a process that eventually contributed to a series of small bank failures in the early 1990s. At the same time, actual supervision of small and large banks did not always keep pace with formal changes in regulation. The persistence of informal regulation encouraged a variety of management abuses that contributed to a serious deterioration of the banks' balance sheets, bankruptcies, and a rise in systemic risk throughout the Japanese financial system (Schaede 2000b).

As early as 1992, the first signs of serious problems began to surface with NPLs. However, because of informal bank monitoring and lenient disclosure rules, banks found many ways to hide their problem loans. Still, no one would have forecast the eventual scope of the problem. In 1995 alone, more than 15 small and medium-size banks went bankrupt. In 1998, the crisis forced the government to provide ¥60 trillion in public funds to recapitalize major banks and to shore up the Deposit Insurance Corporation—at the time, nonperforming loans were conservatively (and unrealistically) estimated to total ¥35 trillion.[9] Despite the capital infusion, two major banks were closed down in October 1998. As of the end of fiscal year 2000 (March 31, 2001), the total NPL burden was officially estimated to have risen to ¥43 trillion ($368 billion); despite ¥11.6 trillion ($100 billion) in write-offs over the previous three years (FSA 2001a, 2001b).

Two factors are important when considering these numbers. First, the total extent of the bad loan problem becomes clear only when adjusting figures for bad loans already written off by banks throughout the 1990s, a number which may never become fully known. Second, the definition of what constitutes an NPL, while revised several times throughout the 1990s, remained much more forgiving and lenient than in the United States. Roughly, whereas U.S. banks have to report all loans as "nonperforming" that are not current on interest and principal, in Japan a "risk management loan" was one where no interest payments had been made for more than three months (Schaede 2000b).[10]

The bad loan problem was proving to be a sinkhole both for government funds and for private savings, and was likely to constrain both public and private action for years to come. It also reflected a regulatory struggle that occupied the attention of all players in the political economy, with deeply entrenched interests in both the public and private sectors. What compounded the problem even further was a large number of small finance, leasing, and real estate firms that were subsidiaries of banks and continued to provide pockets in which to hide loan positions, in the hope that the borrower could turn itself around. Finally, the problems of banking were mirrored in the securities firms and in the life insurance companies, which had succumbed to the bubble frenzy just as much as the banks.

In addition to the enormous cost and ramifications for the real economy in cleaning up the banking problem, the banking crisis was further fueled by concerns about the banks' ability to meet the BIS capital-asset ratio of 8 percent required for banks engaging in international finance.[11] The stock market slump of the late 1990s and early 2000s had significantly reduced the value of the stocks held by banks, forcing banks to cut their lending, regardless of the creditworthiness of the company or quality of the business proposal. In combination with the economic downturn and slowed demand for products, this led to a credit crunch, in which companies were unable to secure loans from banks, simply because banks would not lend. Unable to obtain funds, many small or weak companies looked to the state for help—but, as we have seen, the government's ability to protect and compensate was dwindling.

Challenges of Monetary Policy

The issues of stimulatory policy, stagnant growth, and the weak financial sector converged into serious challenges for monetary policy. The single biggest problem was deflation: As of summer 2001, wholesale and land prices had been in decline for about a decade, while consumer prices had been more or less stagnant, creating a clear case for loosening monetary policy.[12] Yet, by 1995, nominal interest rates were so close to zero that it was impossible to lower them any further.

From 1995 onward, short-term interest rates had stayed consistently below 0.5 percent, and in February 1999, the Bank of Japan (BOJ) (Japan's central bank) decided to guide the overnight call rate (an interbank lending rate that was the main vehicle of monetary policy operations) down to about 0.01 percent, or essentially zero, in a desperate attempt to reverse a worsening economic situation. By the fall of 2001, this "Zero Interest-Rate Policy" had been in effect for more than two years (with the exception of a 0.25 percentage point increase between August 2000 and March 2001). Still, real interest rates remained too high to produce a meaningful stimulus to the economy, prompting some economists to call for "quantitative easing"—flooding markets with more money to try to push down long-term rates.[13] In March and August 2001, the BOJ made important concessions toward quantitative easing, but the effects were still unclear as of fall 2001.

The difficulties of stimulating the Japanese economy through monetary policy made economic recovery much more difficult. Under the circumstances, fiscal stimulus would have been the obvious choice, had it not been for the huge fiscal constraints. Faced with massive budget deficits, Prime Minister Koizumi focused his attention on regulatory and administrative reform in 2001, despite the likelihood that these would have negative short-term effects on employment and economic growth. Corporations, along with the bureaucrats and politicians, had little choice but to turn to innovative new policies of permeable insulation in order to protect their livelihoods. In the face of seemingly incurable economic stagnation, each firm or sector was forced to explore avenues that would be best for it, if not for the Japanese economy.

Changes in the Corporate System

For most of the postwar period, the Japanese corporate system had proven remarkably flexible in dealing with change. Ironically, some of this flexibility was in fact rooted in rather rigid, long-term relationships of firms with owners, creditors, suppliers, customers, and labor (Dore 1986). These relationships insulated large firms from cyclical downturns and allowed them to pursue long-term investment objectives, at least at a time when imports of new technologies and mass production of high-quality manufacturing goods were key to economic success.

However, by the 1990s the major pillars of the Japanese corporate system were being challenged by globalization. In finance, the main bank system came under pressure with the deregulation of capital markets in the 1980s, which afforded large firms alternative means of external finance in the form of stocks, bonds, or commercial paper. Combined with rising retained earnings, this meant that large corporations were less dependent on bank loans. Banks therefore increasingly turned to other clients, including real estate companies, which exposed them to the speculative bubble of the late 1980s. With the depressed stock market and the banks' need to boost their capital-asset ratios, in the 1990s some banks began a partial and quiet sell-off of what used to be stable "relationship" shareholdings (Hoshi and Kashyap 1999).

At the same time, as the long-term relationship between firms and banks generally became less fixed, cross-shareholdings with corporate groups also came to look less stable. Among the most distinctive features of the Japanese private sector in the postwar period have been the corporate *keiretsu* groups, in which major companies were linked by multiple, overlapping relationships that included cross-shareholding, preferential trading, and lending (Gerlach 1992). *Keiretsu*, once hailed as the backbone of Japan's closed trading system, changed in nature as cross-shareholdings among *keiretsu* firms seemed to decline and, perhaps more importantly, some of the formerly competing main banks—such as Sumitomo and Sakura (a descendant of Mitsui Bank)—merged. While data on *keiretsu* shareholdings were often ambiguous, according to Tōyō Keizai in 1986 the six largest horizontal *keiretsu* groups (Mitsui, Mitsubishi, Sumitomo, Fuyō, Sanwa, and Dai-Ichi Kangyō) held on average 19.15 percent of outstanding group shares in mutual relations within the group. In other words, group firms owned 19.15 percent of all outstanding group shares in a stable, friendly arrangement. By 1997, this ratio had dropped to an average of 17.9 percent, indicating that some firms had sold their group stakes (Tōyō Keizai 1988, 1999). Although this still seemed to be a ratio indicative of extensive cross-shareholdings, some analysts predicted that the *keiretsu* model of the postwar period had come to an end, and would be replaced by more open, arm's-length financial relationships (Hoshi and Kashyap 2001).[14]

Lifetime employment, long considered a valuable source of

Japan's manufacturing prowess, also came under pressure. True, only 25 to 30 percent of the labor force ever enjoyed lifetime employment, which was not contractually guaranteed, but rather assured by custom. The practice of keeping the core workforce within the company for a whole career had helped Japan's economic development, in that companies could invest in employee training, often including at universities abroad, without having to fear losing these employees to competitors. Overall, lifetime employment resulted in a well-trained, loyal workforce (Aoki 1988). After the prolonged recession of the 1990s, however, firms came increasingly under pressure to "restructure"—in other words, to lay off workers. Throughout 2001, firms in the electronics, information technology, and construction industries, among others, announced the need for large-scale layoffs. More important than the actual numbers of layoffs during that time, however, was the fact that at the turn of the century a profound revision of the lifetime employment system was widely discussed, undermining the previous general sense of job security and challenging one of the core features of Japanese business practices.

The combination of recession and globalization left few aspects of Japanese industrial organization untouched. Large companies felt pressure to adapt to global financial rules, while small firms struggled to attract loans domestically. Deregulation had brought new accounting and disclosure rules that put many companies under pressure. The stock market slack forced firms to engage in a debate over corporate governance reform (see Chapter 9). Yet, just how decisive changes in these areas would eventually be seemed to depend importantly on how long economic stagnation was to continue. While few firms had indeed changed their practices as of 2001, it was unclear just how long they could continue the traditional management patterns.

Bringing Competition Back Home

In addition to domestic pressures for change caused by the recession, Japan's companies also feared increasing global pressure in the form of more foreign participation in their domestic marketplace. Until the 1980s, foreign direct investment into Japan had been negligible, due to strict legal limitations on joint ventures and foreign investment in Japanese firms. The formal restrictions were compounded by existing "business practices" that often made it prohibitively expensive for a foreign firm to engage in full-scale business operations in Japan. The distribution system added further obstacles in almost all intermediate and end product markets. Beginning in the 1980s, foreign trade pressure (*gaiatsu*), especially as exerted by the U.S. government, had opened access for foreign firms to a number of industries, including in finance and semiconductors. Sectoral negotiations continued, especially in the early 1990s, with agreements regarding automobiles and auto parts, construction, insurance, and others. Yet, while the trade negotiators celebrated partial success in a few product markets, *gaiatsu*-induced changes generally left the underlying structures within Japan intact.

This situation began to change somewhat in the late 1990s. A series of revisions, beginning in 1980, of the Foreign Exchange Law eventually allowed fundamentally free inflows and outflows of foreign exchange. The decline in Japanese stock prices after 1990 invited acquisitions by and mergers with foreign firms. To be sure, most foreign takeovers in the late 1990s occurred where the Japanese target firm was either beyond salvation or in such bad shape that no "white knight" could be found within Japan. Prominent examples included the 1998 joint venture between GE Capital and Nippon Lease, the effective purchase of Mitsui Trust by Prudential in 1998, and the absorption of the Long-Term Credit Bank of Japan, a former flagship bank, by a U.S. financial consortium after the Japanese government allowed a partial write-off of the bank's major debts. As of 2001, it remained unclear whether foreign acquisitions of major healthy companies would ever be accepted by the Japanese business community. Nevertheless, the foreign firms had arrived, and Japan's financial industry had most certainly turned international in the 1990s.

The one truly global manufacturing sector, automobiles, was also affected by this trend. By 2001, the Ford Motor Company had increased its previous, smaller stake in Mazda to a controlling 33.4 percent, and had assumed management leadership of the failing automobile maker. In an even more surprising move, in 1999 French automaker Renault saved Nissan, Japan's former flagship auto company, from certain bankruptcy by purchasing a controlling stake of 36.8 percent and launching a remarkable turnaround. Finally, in 2001, DaimlerChrysler acquired a 34 percent controlling stake in Mitsubishi Motors. As a result of these developments, only two major Japanese car companies—Toyota and Honda—were still domestically controlled in 2001.[15]

Foreign penetration not only meant more domestic competition and challenges to informal regulation and deal making; it also provided alternative models of corporate management and governance (see Chapter 9). Moreover, the increasing foreign role in finance—particularly in the securities markets—meant that old-style relationship management was increasingly under attack. Nevertheless, when looking at all Japanese industries, as of the late 1990s Japan's import ratio (the market share of foreign products) continued to be below 5 percent in most intermediate and end-product markets. Manufactured goods' import penetration was less than half that of any other industrialized nation, even in 1998 (Lincoln 2000, p. 10). In spite of the new sales venues of Internet sales, mail order, and the advance of foreign retail stores into Japan, the overall data indicated that many of Japan's product markets remained difficult to crack. As of 2001 there was still little evidence of a fundamental, comprehensive opening of the Japanese economy. Thus, globalization and insulation coexisted in striking, and sometimes uneasy, patterns.

Conclusions: Reluctant Globalization

In the face of globalization pressures and economic stagnation, Japanese firms and policy makers were forced to pursue innovative new strategies that aimed concurrently at both growth and insulation. While this was not a completely new fact of life, the new multilateral, globalized environment had joined with a shifting domestic political scene to limit the choices and tools at their disposal.

Possibly most affected by these new constraints were the bureaucrats. A growing atmosphere of legalism at the international level reduced the policy tools available to promote the interests of increasingly diverse domestic firms versus foreign firms. Meanwhile, heightened legalism at home, coupled with reduced leverage as firms became less dependent, made informal regulation ever more contingent on the cooperation of the regulated firms. While this could sometimes be induced by providing resources, resources were increasingly difficult to come by, given Japan's stagnant economy and alarming fiscal deficits. Both past successes and recent failures increased the level of public scrutiny on bureaucrats. Success in fostering strong firms and markets over the postwar period meant that firms were less dependent on the state. Meanwhile, the policy failures of the 1990s triggered calls for heightened oversight over bureaucrats' decisions.

Perhaps most importantly, the notion of the "public interest" equaling "economic national interest" had finally become untenable.[16] Corporate interests differed between the competitive multinationals and the unproductive domestic firms dependent on protection. This bifurcation caused fissures in party politics as well, especially in the ruling LDP. Perhaps for the first time, politicians were seriously confronted with a choice between forcing reform that would hurt some traditional backers, and maintaining compensation politics that would hurt other key current and future constituencies. Election results and rhetoric in 2000 and 2001 suggested that the long-predicted rift between rural and urban interests was finally becoming decisive in Japanese politics. While the long-term impact on party politics was still unclear in 2001, the persistence of this basic cleavage within and among parties was bound to make Japanese politics and policy making more complicated and more multi-faceted than they had been in most of the postwar period.

In the face of declining competitiveness, expanded global networks, and weak government finances, both firms and policy makers were being forced to design innovative, low-cost strategies either to promote meaningful change for firm or country, or to gain protection from the ravages of the outside world. Naturally, policy makers sought to do so in a way that would serve most interests—but the environment had changed. Not only were there deep divisions between those industries that were competitive on the global stage and those that were not, the Japanese government had no choice but to appear to be a responsible participant in multilateral economic organizations. Sectorally differentiated permeable insulation was the result.

Notes

1. The term *zoku* describes politicians who have special expertise in a certain policy area and are able to influence the bureaucracy toward their preferred policy directions. Before the early 1980s, politicians had often been characterized as a rubber stamp for policies formulated by the bureaucracy.

2. On the long period of Liberal Domestic Party (LDP) rule, see, for example, Curtis (1988, 1999) and Calder (1988).

3. The electoral system revision of 1994 mandated 200 (reduced to 180 in 2000) proportional representation seats, in addition to 300 single-member districts. Success in proportional representation voting depended on strong party identity, but it was difficult for small, niche-oriented parties to win majorities in single-member districts. See Christensen (1996) for details on the new system.

4. The particular structure of Japan's bureaucracy, which forced high-powered bureaucrats to retire around the age of 58 (and less-powerful ones much earlier), created a need for a second career where their skills could be put to further use; given very limited pension provisions, bureaucrats were keenly interested in such further employment. In the *amakudari* (descent from heaven) system, post-retirement jobs for bureaucrats were ranked in a strict hierarchy, with the top former civil servants occupying a series of highly prestigious positions until final retirement. For example, retired Ministry of Finance (MOF) officials often became leaders of such key institutions the Fair Trade Commission, the Tokyo Stock Exchange, and the Bank of Japan (BOJ). The private sector also offered many post-retirement options. While firms hired former bureaucrats for various reasons, one important effect of the *amakudari* system was to smooth out the flow of information between government and business (Schaede 1995; Tsutsumi 1997).

5. Although annual deficits had been declining throughout the 1980s, they still required new government borrowing. Thus, debt had continued to grow despite declining deficits. Since debt grew slightly faster than the gross domestic product (GDP), on average, the ratio of debt to GDP also increased.

6. While much has been made of the effects of fiscal stimulus packages, such packages contributed only marginally to deficits prior to 1998, as shown in Posen (1998) and Grimes (2001).

7. In the short to medium term, high deficits helped provide the needed economic boost in the face of depressed demand in the face of economic stagnation. The long-term dangers of high deficits were (a) that future growth would be blunted by the need to repay large amounts of debt, and (b) the more remote possibility that large-scale borrowing would someday become difficult to repay fully. The main short-term policy problem posed by high deficits in 2001 was that Japanese citizens might reduce their current spending in order to save for the future tax increases necessary for the state to pay off the debt, thus wiping out the intended economic stimulus. Short-term sustainability of deficits is seldom a problem for major economies, as seen also in the lack of serious side effects from the high U.S. deficits of the Reagan era.

8. For details, see Calder (1990), Miyawaki (1993), Grimes (2001), Lincoln (2001), and Solís (chapter 5, this volume).

9. FSA (1998). An MOF estimate from earlier that year had put the number at ¥76 trillion, or nearly 15 percent of all loans outstanding. For the sake of consistency, we use only the FSA numbers here.

10. The bankruptcy of the large retailer MyCal in September 2001 was instructive in this regard. Not one of MyCal's major lenders had classified its loans as problematic up to the day it went bankrupt.

11. In calculating this ratio, "capital" consists of the banks' equity and subordinated debt, whereas "assets" consist of loans; the latter have to be evaluated by their risk level, and all corporate loans fall in the highest risk category.

12. Figures from the BOJ and National Land Agency databases. There were some minor blips of positive inflation in the price indexes—most notably in 1989–90 in the wholesale price index—but the long-term trend was downward.

13. Quantitative easing is actually rather difficult. With zero interest rates, the securities the BOJ might try to sell in exchange for cash carried essentially no

interest—making them functionally equivalent to the money for which they would be sold. The central bank also tried to leave large amounts of credit available in interbank markets, but with limited effects. Two other possibilities were often mentioned. One was large-scale unsterilized intervention in currency markets (in other words, trying to lower the value of the yen by selling large quantities of yen for dollars, without simultaneously reducing the amount of yen outstanding in domestic financial markets). The other was that the BOJ could purchase large amounts of long-term government bonds—essentially acting as a credit line (or printing press) to the government. The purpose of the latter strategy would be to lower long-term interest rates, rather than just the short-term ones with which monetary policy usually deals. See, for example, Itō, et al. (2001).

14. Different types of stable shareholders faced varying incentives in deciding whether or not to sell off holdings in affiliated companies. Insurance companies, which depended the most on current earnings, were often willing to sell off first. Banks were generally next, but were hesitant to sell off shares of firms to which they also had loans outstanding. Distributors and suppliers were typically most hesitant to sell off shares that supported long-term business relationships with buyers.

15. Daihatsu and Hino were controlled by Toyota. Mitsubishi, Nissan, Isuzu, and Mazda were all controlled by foreign firms, while Fuji Heavy (Subaru) and Suzuki both had a foreign firm as their largest shareholder.

16. See Schaede (2000a, chap. 3) for a discussion on how this equation guided industrial policies in the immediate postwar years.

References

Aoki, Masahiko. 1988. *Information, Incentives, and Bargaining in the Japanese Economy.* Cambridge: Cambridge University Press.

Calder, Kent. 1988. *Crisis and Compensation: Public Policy and Political Stability in Japan, 1946–1986.* Princeton: Princeton University Press.

———. 1990. "Linking Welfare and the Developmental State: Postal Savings in Japan." *Journal of Japanese Studies* 16, no. 1: 31–59.

Christensen, Ray. 1996. "The New Japanese Electoral System." *Pacific Affairs* 69 (Spring): 49–70.

Council of Economic Advisers. 2001. *Economic Report of the President.* Washington: U.S. Government Printing Office.

Curtis, Gerald. 1988. *The Japanese Way of Politics.* New York: Columbia University Press.

———. 1999. *The Logic of Japanese Politics: Leaders, Institutions, and the Limits of Change.* New York: Columbia University Press.

Dore, Ronald. 1986. *Flexible Rigidities: Industrial Policy and Structural Adjustment in The Japanese Economy, 1970–80.* London: Athlone Press.

FSA (Financial Supervisory Agency). 1998. "The Current Status of Risk Management Loans Held by Deposit-Taking Financial Institutions" (July 17). Tokyo: FSA. Available at www.fsa.go.jp/p_fsa/news/newse/news-e-717.html.

FSA (Financial Services Agency). 2001a. "Loss on Loan Disposal of Bad Loans

of All Banks" (August 2). Tokyo: FSA. Available at www.fsa.go.jp/news/newse/
e20010802-1b.html.

———. 2001b. "Status of Risk Management Loans Held by All Banks in Japan (as
of the end of March 2001)" (August 2). Tokyo: FSA. Available at www.fsa.go.jp/
news/newse/e20010802-1b.html.

Gerlach, Michael. 1992. *Alliance Capitalism: The Social Organization of Japanese
Business*. Berkeley: University of California Press.

Grimes, William W. 2001. *Unmaking the Japanese Miracle: Macroeconomic Politics, 1985–2000*. Ithaca: Cornell University Press.

Haley, John. 1987. "Governance by Negotiation: A Reappraisal of Bureaucratic Power
in Japan." In Kenneth Pyle, ed., *The Trade Crisis: How Will Japan Respond?*,
177–91. Seattle, WA: Society for Japanese Studies.

———. 1991. *Authority Without Power: Law and the Japanese Paradox*. New York:
Oxford University Press.

Hoshi, Takeo, and Anil Kashyap. 1999. "The Japanese Banking Crisis: Where Did
It Come From and How Will It End?" In Ben Bernanke and Julio Rotemberg,
eds., *NBER Macroeconomics Annual 1999*, 129–201. Cambridge, MA: National
Bureau of Economic Research.

———. 2001. *Corporate Financing and Governance in Japan: The Road to the
Future*. Cambridge: MIT Press.

Inoguchi, Takashi, and Tomoaki Iwai. 1987. *"Zoku giin" no kenkyū: Jimintō seiken
gyūji shuyaku toshite* (Research on "Zoku" Politicians: The Lead Actors Dominating LDP Government). Tokyo: Nihon keizai shimbunsha.

Itō, Takatoshi, Kōichi Haji, Mitsuhiro Fukao, Mikio Wakatsuki, and Tsutomu
Watanabe. 2001. "Kin'yū seisaku de defure o kōfuku dekiru ka? (Can Deflation
Be Conquered by Monetary Policy?)." *Economics and Policy*, no. 5, 10–29. To-
kyo: Tōyō keizai shimpōsha.

Johnson, Chalmers. 1978. *Japan's Public Policy Companies*. Washington: American Enterprise Institute.

———. 1982. *MITI and the Japanese Miracle: The Growth of Industrial Policy,
1925–1975*. Stanford: Stanford University Press.

———. 1990. "The People Who Invented the Mechanical Nightingale." *Daedalus*
(Summer): 71–90.

Katō, Kan. 1997. *Kanryō shudō kokka no shippai* (The Failures of the Bureaucratic
Dominant State). Tokyo: Tōyō keizai shimpōsha.

Katz, Richard. 1998. *Japan: The System That Soured*. Armonk, NY: M.E. Sharpe.

Kim, Hyung-Ki, Michio Muramatsu, and T.J. Pempel, eds. 1995. *The Japanese Civil
Service and Economic Development: Catalysts of Change*. Oxford: Oxford University Press.

Laurence, Henry. 2000. *Money Rules*. Ithaca: Cornell University Press.

Lincoln, Edward. 2000. "Japan: A Continuing Dilemma for Open Trade Ideals."
Washington: U.S. Trade Deficit Review Committee. Available at ustrdc.gov/
research/japan.pdf.

———. 2001. "Time to End Postal Savings." *Sentaku* (June 2). English version
available at www.brookings.com.

Mabuchi, Masaru. 1997. *Ōkurashō wa naze oitsumerareta no ka?* (Why Is the Ministry of Finance on the Run?). Tokyo: Chūō kōronsha.

MacLachlan, Patricia. 2000. "Information Disclosure and Center-Local Linkages in Japan." In Sheila A. Smith, ed., *Local Voices, National Issues: The Impact of Local Initiatives on Japanese Policy*. Ann Arbor: Michigan University Press.

McMillan, John. 1991. "Dango: Japan's Price-Fixing Conspiracies." *Economics and Politics* 3, no. 3; November: 201–18.

MOF (Ministry of Finance). 2001a. *FILP Report 2000* (February). Tokyo: MOF. Available at www.mof.go.jp/english/zaito/zaito00e.html.

———. 2001b. *Highlights of the Budget for FY 2001* (April). Tokyo: MOF. Available at www.mof.go.jp/english/budget/e1b061.pdf.

MPM (Ministry of Public Management, Home Affairs, Posts and Telecommunications). 2000. *Labour Force Survey: 2000 Annual Average Results*. Tokyo: MPM. Available at www.stat.go.jp/english/154b.htm.

Miyawaki, Atsushi. 1993. "The Fiscal Investment and Loan System Towards the 21st Century." *Japan Research Quarterly* 2, no. 2: 15–66.

Murakami, Yasusuke. 1982. "The Age of New Middle Mass Politics: The Case of Japan." *Journal of Japanese Studies* 8, no. 1 (Winter): 29–72.

Nikkei, ed. 1994. *Kanryō: Kishimu kyodai kenryoku* (Bureaucrats: Creaking, Massive Power). Tokyo: Nihon keizai shimbunsha.

Ozawa, Ichiro. 1994. *Blueprint for a New Japan*. New York: Kodansha.

Pempel, T.J. 1998. *Regime Shift: Comparative Dynamics of the Japanese Political Economy*. Ithaca: Cornell University Press.

Posen, Adam. 1998. *Restoring Japan's Growth*. Washington: Institute for International Economics.

Satō, Seizaburō, and Tetsuhisa Matsuzaki. 1986. *Jimintō seiken* (LDP Rule). Tokyo: Chūo kōronsha.

Schaede, Ulrike. 1995. "The 'Old Boy' Network and Government-Business Relationships in Japan." *Journal of Japanese Studies* 21, no. 2: 293–317.

———. 2000a. *Cooperative Capitalism: Self-Regulation, Trade Association, and the Antimonopoly Law in Japan*. Oxford: Oxford University Press.

———. 2000b. "The Japanese Financial System: From Postwar to the New Millennium." Boston: Harvard Business School Case 9-700-049.

Schoppa, Leonard. 1997. *Bargaining with Japan: What American Pressure Can and Cannot Do*. New York: Columbia University Press.

Shindō, Muneyuki. 1992. *Gyōsei shidō: Kanchō to gyōkai no aida* (Administrative Guidance: Between Agencies and Industries). Tokyo: Iwanami shinsho.

Smithers, Andrew, and David Asher. 1998. "Japan's Key Challenges for the 21st Century: Debt, Deflation, Default Demography, and Deregulation." SAIS Policy Forum Series (March). Washington. Available at www.sais-jhu.edu/pubs/policyforum/asher.html.

Suzuki, Takaaki. 2000. *Japan's Budget Politics: Balancing Domestic and International Interests*. Boulder: Lynne Reinner.

Takenaka, Heizō. 1999. *Keisei saimin: Keizai senryaku kaigi no 180 hi* (Government for the Good of the People: The 180 Days of the Economic Strategy Council). Tokyo: Diamond-sha.

Tōyō Keizai, ed. 1987. *Kigyō keiretsu sōran 1988* (Tōyō Keizai Data Bank 1988). Tokyo: Tōyō keizai shimpōsha.

———, ed. 1999. *Kigyō keiretsu sōran 1999* (Tōyō Keizai Data Bank 1999). Tokyo: Tōyō keizai shimpōsha.

Tsutsumi, Kazuma. 1997. *Amakudari hakusho* (Amakudari White Paper). Iwanami Booklet 425. Tokyo: Iwanami shoten.

Upham, Frank K. 1987. *Law and Social Change in Postwar Japan*. Cambridge: Harvard University Press.

Vogel, Steven. 1999. "Can Japan Disengage? Winners and Losers in Japan's Political Economy, and the Ties That Bind Them." *Social Science Japan Journal* 2, no. 1: 3–21.

Vogel, Steven, and John Zysman. 2002. "Technology." In Steven Vogel, ed., *U.S.- Japan Relations in a Changing World*. Washington: Brookings Institution.

Woodall, Brian. 1996. *Japan Under Construction: Corruption, Politics, and Public Works*. Berkeley: University of California Press.

Part II

International Political Economy
and
Permeable Insulation

——— 3 ———

Internationalization as Insulation

Dilemmas of the Yen

William W. Grimes

The Asian financial crisis of 1997–98 was a shock to Japan and the world. The rapidity with which fast-growing economies were hit by currency attacks and then economic chaos, the spread of the crisis first among disparate regional economies and then as far as Brazil and Russia, and the seeming inability (or perhaps unwillingness) of the United States and the International Monetary Fund (IMF) to fix the problem left a huge impression around the globe. The size and rapidity of the capital movements appeared to make for a qualitatively different kind of currency crisis from those of previous decades, and presented global finance with a serious new challenge. Unlike those in most other countries, however, policy makers in Japan saw themselves as being in a position to reduce about the possibility of a repeat performance—particularly a repeat performance that would have a direct effect upon Japan itself.

The Asian financial crisis brought home to Japan both the desirability of insulation from external financial shocks, and the essential permeability of all national financial systems in the face of economic globalization—including its own. In searching for a viable strategy of permeable insulation, one of the responses to the new problem of the "capital-account crisis" (Yoshitomi and Ohno 1999) was the resurrection of an older policy prescription: the internationalization, or regionalization, of the yen. Despite the name, the basic motivation was to insulate Japan from the perceived dangers of globalization, including severe currency fluctuations (Grimes 2003). Internationalization of the yen means increasing its use outside of Japan and, in particular, expanding its weight in the currency management of its Asian trading partners; by promoting internationalization, policy makers hoped to make Japan and the rest of Asia less vulnerable to the effects of fluctuations in global financial markets. But the strategy of insulation through internationalization of the yen contains interesting internal contradictions. As Japan seeks to maintain stability in its external environment, it is forced to face the constraints posed by globalization and its own severe government debt problems. The result, as of 2001, was an unresolved tension between the goals and side-effects of the policies of yen internationalization.

The problems and process of internationalizing the yen reflect the broader problem of change in Japan's political economy in response to pressures of globalization, and toward structural reform. As in other areas, and as seen particularly in Chapters 5 and 6, the goal of insulating Japan or Japanese firms in the face of rapid economic change coexists uncomfortably with the need for structural change. And also, as in other areas, the policy tools or "scripts" of the Japanese government in promoting change tend toward control, even as control becomes more difficult.

In the issue of yen internationalization, we see clearly the dynamic—and difficulties—of permeable insulation. This is a fundamentally different kind of insulation than traditional forms of protection in which specific sectors are insulated from foreign competition, or even from the sort of trade protection that Pekkanen (Chapter 4) and Schaede (Chapter 8) argue persists, despite adherence to World Trade Organization (WTO) rules. Rather, policies in this case have sought to insulate the entire Japanese economic system from the perceived dangers of financial globalization by stabilizing Japan's external economic environment. The difficulties are best exemplified in a series of dilemmas that are the main focus of this chapter, and that derived from the problem of permeability. The basic problem for Japan was that insulation from global financial fluctuations could not practically be accomplished through restrictive regulations, as in the early postwar years; not only was there already considerable openness or permeability in Japanese finance at the turn of the century, but increasing the attractiveness of the yen as an international currency actually called for greater permeability. Whether or not yen internationalization would succeed (in terms of either increasing international use of the yen or actually stabilizing Japan's economic environment), it was a new way of trying to guide the Japanese economy through a potentially dangerous world.

While currency usage may be viewed as an economic issue, in this story politics looms large. At the international level, Japan's economic stagnation and financial crises from 1992 to 2001 meant that it no longer faced global finance from a position of power, so its choices were fundamentally constrained. Not only did the debates over yen internationalization derive from differing ideas of how Japan should be positioned in the international system, but they necessarily also engaged important domestic values and interests—in particular, with respect to seemingly technical economic questions of financial regulation and means of taxation. Key structural changes within Japan, including the growth of government deficits and the increased autonomy of the Bank of Japan (BOJ), also shaped the payoffs and possibilities available to policy makers. In the end, the political dynamics appeared likely to be as important as economic variables in determining whether this ambitious project could succeed.

Internationalization as Insulation

Discussion of internationalization of the yen dates back to the mid-1970s in Japan, but it was only in the 1980s that the term emerged as a centerpiece of a meaningful policy debate. The dimensions of that debate changed considerably over time, in particular tracking the perception (and self-perception) of Japan first as a rising power in global finance, and then a declining power. In the aftermath of the Asian crisis, despite the relatively modest economic effects on Japan, recognition of declining strength shifted to a heightened perception of vulnerability, and increased the urgency of the debate over yen internationalization.

Starting as early as the late 1970s, it was becoming clear that excess savings in the Japanese economy, reflected in growing trade and current account surpluses, needed to be invested outside the country. However, funds remained subject to development-era rules that obstructed easy movement of capital across Japan's borders. In negotiations such as the 1983 Yen-Dollar talks, and in policy initiatives such as the 1986 estab-

Figure 3.1   **Yen Denomination of Japanese Trade**

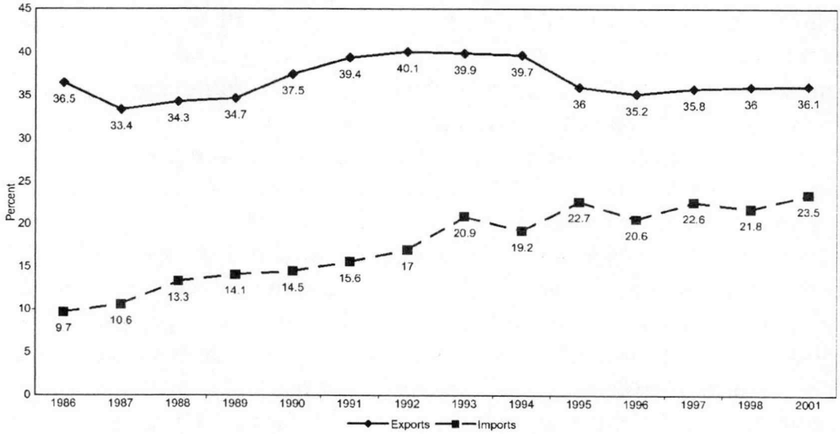

Source: Foreign Exchange Commission 1999, table 1-2(1).
Notes: 1986–91 figures reported annually; 1992–97 figures reported in September;
1998 figures reported in March; and 2001 figures reported in January.

lishment of a Tokyo offshore banking facility, the pent-up pressures for a degree of opening were evident (Rosenbluth 1989).

At that time, the catchphrase "internationalization of the yen" pointed to the apparent desire for a rising Japan to take a larger role in international finance, just as it had already done in world trade. During most of the 1980s, internationalization of the yen was seen to be primarily an issue of internationalization of Japanese finance, rather than increased international use of the yen *per se*. In practice, this meant rapid expansion of the activities of Japanese financial firms (especially banks and securities firms) outside the country, but a much more limited exposure of the domestic financial system to outside influences. The Tokyo offshore market exemplified the latter focus of policy makers, by trying to provide international outlets for regional Japanese banks without opening up international competition in the provision of domestic Japanese banking services. Despite the rapid increase in Japanese financial firms' international activities, however, internationalization of the yen itself advanced only slightly (see Figure 3.1 and Table 3.1). Even the burgeoning euro-yen market (trade in yen-denominated bonds located outside Japan, and thus outside the reach of Japanese regulators) was accessed primarily by Japanese firms as both buyers and sellers—in other words, it was primarily domestic

Table 3.1

Currency Denomination of Japanese Banks' International Loans

End of year	Total ($ billion)		Share (%)	
	Yen	Other	Yen	Other
1985	35.2	134.4	20.8	79.2
1986	57.2	169.1	25.3	74.7
1987	80.4	218.2	26.9	73.1
1988	99.7	275.5	26.6	73.4
1989	108.3	337.3	24.3	75.7
1990	93.8	392.8	19.3	80.7
1991	101.5	399.7	20.3	79.7
1992	93.8	403.9	18.8	81.2
1993	96.5	384.6	20.1	79.9
1994	105.8	386.8	21.5	78.5
1995	131.9	418.6	24.0	76.0
1996	108.1	426.2	20.2	79.8
1997	94.4	398.8	19.1	80.9

Source: Foreign Exchange Commission 1999, table I-5.

Japanese finance conducted in a market with fewer restrictions, rather than an actual increase in the international use of the yen (Oka 1996, chap. 2).

The yen itself came back into focus in the mid-1980s as the Group of Five, and later the Group of Seven (G-7), countries sought to reduce payments problems by altering currency values (Funabashi 1989; Volcker and Gyohten 1992; Gyohten 1986). The rapid rise of the yen after 1985 meant that Japan's massive amounts of surplus capital were all the more massive in foreign currency terms—and soon, Japanese banks and securities firms became dominant in world markets, at least in size. The apparent retreat of the dollar raised both economic and political issues. Economically, would decreased confidence in the dollar increase international use of the yen as a vehicle currency and store of value? And politically, would international use of the yen increase Japan's power in setting and maintaining the world economic system? If the answers to either or both of these questions were "yes," then it was time for Japan—as a rising power—to step up to the plate and seek to move from internationalization of financial institutions, to internationalization of the yen itself.

Whatever the goals of policy makers, however, use of the yen outside of Japan's own borders did not grow as rapidly as had other aspects of Japan's international economic role. Internationalization of the yen did progress in the 1980s, but via channels other than the offshore market, on which yen internationalizers had concentrated so much of their energy. As Table 3.2 suggests, these channels included the rapidly increasing investment and trade activities of Japanese firms in East and Southeast Asia (Oka 1996, pp. 73–74; Kohsaka 1996), in addition to the burgeoning euro-yen markets. In any event, international use of the yen soon leveled off and, in a number of measures, began to decline after the mid-1990s (FEC 1999). Moreover, a survey released in 2000 by an organization of top Japanese executives found little interest among firms in expanding the yen denomination of their international activities (Keizai Dōyūkai 2000).

Meanwhile, the liberalization of Japan's financial markets also proceeded slowly; unlike the internationalization of the yen, however, that progress continued through the 1990s, culminating in the Big Bang of 1998–2001. Even though Japanese finance was substantially "free, fair, and open" by the beginning of the twenty-first century, Japan's international transactions were ironically still primarily conducted in dollars.

The Asian Financial Crisis

The Asian financial crisis that started in 1997 substantially changed the parameters of the debate. In the wake of the crisis, a number of studies sponsored by leaders of the Japanese economic policy establishment asserted that the worst effects of the crisis might have been averted had countries in the Asian region made greater use of the yen in setting their currency values (FEC 1999; IIMA 1999; Nihon keizai chōsakai 1998; Kwan 1997). Most regional currencies, including those of the hardest-hit countries such as Thailand and South Korea, had maintained a high degree of correlation with the U.S. dollar—in other words, they were following a *de facto* nominal dollar peg, despite official lip service to the notion of managing their currencies based on more balanced currency baskets (see Table 3.3). Note that non-Japanese East and Southeast Asian extra-regional trade has been divided approximately evenly among the world's three major currency areas—Europe, North America, and Japan (IMF [various years]). Thus, when the yen depreciated rapidly against the dollar, starting in 1995–96, those countries' currencies experienced an

Table 3.2

Currency Denomination of Japanese Trade (percent)

Exports	To World			To United States			To European Union			To Asia (not China)		
	Yen	U.S.$	Other	Yen	U.S.$	Other	Yen	U.S.$	Other	Yen	U.S.$	Other
Sept. '92	40.1	46.6	13.1	16.6	83.2	0.1	40.3	11.1	48.4	52.3	41.6	5.9
Sept. '93	39.9	48.4	11.7	16.5	83.3	0.2	41.0	7.5	51.5	52.5	44.3	3.2
Sept. '94	39.7	48.3	12.0	19.0	80.8	0.2	36.6	9.0	54.4	49.0	47.9	3.1
Mar. '95	37.6	51.5	10.9	17.5	82.3	0.2	37.2	11.3	51.5	47.2	49.9	2.9
Sept. '95	36.0	52.5	11.5	17.0	82.9	0.1	34.9	12.2	52.9	44.3	53.4	2.3
Mar. '96	35.9	53.1	10.9	15.9	83.9	0.2	36.1	12.5	51.3	44.1	53.5	2.3
Sept. '96	35.2	53.3	11.5	14.5	85.4	0.1	33.3	12.4	54.4	46.3	51.3	2.4
Mar. '97	35.8	52.8	11.3	16.6	83.2	0.2	34.3	13.4	52.3	45.5	51.7	2.7
Sept. '97	35.8	52.1	12.1	15.3	84.5	0.2	34.2	12.3	53.5	47.0	50.2	2.7
Mar. '98	36.0	52.1	12.9	15.7	84.1	0.1	34.9	13.2	51.9	48.4	48.7	2.9
Jan. '01	36.1	52.4	11.5	13.2	86.7	0.1	33.5	13.0	53.5	50.0	48.2	1.8

Imports	From World			From United States			From European Union			From Asia (not China)		
	Yen	U.S.$	Other	Yen	U.S.$	Other	Yen	U.S.$	Other	Yen	U.S.$	Other
Sept. '92	17.0	74.5	8.5	13.8	86.0	0.2	31.7	17.9	50.4	23.8	73.9	2.3
Sept. '93	20.9	72.4	6.7	13.8	86.1	0.1	45.0	18.2	36.8	25.7	72.0	2.3
Sept. '94	19.2	73.9	7.0	13.3	86.4	0.3	38.6	21.9	39.5	23.6	74.2	2.2
Mar. '95	24.3	68.9	6.8	18.4	80.9	0.6	40.6	20.2	39.2	34.1	64.2	1.7
Sept. '95	22.7	70.2	7.1	21.5	78.4	0.2	44.8	16.1	39.2	26.2	71.9	2.0
Mar. '96	20.5	72.2	7.3	17.5	82.7	0.1	40.9	15.3	43.0	23.9	74.1	2.0
Sept. '96	20.6	72.4	6.9	16.4	83.2	0.4	46.1	12.5	41.5	24.0	73.8	2.3
Mar. '97	18.9	74.0	7.1	14.2	85.6	0.2	41.3	17.0	41.7	23.3	74.9	1.7
Sept. '97	22.6	70.8	6.6	22.0	77.8	0.2	49.3	13.1	37.7	25.0	73.0	1.9
Mar. '98	21.8	71.5	6.7	16.9	83.0	0.1	44.3	14.3	41.4	26.7	71.6	1.7
Jan. '01	23.5	70.7	5.8	20.8	78.7	0.5	49.7	17.5	32.8	24.8	74.0	1.2

Source: Study Group for the Promotion of the Internationalization of the Yen 2001, table 3.

Table 3.3

Currency Composition of Official Foreign Reserve Holdings
(percentages of total identified official holdings)

End of year	World		Developed countries		Developing countries	
	Yen	U.S.$	Yen	U.S.$	Yen	U.S.$
1976	2.0	76.5	1.8	87.0	2.2	68.8
1980	4.4	68.6	3.3	77.2	5.4	59.9
1985	7.3	55.3	7.6	50.1	6.8	62.5
1990	8.0	50.6	8.8	45.5	6.4	61.1
1991	8.5	51.1	9.7	43.6	6.6	62.8
1992	7.5	55.1	7.6	48.8	7.5	63.9
1993	7.6	56.4	7.8	50.2	7.4	63.8
1994	7.8	56.4	8.2	50.8	7.5	62.7
1995	6.8	56.8	6.6	51.8	6.9	61.9
1996	6.0	60.1	5.6	56.1	6.5	64.0
1997	5.3	62.1	5.8	57.9	4.9	65.8
1998	5.3	65.7	6.6	66.7	4.3	65.0
1999	5.1	66.2	5.8	68.3	4.5	64.6

Source: Study Group for the Promotion of the Internationalization of the Yen 2001, table 6.

overall appreciation, making their goods more expensive relative to Japanese products, and causing deterioration of their trade and current accounts. Given their high degree of openness to capital flows, the argument went, the economies were sitting ducks when enough international investors decided that those current accounts were unsustainable.

This interpretation is actually not entirely convincing. It ignores the effects of Japan's own economic stagnation (and thus lack of demand for imports from Asia), as well as the fact that relatively high inflation in Thailand and other Southeast Asian economies meant real appreciation against the dollar, even though the nominal value of the local currency did not change. Moreover, Thailand's trade and current account deficits were actually widening during the period of yen appreciation. Thus, it is probably most accurate to describe yen appreciation in 1994–95 as acting only partially to shield Thailand from the real appreciation caused by maintaining a nominal peg at the same time as relatively high domestic inflation. Still, it was a commonly held belief among Japan's top economic policy makers that greater use of the yen in managing regional exchange rates might have prevented the crisis (author's interviews 1999, 2000, 2001).

In any event, if broader use of the yen in Asian exchange rate management was to be seen as an essential pillar of regional stability, then there was a clear rationale for more actual use of the yen in invoicing, in settling accounts, and as a store of value—in other words, internationalization of the yen. In particular, the latter two functions are essential. The primary public use of a foreign currency as a store of value is in foreign exchange reserves management—holding foreign currency assets that can be drawn upon in order to defend the value of the home currency. In practice, these assets are held almost entirely in major currency-denominated short-term government securities in major financial centers. The reason is that currency attacks can happen in a very short time-frame, and it is essential to have highly liquid assets with highly stable values in order to ensure the ability to respond effectively. Thus, an increase in the emphasis on yen in exchange rate management would call for East and Southeast Asian central banks to hold substantial amounts of short-term Japanese government securities.

As for settling accounts, the main question is how easy it is to transfer funds from yen to the home currency. As of 2001, most such foreign exchange transactions in Asia went from yen to dollar, and then from dollar to home currency, rather than directly from yen to home currency. This process naturally meant greater transaction costs (since each trade incurs costs) and lower liquidity, and correspondingly fewer incentives to use yen for safety reserves.

The Japanese argument carried within it a call for broader regional use of the yen, not only for Japan's benefit, but also for the benefit of East and Southeast Asia generally. It argued that internationalization of the yen would contribute at the regional level to insulation from international market threats. Japanese firms' vast regional production networks in East and Southeast Asia presumably raised Japan's interests in regional stability and well-being as well (see Chapter 6; Hatch and Yamamura 1996; Pempel 1997; Ernst 1994).

"Crisis of Global Capitalism" and Fears of Globalization

At least for some observers, the Asian financial crisis was not just an important regional issue, but also what a former Japanese vice-minister of finance for international affairs, Eisuke Sakakibara, called the first major "crisis of global capitalism" (Sakakibara 1998; Shinohara 1999). In this interpretation, it was not the specific circumstances of the affected countries that led to the extraordinary extent of the crisis, but rather the ability of money to move rapidly, in massive quantities and without limits. Given the resources at the disposal of international speculators, as well as their tendency toward herd behavior, virtually no developing country could possibly hold enough reserves to defend its currency from concerted attack—no matter how misinformed or irrational the reason for the attack in the first place.

This analysis implied that international financial rules and institutions should be redesigned to allow for much larger and more rapid rescue efforts for currencies under attack, as well as perhaps some restrictions on the activities of hedge funds and the mobility of capital.[1] But it also created additional impetus for Japan to try to expand use of the yen, both regionally and globally. Among the many risks highlighted in Sakakibara's analysis of global finance were the likelihood of large swings in exchange rates even for major currencies, and the possibility of a return of the "Japan premium."[2] Internationalization of the yen sought to address both these fears.

Greater use of the yen in invoicing and lending could reduce currency risks for Japanese firms that are directly involved in international transactions; if nothing else, it should reduce the costs of hedging against currency fluctuations. Moreover, as long as global product markets are invoiced mostly in dollars, there is a risk to Japanese firms of large price swings; if more products are invoiced at least partly in yen, yen price swings might be less abrupt, and thus may create fewer painful distortions for Japanese participants in world markets. As for a new "Japan premium," here the case was less convincing; but at least some seemed to believe that if Japanese banks had been accessing international financial markets in yen rather than in dollars in 1998, they would not have faced higher interest rates than banks based in other countries—presumably because the BOJ would have been standing by as a lender of last resort in yen.

A final idea that appealed to some Japanese thinkers was that internationalization of the yen could help to stabilize the values of major world currencies (FEC 1999; Nihon Keizai Chōsakai 1998). Some Japanese policy makers believed that U.S. policy makers would have to act more responsibly in terms of currency management and economic policy if there were viable alternatives to the dollar—in other words, if the euro and yen were used as key international currencies. One prominent former Japanese Ministry of Finance (MOF) official suggested that having a more international yen would give Japan more influence at the G-7 table as well (Utsumi 1999).

Policies of Internationalization

Regardless of the rationale for internationalizing one's own currency, actually doing so is by no means a simple proposition. A variety of issues color the question of which currencies are most attractive for international transactions, whether for foreigners or even Japanese economic actors. In an era of globalized finance, one of the most important of these issues is ease of use, which is best addressed through what I describe below as "liberalizing measures." But just as in any other economic decision, actors behave not only based on price (in this case, largely transaction costs), but also other factors such as reputation and size of markets. Perhaps the most effective step in increasing the attractiveness of the yen would be to increase confidence in Japan's economic growth prospects and financial system; this imperative is obviously much more important in its own right than for its effects on internationalization of the yen. More directly, governments can intervene in markets to affect both price and quantity measures, at least for certain types of transactions. These are what I call "active measures."

At issue here is the complementarity or noncomplementarity of liberalizing and active measures. There appears to be an innate tension between a market-oriented approach and an approach based on government intervention. This is particularly true in an era of globalized finance, due to the ubiquitous influence of "market confidence" in maintaining or subverting economic policy and practice.[3] However, given the importance of network effects (the fact that the attractiveness of a currency increases the more widely it is used), and given the large natural constituencies for the U.S. dollar and the euro, it seemed unlikely that effective internationalization of the yen would happen without fairly strenuous efforts on the part of the Japanese government.[4]

Liberalizing Measures

The rationale behind liberalizing measures is that market participants and foreign governments make portfolio decisions based on economic rationality. Therefore, in order to make yen-denominated assets more attractive to non-Japanese investors, it is essential to reduce transaction costs and increase liquidity of investment instruments. Most important, at least for the purposes of encouraging foreign central banks to hold more of their reserves in yen, would be to ensure a broad and liquid short-term government debt market. Additionally, hedging currency risk can be made easier by increasing the availability of default-risk-free (i.e., government) debt over a broad continuum of maturities. Reducing transaction costs and increasing efficiency of settlement for other types of securities trading are also important.

As of 2001, the Japanese government and the BOJ had in fact made meaningful efforts in all these directions. With respect to overall transaction costs and efficiency, not only had the Securities Transaction Tax (formerly levied on all securities trades) been eliminated, but the BOJ and private actors also were working to improve the speed and accuracy of settlements. Moreover, foreigners were—at least in theory—no longer required to pay withholding tax on interest from government securities (FEC 1999; author's interviews 2000, 2001). In 1999, the MOF began to issue bonds across a wider spectrum of maturities, which was important not only in opening up Japan's government debt market (not to mention financing the nation's ballooning public debt), but also in easing the problem of hedging currency risk—the greater the diversity of the available debt instruments, the easier it is to use them as a hedge against fluctuations in the value of the yen.[5] Finally, to allow foreign currency authorities access to default-risk-free, highly liquid securities with which to carry out rapid and effective exchange market interventions, yen internationalization advocates pushed for—and won—a substantial liberalization of the short-term government securities market.

Most of these measures were relevant not only to yen internationalization, but also to domestic politics and policy. Since at least the early 1980s, the most dedicated adherents of financial deregulation in Japan were financiers and bureaucrats who dealt directly with the world of global finance. These were the actors who pushed the Japanese government on the domestic front to accept the proposals of U.S. negotiators in the Yen-Dollar talks of 1983–84, which sought to open the door to easing restrictions on foreign transactions by Japanese financial institutions and domestic market participation by foreign financial institutions. They were also involved in the (largely failed) attempt to set up a world-class offshore market in Tokyo in the mid-1980s (Frankel 1984; Rosenbluth 1989, chap. 3; Oka 1996, chap. 2).

By the early 1990s, consensus had seemingly been reached among elites on the desirability of expanding competition in Japanese finance—at least that was the public face. But key elements of 1993's major financial regulation reform continued to stifle competition (Vogel 1996, chap. 8; Nakakita 1999, chap. 1). Even the 1998–2001 Big Bang, which aimed to make Tokyo a global financial center, retained special privileges for the smallest and weakest financial institutions, especially credit cooperatives. Moreover, the powerful budget and tax bureaus in MOF resolutely opposed eliminating the Securities Transaction Tax and withholding tax on interest income, which would make the Tokyo market more attractive to outsiders. Meanwhile, the ministry's long-term opposition to offering short-term government debt in public auction had the dual effects of lowering government financing costs and making monetary open market operations very difficult.[6] This made the additional liberalizing measures of 1999–2001 even more significant.

Active Measures

In addition to efforts to make the yen more attractive through liberalization, the Japanese government also advanced some more activist policies. The main policies and proposals in this category were expansion of yen-denominated official financing (including the $30 billion New Miyazawa Plan),[7] loan and bond guarantees for new yen-denominated sovereign debt (also including provisions of the New Miyazawa Plan), specific payment arrangements, and the proposed Asian Monetary Fund (AMF) concept. The first three of these plans had the objective of directly increasing use of the yen in Asia, while the AMF potentially involved much broader guarantees of liquidity and a much more ambitious Japanese role in providing regional public goods.[8]

It will probably strike many readers as bizarre that large portions of Japanese official lending were lent in dollars rather than in yen, especially since most aid lending is by convention called "yen loans" (*en shakkan*). This was true even for loans to major Japanese trading partners. Yet Japan's official policy for around a decade had been to provide aid and financing in the currencies preferred by recipient states, although the invoicing was in yen. Many concessional loan recipients preferred dollars, due to their dollar-pegged exchange rates and the ease and attractiveness of dollar-denominated markets. The easy way to decrease political friction was to let the recipients choose their desired denomination.

In a shift of policy, from 1999 onward the Japanese government insisted on denominating most official international lending in yen, including virtually all lending to Asia by the Japan Bank for International Cooperation (JBIC).[9] The rationale was to increase the amount of yen in circulation in Asia. By doing so, officials hoped to create a viable yen-denominated flow of funds in the region, partly through official lending and partly by leveraging JBIC participation in syndicated loans to entice Japanese banks to do more yen-denominated lending.

While the decision to move toward more yen-denominated official lending seemed unsurprising and uncontroversial in almost any terms, the 1999 decision to offer Japanese government guarantees on sovereign yen-denominated bonds and loans moved into somewhat different territory, for two reasons. First, guaranteeing the debt of developing countries is a policy that carries potential economic costs for the donor, and that could put it into a difficult political position in the future if participants in the program start defaulting. Second, it was not decided purely on the basis of whether a state needed new money and could pay it back—or even whether the state was politically important—but rather on the denomination of the bond or loan. Thus, it moved Japanese aid policy explicitly into promotion of yen internationalization as a national priority. A number of prominent Liberal Democratic Party politicians, including the then-ascendant Kōichi Katō, were involved in pushing forward this policy, with the stated intention of contributing to resolution of the aftermath of the crisis; however, the relative tardiness of the policy and its insistence on yen denomination should give us pause in accepting that explanation purely at face value. Interestingly, as of 2001, few countries had taken Japan up on the offer, for fear of being seen as a poor credit risk by investors. However, yen internationalization advocates pointed to a near tripling of samurai bond issues (yen-denominated sovereign debt) from 1999 to 2000, particularly in Southeast Asia, as a hopeful sign of increased attractiveness of yen-denominated assets to governments (SGPIY 2001, p. A-14; author's interviews 2000).

Both the expansion of yen-denominated financing and the establishment of bond and loan guarantees for Asian governments fell largely under the New Miyazawa Plan.[10] The plan was put forward in October 1998 as a means of providing official funding to help countries struggling in the Asian financial crisis to obtain necessary short, medium, and long-term financing. The $30 billion in funds was originally divided in such a way that half would be available for short-term uses (including through the new Asian Currency Crisis Support Facility in the Asian Development Bank), and the other half for medium and long-term financing. As time went by, more funds were moved into medium and long-term activities. The New Miyazawa Plan was very popular within Japan, where it was seen as a positive response to the needs of the region (and perhaps as a lifeline by some Japanese firms that had lost private financing for major investments in the region).

One step further along the continuum toward interventionist economic policy were government efforts to arrange specific deals to encourage use of the yen in regional transactions. There was not much evidence, as of 2001, that such deals were at all important, and they seemed unlikely to be very successful in any event; but, the following instance may serve as an indicator of the general idea.[11] The deal in question centered on an Export-Import Bank (now JBIC) loan to a joint drilling venture between Vietnam's national oil company and a Japanese firm. The yen-denominated loan was to be used for purchase of exploration and drilling equipment; the deal was structured in such a way that oil would be purchased in Japan in yen, which would be used to pay back the loan. Even though yen prices would presumably shadow world dollar-denominated prices, the deal was meant to increase the amount of trade settled in yen at least marginally—and, of course, if there were to be more such deals, they could eventually have a more meaningful effect.

Finally, there was the proposal for an AMF. The idea was unofficially floated by the vice-minister of finance for international affairs, Eisuke Sakakibara, in the fall of 1997 before being shot down by opposition from the United States, China, and the IMF. Nonetheless, it remained a live idea inside the Japanese bureaucracy (author's interviews at MOF 1999, 2000, 2001). The AMF idea gained a new lease on life with the Chiang Mai Initiative, announced in May 2000 by the finance ministers of the Association of Southeast Asian Nations (ASEAN) plus Japan, China, and South Korea. In it, the so-called ASEAN+3 countries agreed to establish swap lines—agreements to lend reserves to each other in the event of currency crisis (Bergsten 2000). While details were still being hammered out as of fall 2001, and the actual amounts were far too small to deal with a real crisis, the initiative was of great symbolic importance for the yen internationalizers.[12]

In essence, the original AMF concept called for a well-funded mini-IMF (one figure commonly cited in 1999 was $100 billion, with Japan fronting at least half) that would be able to respond rapidly to regional currency crises. Japanese policy makers reasoned that the IMF was too slow and too strict to be able to deal with the kinds of liquidity crises seen in Asia in 1997–99, and that a kind of rapid response team was needed in the region (Yoshitomi and Ohno 1999; Sakakibara 1998, chaps. 1 and 5). The same rationale reappeared in the Chiang Mai Initiative. By 2001, however, Japanese policy makers were arguing that any regional fund, including the ASEAN+3 swap lines, would have to cooperate with the IMF by serving a bridging function until a proper IMF plan could be formulated and disbursed. Indeed, Japan's bilateral agreements stipulated that no more than ten percent of ASEAN+3 funds could be released without the approval of the IMF. Nonetheless, observers have suggested that ASEAN+3 may be a prelude to more formal and ambitious institutions (Bergsten 2000; author's interviews at MOF and the Diet 2000, 2001). There also remained support for the idea that the AMF would be the first step in a much more ambitious long-term plan to set up an European Union-style common currency and trading system (Kishimoto 1999, pp. 40–48; author's interviews 2000). In this sense, the policy would be complementary to the kinds of private and public actions described by Solís and Nelson (Chapters 5 and 6), although the varying interests of actors involved made it unlikely that there was an overarching "strategy."

Dilemmas of Insulation

The policies of yen internationalization carried within them a number of potential contradictions and dilemmas, both political and economic. These ironies reflected the specific difficulties that Japan faced in effecting economic reforms to respond to globalization and economic change. As we see in the other chapters of this volume as well, Japan has indeed been changing in important ways, but those changes are mediated by the nation's distinctive institutional and political conditions.

The most central dilemma of the efforts at yen internationalization stemmed from the impulse shared by many of its advocates for insulation. Paradoxically, however, all of the policy measures suggested or actually employed would actually increase Japan's exposure to the whims of global finance. Clearly, all of the liberalizing measures were meant to increase the confidence of international market participants in Japanese financial markets and the yen; but, in order to gain that confidence, Japan would have to make itself vulnerable to the cold-blooded rigor of the market. Even the activist measures potentially increased Japan's exposure to external crises—it is easy to imagine losing substantial amounts of taxpayer money on guaranteeing Asian developing country sovereign debt, or as part of an AMF that tried to support an unsupportable currency. Whether the benefits of insulation and stabilization would indeed appear, and would outweigh the potential costs of increased exposure, remained to be seen.

Internal Dilemmas of Liberalization

As I have pointed out, several important tax reforms were carried out in 1999 to promote internationalization of the yen, including the elimination of the Securities Transaction Tax, the Stock Exchange Tax, and some withholding requirements on government debt. With respect to withholding tax on interest income, two important changes were instituted to make government debt instruments more attractive to foreign investors. First, withholding tax requirements for purchasers of short-term government debt (financing bills [FBs] and treasury bills [TBs]) were eliminated as long as the purchase was registered in the Bank of Japan's "book-entry system." Second, withholding tax was eliminated on all purchases of long-term government debt by nonresidents who participated in the BOJ's book-entry system.

There was less there than met the eye, however, as the BOJ's book-entry system proved to be unwieldy for potential investors. Most foreign bondholders in any market keep their bonds in trust with a "custodian" bank, which in the Japanese case needed to be a member of the BOJ book-entry system in order to qualify for the withholding tax exemption. Often, there is an additional layer of intermediation between the actual owner and the local custodian, in the form of a "global custodian," which is another bank (usually in New York or London) that maintains the owner's worldwide accounts. In order to qualify for the Japanese withholding tax exemption, both the global and the local custodians were legally responsible, subject to penalty and prosecution, for certifying that the actual owner of the bond was a non-resident juridical person. In turn, in order to take advantage of the withholding tax exemption, any bank that wished to act as a custodian needed to be certified by the Japanese tax authorities.

This is where complications arose. In the first two years of the exemption, the National Tax Agency criteria (written by the MOF Tax Bureau) were drawn so tightly that only a small number of banks could actually take advantage of it; moreover, the book-entry system was also seen as unwieldy. As of April 1, 2001, the rules had been considerably eased, and the number of qualified global custodians had risen from one to twenty-four (MOF 2001; author's interviews at MOF and among foreign bankers in the Tokyo markets 2000, 2001).

Beyond the custodian issue, another issue remained. The exemption was explicitly only for nonresident "juridical persons," such as corporations or nonprofit organizations. Thus, mutual funds and many pension funds—which are owned by their account holders and are among the largest potential investors in Japanese government bonds (JGBs)— were barred from the tax exemption. The reason for this restriction was that a Japanese citizen might buy shares of a foreign mutual fund that invested in Japanese government debt and thus evade taxes. There are probably very many situations where a waiver was in principle possible; but, at least as of 2001, applying for the exemption remained a time-consuming case-by-case process. Thus, foreign financial institutions were not quick to shift their portfolios into JGBs. The lack of success in attracting foreign interest in JGBs and other Japanese bonds demonstrated the difficulties of the project of yen internationalization, and particularly of the juxtaposition of permeability and insulation.

While the withholding tax issue may appear technical and esoteric, it was at its core a political dispute over fairness and control. The major objection to relaxing some of the rules to make government debt more attractive to foreigners was that it would degrade tax system fairness. The objection was not only that foreigners would get preferential treatment, but that loosening up the system would also provide opportunities for tax evasion by Japanese nationals. This was stated quite passionately by a number of officials of the Tax Bureau (author's interviews 2000).

More broadly, this debate pointed to the continuing relevance of control as an operating principle in Japanese bureaucratic behavior, and as such is a good example of the impulse toward insulation. In particular, despite the efforts of liberalizers, even within the MOF the

tax bureaucracy remained focused on the mechanism of specific per-
missions in order to control the problem of tax evasion. While preventing tax evasion and money laundering is admittedly a difficult
challenge, at issue here is that in weighing the costs and benefits of
liberalization versus control, the bureaucratic instinct continued to
veer toward control.

Political Economy of Government Debt

Beginning in September 1999, there were also significant changes in
government debt issuance. All short-term government debt was to be
offered in public auction, rather than privately placed with the BOJ,
thus for the first time creating the possibility of a viable market in
short-term default-risk-free debt. Such a market is essential not only
for internationalization of the yen, but also for enabling effective open
market operations by the BOJ (Eijffinger and van Rixtel 1992). This
had important implications for government finance, since the previous system had made it easier and cheaper for the government to issue
debt and had thus been very popular within the MOF, despite the difficulties it caused elsewhere.

In addition, the MOF began issuing debt in a variety of maturities
all the way up to thirty years.[13] One reason for this change was to improve the ability of the MOF Financial Bureau (i.e., treasury) officials
to make better choices concerning the term structure of Japan's massive and rapidly increasing national debt. The yen internationalizers
also lobbied heavily for this change, because having a full spectrum of
default-risk-free government debt would provide a full set of natural
hedges for both foreigners with yen-denominated business and Japanese
with foreign-currency-denominated business. While at least some foreign financial professionals still felt in 2001 that the JGB yield curve
was distorted, these measures were clearly a move in the right direction
(author's interviews and personal communications 2000, 2001).

The massive increases in Japanese public debt during the 1990s (especially from 1998 onward) made it much easier to promote substantial opening-up of the short-term government debt market. The BOJ,
with vastly increased autonomy under the revised BOJ Law that took
effect in April 1998, was increasingly unwilling to purchase 100 percent of central government TBs and FBs at low, uncompetitive interest
rates.[14] Together with the increasing need on the part of the MOF Fi-

nancial Bureau to place short-term debt, the result of the change was slippage in the relative power of the ministry in that issue area. In the face of pressures for yen internationalization, it was perhaps not surprising that this long-term irritant of the financial community and BOJ officials disappeared so abruptly.

The most severe constraint on Japanese policy makers in 2001 was the extremely strained fiscal situation. With Japan suddenly the largest issuer of government debt in the world, it was important that there be purchasers of that debt, but estimates of foreign ownership of JGBs were quite low, particularly for private investors.[15] As Japanese financial institutions continued to diversify their holdings and the government's need for financing continued to grow, there was an increasing urgency for more foreign purchases of JGBs. The result was irony. MOF officials had long focused on placing domestic debt almost entirely domestically, which retarded the internationalization of the yen. By 2001, the very lack of liquidity they had fostered in earlier years threatened to make their jobs harder.

Perhaps most surprising among the liberalizing measures were the tax issues. Neither the abolition of the Securities Transaction Tax nor the new withholding tax exemptions were intended as stimulatory tax cuts. Thus, at a time when tax reduction for stimulatory purposes was a hotly-debated issue, it seemed particularly odd that fiscal conservatives would allow tax reductions that had not even been tabled for that purpose. Moreover, each of the tax law changes had previously been challenged for specific reasons by the tax authorities. The continuing problems concerning the administration of the withholding tax exemption as of 2001 suggested just how politically sticky these issues could be—even an apparent victory by the liberalizers proved to be only partial, and subject to continuing negotiation.

There was not much reason to believe that the withholding tax exemptions would lower tax revenues, since taxation at the source essentially changes only the timing, rather than the amount, of the tax payment. The rationale behind the new system was rather to prevent tax evasion by Japanese nationals—a surprisingly difficult technical task. What was most striking about the exemption for longer-term government debt was that it applied only to foreign firms. In other words, it was a preferential tax measure that favored foreigners and, as such, was probably a first in Japanese financial regulation (with the possible exception of "third-sector" insurance entry, which favored foreigners as a partial *quid pro quo* for keeping them out of the life and liability insurance markets). One can only be impressed that a financial system that had for years been characterized as rigged for the benefit of domestic players took such a step, especially given the weak condition of many domestic firms relative to the foreign firms.

The Tax Debate

The tax reforms were not simply a logical extension of the Big Bang, nor an attempt to repair defects in the original legislation. While such an interpretation may seem logical from an economic standpoint, in reality the reforms were contested. In interviews, even the most cynical observers agreed that the success of the tax reforms was both surprising and significant.

The strength of bureaucratic opposition to changes in withholding taxes is clear from Tax Commission reports for the period 1996–98, which explicitly opposed altering the existing system, despite acknowledging the benefits for internationalization of the yen and strengthening Japan's financial markets.[16] As the FY1999 report put it, "In order to implement appropriate and fair taxation for interest that is issued frequently and in large amounts, it is necessary to have an enforceable system of income determination. Taxation at the source is an efficient and simple mechanism, and it is the basis of Japan's collection of taxes on interest" (Tax Commission 1998).

Various outside observers applauded the changes for their likely effects on the international use of the yen (Nikkan Kōgyō Shimbun 1999, pp. 73–76; author's interviews 1999, 2000). But the political loss for the orthodox tax officials was considerable. It is true that the elimination of tax withholding was strictly limited to actors for whom there already existed alternative measures to prevent tax evasion (i.e., direct participation in the BOJ book-entry system). However, prevention of tax evasion by nonresidents had only been a part of the original objection. Although not stated explicitly, tax officials were also concerned about the possibility of further change. Withholding taxes for nonresident holdings of government debt was an early battleground in eliminating the whole system of tax withholding for financial transactions —once an exception had been made to the overall logic in the system, the system itself would be more permeable and vulnerable to attack (author's interviews 1999).

Contradictions and the Possibility of Coalition Breakdown

Whereas the liberalizers saw these tax measures as a foot in the door, their actual ability to shepherd through further market-opening measures appeared to rest on their ability to maintain cooperation with economic nationalists, for whom liberalization *per se* was not a goal. Political cleavages remained that threatened continued cooperation.

While Tokyo financial market revitalization was undoubtedly a goal for most Japanese policy makers, full liberalization was not necessarily the only possible course to follow. First, the liberalizers, at least in theory, were willing to have a revitalized Tokyo financial market in which the major players would not be Japanese. (Some called this a "Wimbledon system," after the famed English tennis tournament that has not seen English champions in decades.) As long as money were to be moved through Tokyo and profits were to accrue to Japanese workers and shareholders, liberalizers claimed they would be happy and that the goal of yen internationalization would be furthered. Such a world would be anathema to more conservative nationalists.[17] Thus, if further liberalization were seen to benefit foreign firms more than domestic ones, cooperation appeared likely to break down.

Second, the reforms that had already been carried out as of 2001 were the most logically consistent ones, as well as in some ways the easiest. The intellectual argument that foreign central banks would not hold yen unless they had a liquid, default-risk-free market was undeniable, and the connection between that intermediate goal and the reforms already carried out was clear. It may not have been as clear to legislators why revamping the entire securities tax system for the benefit of foreigners was necessary to Japan's national interest. An additional irony of liberalizing measures was that most of the foreigners to benefit would be American and European firms, while virtually everyone agreed that internationalization of the yen primarily meant greater use of the yen within the Asian region. Thus, the liberalizers were likely to be vulnerable to nationalist rhetoric wielded by those who wanted to protect Japanese financial institutions.

Third, further financial-sector tax reforms for the purposes of yen internationalization were likely to be much more costly in terms of lost tax revenue than those already accomplished as of 2001. This would presumably become a more pertinent issue as the former environment of stimulatory tax cuts faded—regardless of whether these tax cuts were ever seen as part of economic stimulation. Not only might the Japanese government (and especially tax officials) be expected to try hard to find new revenues to cover the immense deficits that had developed in the 1990s, but the idea of making financial market players sacrosanct while hitting wage earners or consumers harder would likely be less than politically attractive. For all these reasons, it was not clear whether internationalization of the yen would be sufficient as a battle standard to keep together the loose "coalition" that succeeded in the reforms of 1998–2001.

Dilemmas of Active Measures

The internal ironies of active measures are relatively obvious, inasmuch as they concern the costs of funding insulation versus the actual benefits. More intriguing are the ironies that might arise from the combination of liberalizing and active measures. While it was unlikely that liberalizing measures alone would lead to rapid internationalization of the yen, combining them with activist measures made for potentially serious mutual contradictions, and thus dilemmas for Japanese policy makers.

For one thing, the two types of measures appear to clash philosophically, in a way that mirrors various other dialectics of change in the Japanese political economy in recent years. As discussed by Grimes and Schaede (Chapter 2), the impulse toward controlled liberalization had underlain economic reforms from trade liberalization to financial regulation to competition policy, and in each case the fundamental contradiction had created a painful and involved process of stop-and-go reform that had frustrated both domestic and foreign participants.

A more specific problem was that of market confidence. Liberalizing measures could only be effective in increasing international use of the yen if they inspired the confidence of global financial market participants. Financiers' decisions would affect yen internationalization not only directly, but also indirectly through government reserves policies and funding decisions by importers and exporters. At the same time, however, activist measures created concern among global financial market participants that the Japanese state would be more broadly interventionist in financial markets, and thus would work against internationalization. In particular, the

AMF and micro-deal-making approaches, which were quite popular among nationalist promoters of the internationalization of the yen, were likely to create serious contradictions when placed next to liberalizing measures. For example, in the case of deal-driven internationalization, the fear was that it would invite more extensive intervention—for example, administrative guidance to "persuade" Japanese financial institutions to emphasize yen-denominated transactions against their will—which would make the Japanese financial system more opaque, less efficient, and less attractive to foreigners.

The various levels of emphasis on active versus liberalizing measures to support yen internationalization reflected different visions for the future of the Japanese and regional economies, and appeared to foretell continued tension among policy makers concerned with yen internationalization.

Conclusions: Dilemmas of Permeable Insulation

Fundamentally, promotion of yen internationalization was an effort to stabilize Japan's external environment. The desire for insulation stemmed from an increased sense of vulnerability, which was at least partly due to the decade-long economic stagnation—ironically, a product largely of Japan's own poor policy decisions in the late 1980s and throughout the 1990s (Grimes 2001). But economic stagnation—combined, of course, with financial globalization—itself created constraints on Japan's ability to increase its external stability. In particular, Japan faced fiscal constraints, market confidence constraints, and the constraints of its own slow progress toward financial liberalization.

The motivations for permeable insulation can arise and be expressed in several ways. Generally speaking, permeable insulation can be seen as an attempt at insulation in the face of the constraints of globalization or shifting comparative advantage. In the quest for a more internationalized yen, there was an additional political counter-tendency to preferences for traditional sectoral insulation. That was the desire to revitalize Japan's financial markets by attracting both Japanese and foreign firms away from alternative locations—a goal that required substantial domestic liberalization, and thus a stripping away of insulation from an important sectoral interest. The exclusivity of these goals necessarily generated a political process that interacted with market forces in ways that were likely to undermine the goals of both revitalization and insulation.

The impact of global market forces was much more immediate and often larger in finance than in other fields. Japan's already-extensive financial liberalization at both the domestic and international levels, moreover, meant that any policy actions could potentially be subverted by actors, foreign or Japanese, who found those policies to lower current or future profits. Thus, no matter how much institutional incentives stressed control, the policies of yen internationalization were inherently permeable.

One answer to the dilemma was the attempt to separate incentives for foreigners from those of (potentially tax-evading) domestic investors. This forces us to return to the fact that policies are made in a political process that inevitably leads to compromises—between and within different sectors, and even within MOF. (And while it may be difficult to find many areas in which the restructuring of Japanese ministries from 1998 to 2001 had any practical effects, MOF's loss of its clientelistic Banking and Securities Bureaus in a 1998 spin-off certainly affected the Ministry's stance in finance-related trade-offs.) However, the compromises reached on the liberalizing measures through 2001 had not yet convinced international investors of the attractiveness of either the yen as an international currency, or of Tokyo as an international financial center. While activist measures appeared to be more consistent on their own terms, no one seriously believed that they were in and of themselves sufficient to transform perceptions of the yen. Moreover, the combination of equivocal liberalizing measures with activist measures ran the risk of leading observers and potential investors to believe that the Japanese government still sought insulation based on control.

These dilemmas would perhaps be impossible to resolve. In the end, internationalization of the yen may well be an unachievable goal. Nonetheless, the quest for it appeared likely to be one more potential battleground in the struggle for Japan's political-economic soul.

Notes

1. See the Ministry of Finance (MOF) policy statements on the international financial architecture and internationalization of the yen, available at www.mof.go.jp.

Also, see Sakakibara (1998), Chapter 5. For U.S. views, see Council on Foreign Relations Task Force 1999, Eichengreen 1999, Goldstein 1998.

2. When Japanese banks were looking very weak in 1998, they had to pay a higher rate to borrow in international markets than the banks of other major economies. This "Japan premium" reflected fears of international financial institutions that Japanese banks might be unable to repay their loans.

3. One could argue that the United States, in the immediate postwar period, utilized both liberalizing measures (e.g., maintaining capital-account openness and gold convertibility) and active measures (e.g., massive dollar-denominated aid programs) that supported the role of the dollar, as Kikkawa (1998), Chapter 1, points out. This is undoubtedly true, but is also irrelevant—postwar U.S. policies were not primarily aimed at gaining currency superiority, and in any event there were no other conceivable competitors. Also, globalization of finance fundamentally changes the rules of the game.

4. On network effects and international use of currencies, Cohen (1998) writes, "The larger the size of the money's transactional network—what one analyst calls the 'thickness' of the market—the greater will be the economies of scale to be derived from its use" (p. 13). See also his Chapters 5 and 7. More technically speaking, choice of international currencies is a multiple equilibrium game, as Takeo Hoshi noted in comments on an earlier draft of this chapter. Thus, network effects mean that liberalizing measures alone—which reduce the transaction costs associated with using a given currency—are not sufficient to make rational actors shift from the dominant currency to another one unless many other actors do so as well. What I call activist measures can be seen in this way as a sort of jump-start to increase the size of the transactional network artificially. See also Matsuyama, Kiyotaki, and Matsui (1993).

5. The need for greater diversity is also being addressed by moves to allow STRIPS (i.e., bonds stripped of their final payment of face value, leaving just the payment of coupons through the life of the bonds) and zero-coupon instruments (i.e., bonds stripped of their coupons, leaving only the final payment of face value) based on government bonds.

6. By placing short-term government debt (Financing Bills and Treasury Bills) with the Bank of Japan (BOJ) at below-market interest rates, MOF could lower its direct debt service costs and eliminate the transaction costs involved in issuing them in the financial markets. (Since most BOJ profits are returned to the government in any event, the latter point was more useful as an accounting gimmick than as monetization of government debt. Nonetheless, it did mean less uncertainty, which MOF bureaucrats appreciated.) The more serious effect was that the resulting lack of a deep market in short-term government debt meant that fluctuations in interest rates in that market did not automatically move other rates through the economy, thus making open-market operations by the BOJ much more difficult and less effective.

7. Ironically, the value of New Miyazawa Plan funds, which are supposed to be disbursed entirely in yen, is officially measured in dollars. Presumably, the low status of the yen meant that international announcement effect required a dollar figure. Surprisingly, however, the $30 billion constituted not just a dollar conversion at the time of announcement, but an actual dollar amount for the life of the program—that is, there was no fixed yen amount budgeted for the program, although part of its purpose was to raise the international profile of the yen.

8. A quick overview of these policies can be found in Grimes (2000), pp. 188–90. The MOF web site (www.mof.go.jp) has information on a number of them in both English and Japanese. There are also a number of useful Japanese sources, including Kishimoto (1999).

9. Japan Bank for International Cooperation (JBIC), which was formed in October 1999, combines the former concessional lender known as the Overseas Economic Cooperation Fund with the former Export-Import Bank of Japan. Thus, it is Japan's major official international lender, and covers everything from concessional commodity loans to conventional trade financing, as well as project lending.

10. Details on the plan can be found on the MOF website. See www.mof.go.jp/english/if/kousou.htm for information in English.

11. This is based on an interview with an MOF official who had been involved in the funding for the project, although the agency actually responsible for arranging and structuring it was the (former) Ministry of International Trade and Industry (MITI).

12. As of fall 2001, not all ASEAN+3 members had established agreements. The countries of ASEAN had jointly agreed to $1 billion in mutual support, while Japan had bilateral agreements with Malaysia ($1 billion), Korea ($2 billion), Thailand ($3 billion), the Philippines ($3 billion), and China ($3 billion).

13. Twenty-year bonds were previously the longest-maturity government debt. MOF was hesitant to issue five-year bonds for many years because of the dependence of the three long-term credit banks on their exclusive right to issue five-year debentures. Since two of those banks went under in 1998 and the third merged with two city banks in 1999, this disincentive presumably became less important.

14. The text of the new law can be found on the BOJ home page (www.boj.jp). On the effects of the revisions, see Shiono 2001; Mieno 2000, Chapter 7; and Nakakita 1999, Chapter 2.

15. One internal estimate by the Tokyo branch of a major custodian bank in the summer of 2000 was that perhaps 5 percent of Japanese government bonds (JGBs) were held by foreigners, significantly less than portfolio theory would predict, given the size of Japanese capital markets.

16. The 1997 report actually calls for the strengthening of withholding taxation for residents' holdings of foreign debt (Tax Commission 1996). See also Tax Commission 1997a, section 2.1(3); Tax Commission 1998, Section 2.3(1)b; and Tax Commission 1997b, Section 2.2(2). On the effects of tax reforms on yen internationalization, see Tax Commission, Subcommittee on Finance-Related Taxation 1997, section 4.1(1).

17. Even Kwan (2001), an economist, rejected this as a bad idea, although it is not clear why.

References

Bergsten, C. Fred. 2000. *The New Asian Challenge*. Washington: Institute for International Economics. Available at www.iie.com.

Cohen, Benjamin J. 1998. *The Geography of Money*. Ithaca: Cornell University Press.

Council on Foreign Relations Task Force. 1999. *Safeguarding Prosperity in a Global Financial System: The Future International Financial Architecture*. New York: CFR.

Eichengreen, Barry. 1999. *Toward a New International Financial Architecture*. Washington: Institute for International Economics.

Eijffinger, S., and A. van Rixtel. 1992. "The Japanese Financial System and Monetary Policy: A Descriptive Review." *Japan and the World Economy* 4, no. 4: 291–309.

Ernst, Dieter. 1994. "Mobilizing the Region's Capacities? The East Asian Production Networks of Japanese Electronics Firms." In Eileen Doherty, ed., *Japanese Investment in Asia: International Production Strategies in a Rapidly Changing World*, 29–55. Berkeley: Berkeley Roundtable on the International Economy.

FEC (Foreign Exchange Commission). 1999. *Internationalization of the Yen for the 21st Century: Japan's Response to Changes in Global Economic and Financial Environments* (April 20). Tokyo: FEC.

Frankel, Jeffrey. 1984. *The Yen/Dollar Agreement: Liberalizing Japanese Capital Markets*. Washington: Institute for International Economics.

Funabashi, Yoichi. 1989. *Managing the Dollar: From the Plaza to the Louvre*. Washington: Institute for International Economics.

Ginkō Tsūshinsha. 1976. *En no kokusaika* (Internationalization of the Yen). Tokyo: Ginkō tsūshinsha.

Goldstein, Morris. 1998. *The Asian Financial Crisis: Causes, Cures, and Systemic Implications*. Washington: Institute for International Economics.

Grimes, William W. 2000. "Japan and Globalization: From Opportunity to Constraint." In Samuel Kim, ed., *East Asia and Globalization*, 55–80. Lanham: Rowman and Littlefield.

———. 2001. *Unmaking the Japanese Miracle: Macroeconomic Politics, 1985–2000*. Ithaca: Cornell University Press.

———. 2003. "Internationalization of the Yen and the New Politics of Monetary Insulation." In Jonathan Kirshner, ed., *Monetary Orders: Ambiguous Economics, Ubiquitous Politics*. Ithaca: Cornell University Press (forthcoming).

Gyohten, Toyoo. 1986. "En no kokusaika: Sono nichibei kankei ni ataeru eikyō" (The Internationalization of the Yen: Its Effects on Japan-U.S. Relations). *Finansharu Rebyū*, no. 2: 1–5.

Hatch, Walter, and Kozo Yamamura. 1996. *Asia in Japan's Embrace: Building a Regional Production Alliance*. Cambridge: Cambridge University Press.

Inoguchi, Takashi, and Iwai Tomoaki. 1987. *"Zoku giin" no kenkyū: Jimintō seiken gyūji shuyaku toshite* (Research on "Zoku" Politicians: The Lead Actors Dominating LDP Government). Tokyo: Nihon keizai shimbunsha.

Inoki Takenori. 2000. "Ōshū no shiren, Ajia no kibō" (Lessons from Europe, Hopes" for Asia). *Chūō Kōron*, no. 1339: 34–37.

IIMA (Institute for International Monetary Affairs). 1999. *Internationalization of the Yen: Implications for Stabilization of Financial Systems and Currencies in Asia* (March). Tokyo: IIMA.

IMF (International Monetary Fund). Various years. *Direction of Trade Statistics*.

Keizai Dōyūkai. 2000. *A Private-Sector Perspective on the Internationalization of the Yen: A Study on Japanese and Asian Stability and Growth*. Tokyo: Keizai Dōyūkai.

Kikkawa, Mototada. 1998. *Manē haisen* (Defeat in the Money Wars). Tokyo: Bunshun shinsho.

Kishimoto, Shūhei. 1999. "Shin Miyazawa kōsō no shimei to Ajia tsūka kikin" (The Mission of the New Miyazawa Plan and the Asian Monetary Fund). *Fainansu* (May): 31–48.

Kohsaka, Akira. 1996. "Interdependence through Capital Flows in Pacific Asia and the Role of Japan." In Takatoshi Ito and Anne Krueger, eds., *Financial Deregulation and Integration in East Asia*, 107–46. Chicago: University of Chicago Press.

Kwan, C.H. 1997. "Ajia no tsūka kiki, sono taishitsu to kyōkun" (The Asian Financial Crisis, Its Characteristics and Lessons). *Sekai*, no. 640: 35–38.

———. 2001. *Yen Bloc: Toward Economic Integration in Asia*. Washington: Brookings Institution.

Liberal Democratic Party Subcommittee on the Internationalization of the Yen. 1998. *"En no kokusaika" ni muketa gutai sochi ni tsuite* (Concrete Measures Toward the Internationalization of the Yen). Mimeo (downloaded June 28, 1999). Available at www.jimin.or.jp/jimin/saishin/seisaku-18.html.

Matsuyama, Kiminori, Nobuhiro Kiyotaki, and Akihiko Matsui. 1993. "Toward a Theory of International Currency." *Review of Economic Studies* 60, no. 2: 283–307.

Mieno, Yasushi. 2000. *Ri o mite, gi o omou* (Pursuing Gain, Remembering Duty). Tokyo: Chūo kōronsha.

MOF (Ministry of Finance). 2001. "Withholding Tax Exemption Scheme for Interest on Japanese Government Bonds (JGBs) Held by Nonresident Investors." Tokyo: MOF. Available at www.mof.go.jp/english/bonds/e1b076.htm.

Nakakita, Tōru. 1999. Nihon ginkō: Shijōka jidai no sentaku (Bank of Japan: Choices in the Era of Marketization). Tokyo: PHP shinsho.

Nihon Keizai Chōsakai. 1998. *Ajia no keizai-tsūka kiki to Nihon no yakuwari* (Asia's Economic and Financial Crisis, and Japan's Role) (March). Tokyo: Nihon keizai chōsakai gikai.

Ohno, Kenichi. 1999. "Exchange Rate Management in Developing Asia." *ADB Institute Working Paper* 1. Tokyo: Asian Development Bank Institute.

Oka, Masao. 1996. *En ga kijiku tsūka ni naru hi* (When the Yen Will Become a Key Currency). Tokyo: Kadokawa shoten.

Pempel, T.J. 1997. "Transpacific Torii: Japan and the Emerging Asian Regionalism." In Peter Katzenstein and Takashi Shiraishi, eds., *Network Power: Japan and Asia*, 47–82. Ithaca: Cornell University Press.

Rosenbluth, Frances McCall. 1989. *Financial Politics in Contemporary Japan*. Ithaca: Cornell University Press.

Sakakibara, Eisuke. 1998. *Kokusai kin'yū no genba: Shihonshugi no kiki o koete* (The Arena of International Finance: Moving Beyond the Crisis of Capitalism). Tokyo: PHP shinsho.

Shinohara, Hajime. 1999. "The End of Globalism." *Institute for International Monetary Affairs Newsletter*, no. 8: 9–16.

Shiono, Hiroshi. 2001. *Nihon ginkō no hōteki seikaku* (The Legal Character of the Bank of Japan). Tokyo: Kōbundo.

SGPIY (Study Group for the Promotion of the Internationalization of the Yen). 2000. *Interim Summarization* (June 30). Tokyo: SGPIY.

———. 2001. *Report* (June 27). Tokyo: SGPIY.

Tax Commission. 1996. "Heisei 9 nendo no zeisei kaisei ni kansuru tōshin" (Report on FY1997 Tax Code Revision) (December). Tokyo: Tax Commission. Available at www.kantei.go.jp/jp/zeicho-up/1227tousin.html (accessed February 21, 2000).

———. 1997a. "Korekara no zeisei o kangaeru: Keizai shakai no kōzō henka ni nozonde" (Thinking About the Future Tax System: Confronting Economic and

Social Changes) (January 24). Tokyo: Tax Commission. Available at www.sori-fu.go.jp/council/naisei/think/index.html (accessed February 21, 2000).

————. 1997b. "Heisei 10 nendo no zeisei kaisei ni kansuru tōshin" (Report on FY1998 Tax Code Revision) (December 16). Tokyo: Tax Commission. Available at www.mof.go.jp/singikai/zeicho/tosin/zeicho1.htm (accessed February 21, 2000).

————. 1998. "Heisei 11 nendo no zeisei kaisei ni kansuru tōshin" (Report on FY1999 Tax Code Revision) (December). Tokyo: Tax Commission. Available at www.mof.go.jp/singikai/zeicho/tosin/zeichoc1.htm (accessed February 21, 2000).

Tax Commission, Subcommittee on Finance-Related Taxation. 1997. "Chūkan hōkoku" (Interim Report) (December). Tokyo: Tax Commission. Available at www.mof.go.jp/singikai/zeicho/top.htm (accessed February 21, 2000).

Utsumi, Makoto. 1999. "Yūro ga Nihon keizai to en ni ataeru eikyō" (The Effect of the Euro on the Japanese Economy and the Yen). In Makoto Utsumi, ed., *Yūro to Nihon keizai* (The Euro and the Japanese Economy), 3–12. Tokyo: Tōyō keizai.

Vogel, Steven. 1996. *Freer Markets, More Rules: Regulatory Reform in Advanced Industrial Countries*. Ithaca: Cornell University Press.

Volcker, Paul, and Toyoo Gyohten. 1992. *Changing Fortunes: The World's Money and the Threat to American Leadership*. New York: Times Books.

Yoshitomi, Masaru, and Kenichi Ohno. 1999. "Capital-Account Crisis and Credit Contraction." *ADB Institute Working Paper* 2. Tokyo: Asian Development Bank Institute.

—————— 4 ——————

Sword and Shield

The WTO Dispute Settlement System and Japan

Saadia M. Pekkanen

At its inception in 1995, few predicted that the World Trade Organization (WTO) would be as widely used by its members as it is today. Between 1995 and 2001, the WTO presided over more complaints than its predecessor, the General Agreement on Tariffs and Trade (GATT), had over a forty-year period.[1] Observing this trend at the close of the 1990s, many scholars—supporters and skeptics alike—agreed that ruled-based dispute settlement had moved to the center stage of international economic diplomacy, and that there were significant economic, political, and legal advantages to this progressive "judicialization" from the perspective of national governments (Jackson 1998a, pp. 175, 178–79; Petersmann 1998 [1997], pp. 84–87).

Like most other countries after 1995, Japan moved increasingly toward the use of the legal rules of the WTO as a means to resolve contentious trade conflicts and concerns. To a great extent, this trend went unobserved. In part, this was because Japan's newfound legal activism looked meager in comparison to that of the United States and the European Union (EU), both of which continued to account for the lion's share of WTO dispute settlement invocations. But in larger part, this was also because of the continued media and scholarly attention on the stagnation of the Japanese economy, and widespread perceptions of "little to no change" in the way it conducted its foreign trade diplomacy.

Yet an important change was taking place in Japan's trade diplomacy, in that it was increasingly being conducted on the basis of international law. This chapter discusses Japanese legal activism with respect to the WTO dispute settlement processes, and shows how and in what ways it speaks directly to the conceptual emphasis on permeable insulation. While this strategy was still emerging at the start of the twenty-first century, what Japan was doing even in the early stages after the birth of the WTO, and more importantly the way it was doing it, constituted an extremely important break from Japan's past trade diplomacy. Leaving aside facile concerns with "wins and losses" in this new legalized forum, which every so often galvanize interest in the subject, the more important long-term policy implications have to do with the formation at long last of a distinct Japanese strategy in trade relations. At many levels this strategy, which is based on the use of the existing legal rules overseen by the WTO, has already begun to have repercussions for Japan's external trade relations, and the international trading system as a whole (Pekkanen 2001a).[2]

To spell out this unfolding story in more detail, this chapter is organized as follows. The first part discusses the key institutional and legal innovations in the dispute settlement processes of the WTO. By relying on a survey that I conducted between 1997 and 1999, I then provide evidence on the extent to which these legal-institutional changes have potentially affected the Japanese government's willingness to engage in the new legalized system. The second part focuses more directly on the dispute system activities of the Japanese government at the WTO. Rather than focusing on the "who" or the "why" of the strategy, my goal is to highlight Japan's legal tactics within the WTO, and in this way to provide direct evidence for the relevance of permeable insulation in the area of foreign trade. As a concept, permeable insulation stresses both changes and continuities in Japan's policy measures that are designed to stave off change, or to make its pace more manageable in a post-developmental context. The argument here, in brief, is that Japan has embarked on a strategy of using the WTO rules as both a "shield" for controversial domestic policies and measures, and as a "sword" with which to challenge its trade partners. This policy flexibility, based on the external legal rules of the WTO, allows the Japanese government to continue protecting some sectors from the rigors of market competition, while at the same time attempting to promote the interests of other sectors abroad. Thus, the novel element in this story concerns the efforts of the Japanese government to make WTO law the centerpiece of its foreign-trade diplomacy. In order to show this more concretely, the focus here will be on tracing and highlighting the key legal provisions invoked by Japan and other parties, and then relating them to specific outcomes. The third part draws conclusions and discusses some policy implications.

Changes in the GATT/WTO Dispute Settlement System

The creation of the WTO led to significant legal and institutional innovations that allowed the dispute settlement system to gain both credibility and legitimacy in the global trading system. The innovations that began with the 1989 Montreal Rules, and which became formalized in 1994 with the "Understanding on Rules and Procedures Governing the Settlement of Disputes" in the WTO Agreements, showed a marked concern of all members with improving the legal processes for handling trade conflicts. Overall, this is reflected in the general provisions of the Dispute Settlement Understanding (DSU), which state that the WTO dispute settlement system, overseen administratively by the Dispute Settlement Body (DSB), is the central element in providing security and predictability to the multilateral trading system (DSU 3.2).[3] The DSB has the authority to establish panels, adopt panel and appellate body reports, maintain surveillance of the implementation of rulings, and authorize suspension of concessions (DSU 2).

Because these changes speak directly to the willingness of all governments, not just that of Japan, to approach the WTO dispute settlement system, it is important to understand the actual nature of the changes, and how the new system differs from the old. In discussing the legal-institutional innovations, I will also highlight the extent to which they have had an impact on the Japanese government's willingness to use the new dispute settlement system. This analysis relies on a survey that I conducted between 1997 and 1999, which coded responses from 119 Japanese government officials concerning the importance of the legal-institutional innovations in the WTO. This, then, gives us a good sense of whether the changes deemed to be important by many observers are, in fact, important in the minds of the actual trade policy-making elite in Japan.

As in the GATT, WTO members today continue to affirm their adherence to the main principles for the management of disputes under

GATT Articles 22 (Consultation) and 23 (Nullification or Impairment), and the rules and procedures further elaborated and modified in the DSU itself (DSU 3.1).[4] Like GATT Articles 22 and 23, article 4.5 of the DSU emphasizes the importance of consultations, especially in attempting to obtain "satisfactory adjustment" of the matter before resorting to further actions under the DSU. In that respect, the basic contours and goals of dispute settlement processes, which emphasize resolution and consistency with the underlying rules, have not changed from the GATT to the WTO (Jackson 1995, p. 17).[5]

In general though, the WTO is an impressive achievement that goes well beyond its predecessor, the GATT. As a product of eight years of diplomatic negotiations by well over 120 countries, its establishment is rightly considered one of the most important events in recent global economic history. Its scope and legal architecture are also greatly improved. Today, the bulk of the WTO charter contains four annexes that comprise almost all the substantive and procedural rules.[6] The first annex covers trade in goods, services, and intellectual property. Trade in product goods is governed by GATT 1994 (an updated version of the original GATT 1947) and twelve appended agreements regarding specific sectors such as agriculture, textiles, antidumping, and sanitary and phytosanitary measures. Trade in services, a new area of coverage, is now overseen by the General Agreement on Trade in Services (GATS). Finally, another new area concerns intellectual property, in which trade is governed by the Agreement on Trade-Related Aspects of Intellectual Property Rights (TRIPs). The second annex contains the dispute settlement rules; the third annex focuses on oversight and review mechanisms for members' trade policies; and, finally, the fourth annex has some multilateral agreements of interest to only a few member states (WTO Agreement; Jackson 1998b, pp. 1–11, 36–100).

Apart from these general improvements, there are also more specific legal-institutional innovations in the WTO that mark a significant departure from the old system, namely "coverage" and "automaticity" (Jackson 1998a, pp. 161–80; Schott 1994, pp. 125–32). First, the dispute settlement provisions apply to all the "covered agreements" identified in Appendix 1 to the DSU. Practically, this means that there is a unified dispute settlement system for all parts of the WTO system, including trade in goods, services, and intellectual property, as well as the other more specific agreements described above.[7] This uniform coverage across all agreements is important because, unlike the old GATT system, there can no longer be drawn-out controversies over which procedures to use in a dispute. In cases where the disputes go across several agreements, the chair of the DSB can also step in to determine the relevant rules and procedures (DSU 1.2). In my survey, I found that "coverage" was indeed an important consideration among Japanese trade officials: 44 percent of the respondents mentioned or talked about the expanded DSU coverage as promoting more favorable perceptions of the WTO, as a whole.

Second, there is an element of "automaticity" to the dispute resolution system, which is reflected in both the time-bound and negative consensus properties evident in the procedural rules of the DSU. The time-bound property, which refers to prespecified time limits for each stage of a trade dispute, is an important innovation. From consultations to panel establishment and onto report adoption, each stage of a trade dispute is under strict time guidelines unless the parties agree otherwise. Thus, in contrast to the past, panels are usually convened within a few weeks of the original request, and parties to the dispute have to make the specifics of the dispute, the terms of reference, absolutely clear from the start (DSU 4.3, 4.7, 6.1, 2.4, 7, 8.5). Even more important, panel procedures cannot be dragged on interminably in the new system and panels, unless they are suspended, are also required to make their rulings within pre-specified time limits (DSU 12.8, 12.9, 12.12, appendix 3). Finally, panel reports are adopted automatically by the DSB within sixty days after the date of circulation, unless there is an appeal. If appealed, the case moves to the Appellate Body. The appellate review is also time-bound, and once it is completed the resulting report is to be adopted by the DSB within thirty days following its circulation to the members (DSU 17.5, 16.4, 17.14).

Overall, then, unless the members of a dispute agree otherwise, the rules automatically preset the entire period of a dispute, from the date of establishment of a panel to the adoption of the reports, generally to nine months if there is no appeal, and to twelve months if there is one (DSU 20). In all, parties to a dispute can be certain that a ruling will emerge in an orderly fashion within a one-year period, in most cases. This emphasis on speed is decidedly better than having the dispute drag on interminably with no end in sight, which was often the case in trade disputes involving the United States, Japan, and the EU under the old GATT.

To what extent, though, does the time-bound feature affect Japanese calculations? In my 1997–99 survey, only 37 percent of the respondents touched upon the importance of the time-bound feature. Those who did so, however, stressed how important it was from a diplomatic and practical viewpoint to bring trade disputes to closure within a foreseeable time frame. In particular, the officials emphasized that disputes with the United States would come to a more conclusive end within a set period of time, and that this would be a marked improvement over the historical tendency for U.S.-Japan disputes to continue interminably.

Automaticity is also underpinned by a twist in the emphasis on consensus that has underpinned the functioning of both the GATT and, now, the WTO (WTO Agreement 9, 9.1; DSU 2.4). Historically, this refers to the practice of decision making by consensus, where a formal vote of "one-member one-vote" is necessitated only in the event that a decision cannot be arrived at by consensus. The twist in the WTO is the emphasis on a negative or reverse consensus—that is, a consensus against doing something—or, put simply, requiring a consensus not to carry out an action (DSU 6.1, 16.4, 17.14). For example, instead of requiring a consensus to adopt a report within the DSB, there now must be a consensus not to adopt the report. Because it is highly unlikely that the winner of a dispute would agree to such a consensus, there cannot be a negative consensus. The practical result is that the DSB adopts reports automatically, because "consensus" means the entire DSB, including the parties to a dispute. And presumably, a complainant party would not agree to blocking the adoption of a report favorable to its interests. In a sense, this affords some protection to weaker parties against stronger ones who, in the past, tended to block the adoption of reports that affected them adversely. Thus, in contrast to the old GATT, neither the establishment of panels nor the adoption of reports can be blocked unless there is a negative consensus (DSU 6.1, 16.4, 17.14). The same negative consensus also applies in two other crucial instances, namely DSB surveillance regarding implementation of recommendations or rulings, and DSB authorization of the suspension of concessions (Jackson 1998b, p. 76; DSU 21.6, 22.6).

Again, one wonders what the true relevance of this innovation is in the minds of Japanese policy makers. In my survey, respondents highlighted this as the most important feature. About 54 percent of the respondents stressed the importance of the negative consensus, either directly or indirectly, in terms of facilitating the establishment of disputes and the adoption of reports without blockage by discontented parties, especially powerful ones like the United States or the EU. Again, Japanese government officials talked far more about this in the context of Japan's relations with the United States than with any of its other trading partners.

Japan's Use of the Dispute Settlement System

The 1997–99 survey conveyed a good sense of the importance that Japanese trade officials attach to the WTO's legal-institutional innovations. But this is not the only measure for understanding the centrality of the WTO to Japan's trade diplomacy as a whole. To appreciate even further the substantive significance of Japan's present use of the WTO dispute settlement processes described above, a comparison with Japan's previous GATT diplomacy is critical. Only then do the differences between Japan's pre- and post-WTO legal diplomacy stand out most starkly. From its accession to the GATT in 1955 until around the end of the Uruguay Round in 1994, Japan studiously avoided using the GATT machinery to resolve its trade problems. In the thirty-odd years in which the old dispute mechanism was in effect, a total of twenty-three complaints were recorded against Japan. Japan, however, registered a mere five complaints in return across the same period of time. To increase and encourage Japan's participation in the GATT system, the GATT leadership even launched a major trade round in Tokyo in 1973, but to no avail (Hudec 1993, pp. 12–15, 21–22, 212, 256).

Whether as complainant or defendant, Japan avoided legal embroilment in the GATT dispute settlement processes, preferring instead to reach bilateral settlements with its trade partners behind the scenes in a nonconfrontational manner (Komatsu 1992, pp. 35–37). To some extent, this reluctance can be attributed to the fact that Japan wished to avoid drawing attention to the many protectionist trade measures and policies then in force, so it had little incentive to throw stones from its glass house. But this disaffection can also be attributed to a perception within Japan that the GATT was biased against Japan, and that it would not render fair rulings in the country's favor. Contributing even further to this perception was the fact that fourteen countries invoked Article 35 (Nonapplication of the Agreement between Particular Contracting Parties) at the time of Japan's accession, largely because of the possibility of aggressive exports in traditional sectors like textiles. This allowed the fourteen countries to suspend the application of the agreement with Japan, meaning that the GATT's legal provisions had no force with respect to Japan (GATT BISD 2d suppl. 1956, pp. 7–10; GATT GA 1961/62, pp. 31–32; GATT BISD 10th suppl. 1962, pp. 69–74).

Two GATT cases involving Japan changed these perceptions and attitudes. Both took place while the Uruguay Round was still underway, and both constituted distinct firsts for Japan. In one of these, Japan obtained a favorable legal ruling in the GATT for the first time ever. In 1987 Canada had complained that its spruce-pine-fir (SPF) "dimension lumber" exports to Japan were being discriminated against with an eight percent tariff, whereas exports of "like" coniferous lumber from other countries, such as the United States, were entering Japan duty-free. Canada charged that this constituted a violation of Article 1.1, the general "most-favored-nation" rule that forms the cornerstone of the GATT. Essentially, this rule says that any treatment accorded to one member has to be automatically extended to another member. After extensive deliberations, the panel dismissed the Canadian charges, essentially agreeing with Japan that the category of "dimension lumber" was not universally recognized and, more importantly, was extraneous to the Japanese tariff classification (GATT GA 1988, pp. 79–80; GATT BISD 36th suppl. 1988–89, pp. 167–99). The report of the panel was adopted on July 19, 1989, and it triggered a sea change in perceptions, especially within the then Ministry of International Trade and Industry (MITI), about both the fairness and utility of the GATT rules in advancing Japanese positions.[8]

Yet it took another GATT case, one in which Japan itself invoked dispute settlement proceedings for the first time, to crystallize these views. In that case, Japan successfully challenged a regulation of the European Community (EC), forerunner of the EU, on antidumping or "anti-circumvention." The regulation was aimed at companies that had circumvented antidumping duties by assembling products in the United Kingdom and France using low-priced parts imported from Japan. The targets of regulation were five Japan-related companies operating in the EC, and the products at issue included electronic typewriters, electronic weighing scales, hydraulic excavators, plain paper photocopiers, and ball bearings. Further investigations were also opened concerning dot matrix printers and video cassette recorders. Japan charged that the imposed "antidumping duties" were merely protectionist levies designed to force the companies to use EC parts. As such, they were inconsistent with GATT provisions on antidumping duties. In 1990, the panel found the EC regulation to be specifically in violation of GATT's national treatment obligations, and ruled also that the EC measure could not be justified under the existing exceptions allowed under the GATT. Although the EC forestalled compliance because the Antidumping Agreement was then under discussion at the Uruguay Round, the panel ruling as well as the adoption of the report in May 1990 constituted distinct legal victories for Japan (GATT GA 1988, pp. 68–70; GATT GA 1990, pp. 55–57; GATT BISD 37th suppl. 1990, pp. 132–99).

Altogether, these GATT rulings reinforced emerging domestic opinions and perceptions in favor of the use of international legal rules to handle trade disputes. In no small part, the more formal legal changes from the GATT to the WTO in 1995 also had a strong effect on the Japanese government's desire no longer to succumb to bilateral and results-oriented pressures of the U.S. government, as it had done for most of the postwar period.[9] The concern with how best to handle trade problems in the post–cold war era was widely shared across the Japanese foreign trade policy establishment, and efforts to institutionalize a strategy of cooperation based on legal rules began to take shape at different levels. The efforts were concentrated primarily in MITI (now the Ministry of Economy, Trade, and Industry [METI]), and the Ministry of Foreign Affairs (MOFA). Both of these ministries have proven to be increasingly adept at legitimating their claims and staking out their positions based on the rules of the WTO. In the process, they have also shown how the legal rules of the WTO can serve as both a shield for controversial Japanese measures, and as a sword against contentious foreign ones.

Thus, from 1990 onward, the Japanese delegation began to focus more closely on the dispute settlement setup then under construction at the Uruguay Round. This represented a rigorous effort to formalize the 1989 "Montreal Rules," the predecessor to the present WTO DSU that ran on a trial basis from the beginning of May 1989 to the end of the Uruguay Round in 1994 (Palmeter and Mavroidis 1999, pp. 10–11). The Montreal Rules could be invoked with respect to GATT Articles 22 and 23 on dispute resolution, which are respectively concerned with a flexible form of consultation leading to some resolution and a more legalistic emphasis on nullification or impairment of benefits (Petersmann 1999, pp. 30–33, 59–64). Using these rules as a basis, the goal for Japan, as for the other countries, was to help devise procedural and substantive rules for the WTO framework that allowed flexibility, but were also binding on the disputing parties.

Japan's interest in the dispute resolution procedures stemmed from its concern with handling trade problems with the United States in the post-cold war era. In fact, this concern was foremost in the minds of Japanese government officials, especially since Japan and the United States had been embroiled successively in high-profile and contentious trade disputes over most of the postwar era.[10] From Japan's point of view, the purpose of the new dispute settlement processes was to ensure freedom from arbitrary unilateral U.S. measures like Section 301, a piece of legislation in the U.S. Trade and Tariff Act of 1974 that was updated in 1988. Section 301 came to represent "aggressive unilateralism" on the part of the United States, because it allowed the U.S. government to assess and, if necessary, retaliate against foreign restrictions on U.S. trade (Bhagwati 1990, pp. 1–45). According to a widespread view in the Japanese foreign trade policy establishment, Section 301 had allowed the United States to be both judge and jury in trade disputes with Japan in the 1980s, and the measure had to be countered forcefully.[11] The legitimate way to counter it would be through the rules of the WTO.

By 1995, the Japanese trade policy establishment was fully geared up to use the WTO rules as a functional strategy, not just against the United States, but more generally against Japan's trade partners. In retrospect, what emerged was a distinct rule-based, and thereby entirely legitimate, strategy that allowed Japan to use the legal rules both as a sword with which to challenge the measures and practices of its trade partners, and as a shield for domestic measures and practices—or, in other words, a "permeable insulation" strategy. In keeping with its past, the Japanese government maintained the tradition of protecting its own industries even as, in keeping with future trends, it worked through an external legal framework that constrained its own actions. These changes are best exemplified in two sectors, automobiles and consumer photographic film and paper, which potentially set the benchmark for Japan's actions in similar or other future cases. The automobile cases against the United States, Brazil, Indonesia, and Canada show how the Japanese government has taken up the banner of liberalization abroad on behalf of its industries using the rules of the WTO—the "sword" aspect at work. The consumer photographic film and paper case exemplifies the way in which the rules of the WTO can be used to block changes in controversial domestic measures—the "shield" aspect at play. Both of these cases are discussed below with a focus on the interplay of the legal arguments.[12]

Automobiles

The sword aspect of the strategy comes across most visibly in the automobiles sector, one of the most important and most globalized manufacturing industries in Japan. While automobiles have comprised the major source of trade tensions between the United States and Japan, Japan has not concentrated its legal firepower on the United States alone. Between the 1995 formation of the WTO and 2001, Japan filed four distinct complaints against a range of trade partners in this particular sector: the United States, Brazil, Indonesia, and Canada. Each of these complaints shows how, and in what ways, Japan has relied on the rules of the WTO to confront its trade partners.

United States

The story here begins in 1995, with the United States. After a great deal of frustration with market access issues in Japan, the United States Trade Representative (USTR) launched a highly politicized effort to force open the Japanese market by announcing the imposition of 100 percent retaliatory tariffs on Japanese luxury cars in May 1995.[13] Unlike the past, where Japan generally came to bilateral agreements directly with the United States, this time it was willing to go the legal route in the WTO, both in rhetoric and in action. The Japanese side began with protests from high-ranking officials at MITI about the appropriateness of such U.S. measures and the impact they could have on the newly constituted WTO system.[14] By the end of the month of May 1995, Japan had also moved to file its first complaint at the WTO, protesting the U.S. imposition of import duties on automobiles (WTO WT/DS6).

Japan invoked a range of legal provisions in the GATT, charging violation in each. Specifically, it claimed violation of GATT Article 1, the "general most-favored-nation" treatment clause, a cornerstone of the WTO system as a whole. Next, Japan claimed a breach of Article 2, the "Schedule of Concessions" annexed to the WTO Agreement, which lays out the basic tariff policies agreed upon by all members.

Moreover, Japan accused the United States of contravening Article 11, the elimination of quantitative restrictions, with the argument that the U.S Trade Representative (USTR) actions did not qualify under any of the exceptions laid out for such restrictions. And finally, Japan also invoked Article 13, nondiscrimination in the administration of quantitative restrictions, claiming that the arbitrary U.S. action singled out Japan in direct violation of WTO provisions.

Within a period of two months after the case was filed, Japan and the United States came to an agreement largely favorable to the Japanese side. In the auto agreement that resulted, Japan did not allow any quantitative measures and used the existing legal rules to legitimate its obduracy on that point (ACCJ 1997, p. 101; Lincoln 1999, appendix B). Satisfied with the terms, Japan then informed the WTO on July 19, 1995 that it would no longer pursue the matter under the dispute settlement procedures. Although no panel was established in this particular case and no legal ruling emerged, the case set an important precedent for the way Japan would deal with its most important trading partner, as well as others, particularly in, but not necessarily restricted to, the automobile sector. It was also an important first indicator of how the WTO rules could be effectively wielded as a sword against even the most powerful trading countries.

Brazil

But the Japanese sword was not just wielded against the mighty. The next country to feel Japan's intent to invoke legal rules on behalf of the Japanese automobile industry was Brazil, a less developed country. On July 30, 1996, the Japanese government filed a formal complaint against the government of Brazil regarding some of its automotive investment measures (WTO WT/DS51). At the heart of this dispute was Japan's contention that Brazil was violating numerous WTO rules through an automobile quota that raised duties from 32 percent to 70 percent for manufacturers that did not operate within Brazil.[15] By initiating this complaint, Japan also set in motion similar actions by other developed countries, with the United States weighing in on the same legal issues in August 1996, and further extending them in January 1997 (WTO WT/DS52; WTO WT/DS65). The EU also followed suit with a related complaint in May 1997 (WTO WT/DS81/1).

Japan's specific case involved the Agreement on Trade-Related Investment Measures (TRIMs), one of the twelve agreements attached to GATT 1994. The focus of the dispute was on the trade-restrictive and distorting effects caused by the Brazilian government's investment measures that essentially gave domestic producers tariff breaks.[16] Specifically, Japan alleged violation of Article 2 in the TRIMs, which restricts members from pursuing any measure inconsistent with the rules on national treatment (Article 3) and quantitative prohibitions (Article 11) of the GATT. Along with the most-favored-nation clause, Japan also invoked the same provisions in the GATT directly, charging violation of each. Finally, it also alleged infringement of clauses in the Agreement on Subsidies and Countervailing Measures (SCM), another of the twelve agreements on preferential support and treatment within the territory of a member. Here, Japan targeted two clauses, Article 3 (general prohibition on the use of subsidies) and Article 27:4 (request to developing countries to phase out gradually such subsidies over an eight-year period from the time the WTO Agreement entered into force). Even as it was making this straightforward case for harm, or technically "nullification and impairment of benefits," Japan also alleged a nonviolation claim under GATT Article 23:1(b), which allows a member to assert that its benefits are being harmed by measures that do not, on their face, conflict with WTO provisions.

This specific case was still pending consultations as of 2001. At first blush, it would appear that Japan was moving hesitatingly because of Brazil's status as a developing country. But this seems unlikely, given Japan's harsh legal treatment of Indonesia, as discussed immediately below. Part of Japan's reluctance for moving this case through the formal panel process may well have been because of the complications wrought by the U.S. government's second complaint in early 1997 with respect to the Brazilian measures. In that complaint, the United States claimed that certain Brazilian policies conferred benefits to companies located in Japan, as well as in Korea and the European Union, over U.S.-based firms. Although Japan had a strong case with respect to Brazil, as of 2001 it appeared that it was still in the process of discussing the issue with the other interested parties. However, because Japan had already picked up the legal sword, it was entirely possible that it would move the case to the formal panel process at some stage, irrespective of Brazil's status as a developing country.

Indonesia

In fact, Japan's legal tactics were just as likely to be undertaken vis-à-vis developing countries as developed ones. The Indonesian automobile measures targeted by Japan were a good case in point. In this case, Japan questioned the WTO-legality of Indonesian measures that gave favorable tax and tariff treatment to cars produced by a joint venture between an Indonesian company, controlled by one of President Suharto's sons, and Kia Motors of South Korea.[17] On October 4, 1996, Japan requested consultations with Indonesia with respect to the Indonesian government's measures in the automobile industry.[18] Japan's basic legal claim was that certain measures with respect to motor vehicles and parts, especially those set up in the National Car Program of February and June 1996, violated legal provisions in the GATT, as well as the TRIMs agreement.

Specifically, Japan claimed violation of the national treatment clause in the GATT, because a specific Indonesian luxury tax exemption for domestically produced cars led to discrimination in favor of such cars, over luxury cars imported from Japan. In addition, Japan pinpointed the Indonesian local content requirements and the exemption from customs tariff and luxury sales tax as prohibited by an appendix to the TRIMs agreement. Because of this, Japan could further claim that the Indonesian measures violated TRIMs Article 2, which forbids any measures that are inconsistent with general provisions of national treatment, while also restricting quantitative measures. Moreover, Japan claimed that Indonesia's exemption from customs tariffs and sales taxes applied only to automobiles originating in Korea. This clearly violated the "general most-favored-nation" clause. Finally, to top it off, Japan also claimed there was a lack of transparency with respect to the Indonesian measures, in violation of GATT Article 10, since they were not promptly published and impartially administered.

The WTO established a panel on June 12, 1997. The panel was asked to examine the Indonesian case by Japan, the EU, and the United States. In comparison to the other complainants, Japan presented a more limited case against Indonesia. With respect to the Japanese complaints that targeted the 1996 National Car Program, the panel upheld almost all of the charges and concluded that Indonesia had in fact violated several GATT and TRIMs provisions. By acting inconsistently with the rules of those agreements, Indonesia had harmed the interests of the complainants under those agreements. The panel report was adopted in July 1998. In October 1998, the complainants requested binding arbitration concerning a reasonable period of time for implementation of the ruling by Indonesia. Considering Indonesia's financial situation, the arbitration set the time frame for implementation at twelve months from the date of adoption of the panel report. In July 1999, Indonesia notified the WTO that its 1999 automotive policy implemented the required recommendations and rulings. The outcome in this case again demonstrated that Japan could wield the legal sword effectively against any country that harmed its economic interests.

Canada

Japan's next target was once again a developed country. In this case, Japan went after Canadian import measures that especially favored the big three U.S. automobile manufacturers.[19] Under a 1965 agreement between the United States and Canada, a few auto manufacturers could import vehicles into Canada using an exemption from the generally applicable customs duty, and then distribute them at both the wholesale and retail levels. On July 3, 1998, Japan requested consultations with Canada, but they yielded no agreements. Due to its dissatisfaction with the consultations, Japan ended up requesting the establishment of a panel on November 12, 1998. By March 1999, the terms of the panel had been set, and Japan's legal case was under way.

Japan claimed that the Canadian "duty waiver," which referred collectively to a set of statutory and administrative measures, violated specific legal provisions overseen by the WTO. Japan contended that this duty waiver was contingent upon a Canadian value-added content requirement for both goods and services, as well as a manufacturing and sales requirement. The crux of the legal problem was that the duty waiver violated the most-favored-nation provisions in both the GATT and the GATS. Moreover, because of its domestic content requirement, it violated the national treatment provisions in the GATT, GATS, and TRIMs agreement. And finally, Japan also claimed that the presence of domestic content and manufacturing requirements meant that the duty waiver also contravened the general prohibition against subsidies in the Subsidies and Countervailing Measures (SCM) agreement. After deliberations, the panel report of February 2000 upheld almost all the Japanese claims.

Although Canada went on to appeal the ruling on March 2, 2000, the appellate body largely upheld the rulings, especially with respect to violation of the GATT articles. The only unambiguous reversals concerned the judicial reasoning of the panel with respect to the GATS. The appellate body questioned whether the measure actually affected trade in services, as required under GATS Article 1. More significantly, it reversed the panel's conclusion regarding Canadian inconsistency with GATS Article 2. But for all practical intents and purposes, Japan had won its case against Canada. Both the appellate body and the subsequently modified panel report were adopted by the DSB on June 19, 2000. To sum up, the actions of the Japanese government in the automobile sector clearly indicate a more concerted effort to deal with trade conflicts in a set and stable legal framework.

Other Uses of the Sword

While the sword aspect has been wielded most strenuously in the automobiles sector, it has also made a serious debut in a range of other disputes involving Japan's trade partners. In semiconductors, for example, the Japanese side used the WTO legal regime to argue against the continuation of a controversial quantitative U.S.-Japan bilateral agreement that had been in existence since 1986. The EU had challenged the GATT-legality of this agreement in 1987 (GATT, GA 1987, pp. 63–65; GATT, BISD 35th suppl. 1987–88, pp. 116–63). Japan argued that if there were to be a continuation of such an agreement, trade partners like the EU could challenge its legality more successfully under the tighter rules of the WTO. Even if implemented, the agreement could not remain bilateral in a WTO world. Japan smartly used this argument to undermine the quantitative or results-oriented approach that had come to characterize U.S.-Japan trade relations, and which had been bitterly resented by the Japanese government. Again, the presence of the WTO helped the rhetorical and substantive cause of the Japanese. The resulting 1996 U.S.-Japan agreement, concluded a year after the WTO came into being, made no mention of numerical targets; moreover, it relied on industries, not governments, for data collection and analysis. When that agreement finally expired in the middle of 1999, there was only a loose framework established for consultation, with the EU, Korea, and Taiwan joining the United States and Japan in the arrangement.[20]

Similarly, Japan has taken up the legal sword in the antidumping arena, again most stridently against the United States.[21] Buoyed by successful challenges to U.S. administrative trade practices by the EU and Korea, Japan too moved formally to challenge antidumping measures against some of its steel products in the United States. In February 2000, it requested the establishment of a panel, and deliberations were underway shortly thereafter. By February 2001, the panel report made clear that Japan had prevailed in much of its legal case against the United States. When the United States appealed the panel's ruling, the appellate body similarly found that U.S. actions had violated the key provisions of the Antidumping agreement, as charged by Japan, although not to the extent claimed by Japan (WTO WT/DS184/R; WTO WT/DS184/AB/R).

Consumer Photographic Film and Paper

Complementing the sword aspect of Japan's trade strategy is the shield facet, as well—one which tallies perhaps even better with this volume's emphasis on continued insulation and protection by the Japanese government. Before coming to any general conclusions, it will also be helpful to see how this facet may affect Japan's relations with its trade partners in the future. This is best achieved by examining the legal interplay in a key high-profile case, where the strict judicial deliberations and conclusions set the tone for Japan's actions, or lack of action, in similar cases.

The shield aspect of Japan's use of legal rules is particularly important because it suggests how, and in what ways, market access issues in Japan may well continue to dominate the agenda for some time to come. The case discussed below, known popularly as the "Fuji-Kodak case," best exemplifies how the existing legal rules can also serve as a shield, or cover, for controversial Japanese measures or practices.

On June 13, 1996, the United States requested consultations with Japan regarding a set of measures that, in the judgment of the United States, violated key GATT rules and thereby impaired benefits accruing to it (WTO WT/DS44/R). Because the consultations came to naught, the U.S. side requested the establishment of a panel that was set up formally in October 1996. The United States presented a list of specific "liberalization countermeasures" divided into three categories that were allegedly in contravention of GATT rules: distribution countermeasures, the large stores law, and promotion countermeasures.

The essence of the U.S. legal claim was that certain laws, regulations, and requirements supported by the Japanese government with respect to the distribution and sale of imported consumer photographic film and paper either individually or collectively violated the existing WTO legal provisions, and thereby harmed U.S. interests. For instance, the distribution countermeasures contravened provisions of Article 3, the national treatment clause that calls upon members to give foreign and domestic like goods equal treatment. In addition, the failure of the Japanese government to publish its enforcement actions under the domestic laws and fair competition codes, as well as its guidance for applications for new or expanded stores, directly contravened GATT Article 10, which calls for transparency in the publication and administration of trade regulations. From the start, the United States emphasized a nonviolation claim, something Japan insisted was subsidiary to the straightforward violation claims. What this meant was that the United States was also asking the panel to conclude that U.S. interests were being harmed by Japanese measures that did not, on their face, conflict with WTO provisions.

Within the strict confines of the WTO rules, the panel remained unconvinced and dismissed all of the U.S. claims. In the opinion of the panel, the United States did not demonstrate that the so-called Japanese distribution "measures" accorded less favorable treatment to imported photographic film and paper within the meaning of GATT's national treatment clause. In addition, the United States had not presented clear-cut evidence that Japan failed to publish administrative rulings in violation of transparency clauses in the GATT. Overall, the United States failed to convince the panel of the merits of both its violations and nonviolations claims.

In an interim review on December 19, 1997, both parties requested a review of certain aspects of the panel report, and also presented comments and rebuttals. But even though it lost badly and also requested a review of some of the panel's legal reasoning, the United States did not move to appeal the ruling. This was significant in that it signaled a certain awareness in the United States that, legally, the case had been weak. The panel report was adopted by the WTO in April 1998, and Japan emerged victorious. Contrary to widespread perceptions, a strict legal analysis had shown the world that there were no Japanese government policies or measures that discriminated against or excluded foreigners from the Japanese market—at least not as defined in WTO rules (however, see Schaede [Chapter 8] for a market-based interpretation).

Other cases, such as the long-running leather dispute, also show the Japanese government's intransigence with respect to opening up.[22] Here too, there is a clear indication that the legal rules of the WTO can be used to continue protection for other sectors. Although a 1984 GATT panel dismissed the Japanese reasoning that the import restrictions on leather and leather footwear were justified for complex socio-economic reasons, that conclusion probably served to impress upon Japan the necessity of strategizing within the legal realm. While recalcitrant at the start in terms of making changes, and continuing to make bilateral deals with countries like the United States, Japan then moved from a GATT-illegal quota system to an entirely GATT-legal tariff-quota system, still in effect in 2001, in which amounts above the specified quota limits for various countries are subject to tariffs. Even so, foreign access issues continued to dominate the agenda. In 1998, the EU formally took up consultations with Japan regarding the Japanese tariff-quotas and subsidies affecting leather (WTO WT/DS147/1). That case was still pending consultations in 2001, although it was hard to see how Japan's legal standing could be questioned.

To conclude, the shield aspect of Japan's WTO strategy comes across in both the consumer photographic film and leather cases. The general upshot of outcomes in these cases showed that if a complainant could not pinpoint tangible Japanese government measures or policies in effect, specifically within the confines of the WTO rules, it would be difficult to pressure the Japanese government to make changes or to open up. These cases thus became important reminders of the extent to which the market access problem in Japan would remain controversial.

Conclusions

Let me end with a general point about the use of the WTO dispute settlement processes that also pertains to Japan's activities at the WTO. Once a process of complaint has been initiated at the WTO, a member government seeks to ensure a legal determination that unequivocally declares another states' acts, measures, and practices to be out of line with existing WTO obligations by both the panel, and where relevant, the appellate body as well. In theory, a government that invokes the rules ultimately aims for the removal of the offending act, measure, or practice using .he legal processes available. At the very least, it seeks to ensure that the differences in positions are reduced with respect to the offending measure, such that accruing benefits under the relevant WTO agreements are not nullified or impaired. Thus, in initiating the WTO legal processes, governments aim broadly to harmonize, or to have harmonized in the case of panel proceedings, conflicting perspectives of what is permissible under the existing legal rules. It is also important to note that ensuring compliance and enforcement with legal determinations that lead to such removal are second-stage concerns, which become pertinent only after a state has received a favorable ruling (Keohane 1992, pp. 176–80; Chayes and Chayes 1993, pp. 176).[23]

In practice, however, after registering its complaint a government may also choose not to escalate the process to the panel stage, and come to a settlement that it deems satisfactory with respect to the offending measure.[24] Whatever the particular course, the key point is that a state invokes the legal rules in an effort to forge a cooperative settlement or outcome with the other party within, or based on, a rule-based forum. From the perspective of the initiating government, maneuvering in the WTO framework is of vital importance in and of itself, and gives its complaints moral and legal legitimacy in a multilateral setting.[25]

This is the essence of Japan's legalistic strategy with respect to the WTO, as it emerged in the 1990s. It was instructive because it showed the world that Japan was active, not merely reactive, with respect to the conduct of its foreign trade relations. In invoking the dispute settlement processes at the WTO, Japan essentially used an entirely legitimate set of legal tactics to ward off foreign pressures and to try to preserve its domestic measures to the extent possible—very much in line with the concept of permeable insulation. This pragmatic use of external legal rules set an important benchmark, not an absolute standard, by which to judge the future course of Japan's trade diplomacy. After all, the rule-based diplomacy was not always foolproof. Japan did not always prevail and it lost cases, especially those related to agriculture (GATT BISD 35th suppl. 1987–88, pp. 163–243; WTO WT/DS76/R; WTO WT/DS76/AB/R).

But despite domestic backlashes and international setbacks, the Japanese government chose to center its trade diplomacy on the legal rules of the WTO. This emphasis was important in allowing Japan to confront its trade partners, weak or strong, on an equal legal footing. From the perspective of the Japanese government, the WTO thus provided a means of forging a more forceful foreign trade policy agenda that was in contrast to the nonlegalistic and nonconfrontational one it had pursued for almost fifty years after World War II. From the perspective of Japan's trade partners, the most important policy implication was that dealing with Japan would henceforth be largely a matter of playing by the rules of the WTO.

Notes

1. Compared with the 208 complaints at the GATT during its entire existence, as of July 13, 2001, the WTO had already handled 234 complaints, 180 of which were distinct matters. For an overview of the dispute settlement processes at the WTO see www.wto.org, and Hudec (1993, pp. 11–15) for the litigation history among GATT contracting parties.

2. Although the focus here is on the international level, the impact of the legalistic strategy on domestic politics is equally important, since it affects the relative power of ministries and sectors. In turn, these domestic jurisdictional and sectoral battles will have important consequences for the way Japan can continue down the legalistic path; see Pekkanen (2001b).

3. Technically, the DSU constitutes Annex 2 of the WTO Agreements. In the following section, unless otherwise indicated, all references to specific articles and appendices are as found directly in the text of the DSU.

4. Article 22 (Consultation) and Article 23 (Nullification or Impairment) are the usual means by which countries can initiate dispute resolution processes against other parties under the GATT; but there is a distinction between "power-oriented" and "rule-oriented" diplomacy. Article 22, which emphasizes a consultative approach, leaves a great deal of discretion regarding the dispute resolution to the parties themselves. As such, it is usually seen under the rubric of "power-oriented diplomacy." Article 23, on the other hand, seeks to formalize the complaint process from the start, requiring "written representations or proposals" to establish a complaint of nullification or impairment of benefits and, in the event of no resolution, authorizes suspension of concessions through referral to the contracting parties. This is often referred to as more rule-oriented diplomacy.

5. It is also important to know that despite substantive innovations and improvements in the WTO Agreements regarding dispute settlement, the WTO itself does not have any more real "power" than that which existed for the GATT under the previous agreements.

6. There are also Charter clauses that deal with institutional and procedural matters.

7. When there are special or additional rules in some of the covered agreements, as laid out in Appendix 2, and when these conflict with the general rules in the DSU, the former prevail according to DSU Article 1.2.

8. Interview with senior MITI official, Tokyo (1997).

9. Interviews with senior MITI official, Tokyo (1997, 1998).

10. Interview with senior MOFA official, Tokyo (1998). Along with being re-

sponsible for six of the fifteen negotiation groups during the Uruguay Round, this official also headed the dispute settlement group.

11. Interview with senior MOFA official, Tokyo (1998).

12. The procedural and substantive facts in the cases discussed here are drawn directly from WTO documents, as cited.

13. A brief history of this case can be found on the official USTR Web site at www. ustr.gov/reports/301reports/act301.htm. See also *The Washington Post*, May 11, 1995.

14. Interviews with senior MITI officials (1997, 1998). Both of these officials were heavily involved in forging Japan's WTO-centered strategy, especially in this case.

15. *Financial Times*, November 19, 1996.

16. *Financial Times*, November 1, 1996.

17. *Financial Times*, July 31, 1997.

18. See WTO WT/DS54/R, WT/DS55/R, WT/DS59/R, WT/DS64/R, WT/DS54/ 15, WT/DS55/14, WT/DS59/13, and WT/DS64/12. The complaints regarding the Indonesian National Car Program were also picked up by the EU and the United States. On June 12, 1997, a single panel was established pursuant to requests by Japan and the EC. On July 30, 1997, the U.S. request for a panel was merged with the panel for Japan and the EC, established earlier. While there are three distinct claims, there is a single WTO document, as well as a single WTO arbitration report.

19. See WTO WT/DS139/R, WT/DS142/R, WT/DS139/AB/R, WT/DS142/AB/ R. This complaint was initiated by Japan and then also taken up by the EU. Japan was also the first of the two to request a formal panel. Although a single panel eventually examined the case, the focus here is largely on the Japanese claims.

20. See USTR, Press Release 99–50, "United States, Japan, European Union, Korea and Taiwan Announce New Accord on Semiconductor Trade Practices," June 10, 1999. This accord will be subject to review after five years, in 2004.

21. On Japan's antidumping agenda, see Pekkanen (forthcoming).

22. See GATT BISD 26th suppl. 1978–79, pp. 320–21; GATT BISD 27th suppl. 1979–80, pp. 118–19; and GATT BISD 31st suppl. 1983–84, pp. 94–114. In 1978, the United States filed a complaint against Japanese measures with respect to imports; although a panel was established, the United States and Japan reached a bilateral settlement that gave the United States an increased quota for some products. In 1979, Canada followed suit and settled, with a similar agreement. In 1980, India invoked special 1966 dispute settlement procedures for developing countries with respect to leather products access in Japan, and reached a settlement with Japan before the matter came before the GATT Council. It was not until 1983 that a GATT panel ruled formally against the Japanese import measures in leather, subsequent to a complaint filed by the United States.

23. Although political scientists believe compliance with legal commitments is the most critical factor in analyses of international law, legal scholars disagree. Instead, law scholars merely stress "acceptable" compliance in the interests of safeguarding the treaty, because the empirical verification of compliance is highly problematic across the board. In the case of the WTO, an emphasis on compliance is complicated further by the fact that most disputes are settled in the prepanel stage, and hence long before compliance even becomes an issue.

24. A careful reading of GATT Articles 22 (Consultation) and 23 (Nullification or Impairment), as well as DSU Articles 4 (Consultations) and 5 (Good Offices,

Conciliation and Mediation), suggests that there is a marked emphasis on consultative procedures and prepanel settlements of parties acting in good faith. Parties are urged to give "sympathetic consideration" to requests for consultation regarding the operation of any covered agreement. So dominant is this emphasis on consultative mediation that DSU Article 5.5 allows, if the parties so agree, for good offices, conciliation, and mediation to proceed simultaneously with a panel process.

25. Interview, senior MOFA official, Tokyo (1997).

References

ACCJ (American Chamber of Commerce in Japan). 1997. *Making Trade Talks Work: Lessons from Recent History.* Tokyo: ACCJ.

Bhagwati, Jagdish. 1990. "Aggressive Unilateralism: An Overview." In Jagdish Bhagwati and Hugh T. Patrick, eds., *Aggressive Unilateralism: America's 301 Trade Policy and the World Trading System,* pp. 1–45. Ann Arbor, MI: University of Michigan Press.

Chayes, Abram, and Antonia H. Chayes. 1993. "On Compliance." *International Organization* 47 (2): 175–205.

DSU (Understanding On Rules and Procedures Governing the Settlement of Disputes). 1994. Annex 2, WTO Agreement.

GATT (General Agreement on Tariffs and Trade). *GATT Activities* (GA). Various issues.

———. *Basic Instrument and Selected Documents* (BISD). Various issues.

Hudec, Robert E. 1992. "The Judicialization of GATT Dispute Settlement." In Michael M. Hart and Debra P. Steger, eds., *In Whose Interest? Due Process and Transparency in International Trade,* pp. 9–43. Canada: Centre for Trade Policy and Law.

———. 1993. *Enforcing International Trade Law: The Evolution of the Modern GATT Legal System.* Salem, NH: Buttersworth Legal.

Jackson, John. 1995. "The World Trade Organization: Watershed Innovation or Cautious Small Step Forward?" *The World Economy:* 11–27.

———. 1997. "The WTO Dispute Settlement Understanding: Misunderstanding on the Nature of Legal Obligation." *American Journal of International Law* 91 (1): 60–64.

———. 1998a. "Designing and Implementing Effective Dispute Settlement Procedures: WTO Dispute Settlement, Appraisal and Prospects." In Anne O. Krueger, ed., *The WTO as an International Organization,* pp. 161–80. Chicago: University of Chicago Press.

———. 1998b. *The World Trade Organization: Constitution and Jurisprudence.* London: Royal Institute of International Affairs.

Keohane, Robert O. 1992. "Compliance With International Commitments: Politics Within a Framework of Law." *Panel Proceedings of the 86th Annual Meeting of the American Society of International Law.* Washington, DC: ASIL.

Komatsu, Ichiro. 1992. "Japan and the GATT Dispute-Settlement Rules and Procedures." *Japanese Annual of International Law* 35: 33–61.

Lincoln, Edward J. 1999. *Troubled Times: U.S.-Japan Trade Relations in the 1990s.* Washington, DC: Brookings Institution Press.

Palmeter, David, and Petros C. Mavroidis. 1998. "The WTO Legal System: Sources of Law." *American Journal of International Law* 92 (3): 398–413.

Pekkanen, Saadia M. 2001a. "Aggressive Legalism: The Rules of the WTO and Japan's Emerging Trade Strategy." *The World Economy* 24 (5): 707–37.

———. 2001b. "International Law, the WTO, and the Japanese State: Assessment and Implications of the New Legalized Trade Politics." *Journal of Japanese Studies* 27 (1): 41–79.

———. Forthcoming. "At Play in the Legal Realm: The WTO and the Changing Nature of U.S.-Japan Antidumping Disputes." In Ellis Krauss and T.J. Pempel, eds., *Beyond Bilateralism* (under review).

Petersmann, Ernst-Ulrich. 1998. *The GATT/WTO Dispute Settlement System: International Law, International Organizations and Dispute Settlement*. London: Kluwer Law International.

———. 1999. "International Trade Law and the GATT/WTO Dispute Settlement System 1948–1996: An Introduction." In Ernst-Ulrich Petersmann, ed., *International Trade Law and the GATT/WTO Dispute Settlement System*, pp. 5–122. London: Kluwer Law International.

Schott, Jeffrey J. 1994. *The Uruguay Round: An Assessment*. Washington, DC: Institute for International Economics.

WTO (World Trade Organization). *Report of the Appellate Body* (AB). Various cases.

———. *Report of the Panel* (PA). Various cases.

5

Adjustment Through Globalization

The Role of State FDI Finance

Mireya Solís

One of the greatest puzzles in the debate over Japanese industrial policy—which has been characterized by export promotion, infant industry protection, and strategic policies to influence resource allocation and industrial adjustment—is the fact that, throughout the entire postwar period, the Japanese government provided subsidized loans to outward-bound foreign direct investment (FDI). Why would a government keen on building a home-based industrial juggernaut support the relocation of production abroad?

The answer is quite simply that the Japanese government used preferential FDI credit to serve its own industrial policy goals: to secure the supply of key raw materials for the Japanese market, and to facilitate industrial restructuring by shifting abroad industries with eroding comparative advantage. In this way, the Japanese government aimed to ameliorate the negative effects of one form of globalization—increased competition with foreign producers—with another form of globalization: the multinationalization of noncompetitive industries. For most of the postwar period, large firms that were involved in raw materials processing, or which were rapidly losing export markets, were the main recipients of public credits for overseas investment. Yet, the system for preferential FDI finance did not remain impervious to the forces of change operating in the Japanese political economy of the 1990s. The central purpose of FDI credit policy remained to shelter Japanese firms from unrestrained market competition by reducing the cost of their move to low-cost offshore locations. The system, however, has become more permeable to political meddling, with small enterprises successfully lobbying for the most subsidized FDI loans. In the 1990s, the general trend was one of growing activism by politicians at the expense of the Ministry of Finance's (MOF) control over preferential FDI finance. Outright subsidization of key constituencies, politically engineered institutional mergers of FDI credit disbursing agencies, and structural reform to public finance (whereby MOF lost some of its powers in allocating postal savings) had a significant influence on the future evolution of government FDI finance.

This chapter offers an analysis of the politics of Japanese FDI credit policy, by applying the concept of "permeable insulation" to explain the recent process of change in the FDI finance institutional framework. The first section begins with an inquiry into the reasons behind Japan's unwavering support of overseas investment through FDI credit. The development of a robust system for FDI finance resulted not only from the high priority placed on the goals of resource procurement and industrial adjustment, but also from the absence of significant labor opposition to public finance of private investment abroad. Therefore, this section also addresses the debate over the "hollowing-out" of the Japanese economy, and discusses the factors behind Japanese unions' benign neglect, or tacit approval, of public subsidization of FDI. The second section more explicitly addresses the political uses of FDI credit, demonstrating that during the prolonged economic recession of the 1990s, special programs to finance small-firm FDI were less concerned with industrial adjustment, and more with the demands of a vocal group of small firms for increased subsidization. The third section focuses on the changes introduced to public FDI finance in Japan during the post-bubble recession. Just as the permeable insulation concept would lead us to expect, there were strong continuities with the past, since the central goal of FDI finance continued to be the protection of firms from adverse shifts in comparative advantage. Nevertheless, important changes were also evident in the move toward a more decentralized and politicized FDI credit allocation system.

State FDI Finance and Structural Adjustment

No other country in the world is as active as Japan in financing its corporations' foreign investment. In 1953, Japan became the first country to launch an FDI loan program, administered by Japan's Export-Import Bank (JEXIM). Between 1953 and 1999, the JEXIM disbursed close to $69.5 billion in public loans for overseas investment, equaling almost 10 percent of all postwar Japanese FDI. By comparison, Germany and South Korea, each active in this area as well, recorded $2.6 billion each, equivalent to 0.53 percent of German FDI, and 9 percent of Korean FDI (Solís 2003). Equally striking is the fact that the JEXIM has enjoyed the strongest mandate to finance foreign direct investment. In the United States, for example, unions have successfully lobbied to have strings attached to government FDI finance. For example, the Overseas Private Investment Corporation must verify that a proposed foreign investment project will not have a negative impact on U.S. jobs or exports. In sharp contrast, Japanese labor has not in any way challenged the substantial government support for industries to go multinational.

These observations raise some important questions: Why has the Japanese state committed such a substantial amount of public resources to the expansion of Japanese multinational corporations? In other words, what are the goals behind the selective targeting of FDI credit? And why have the government FDI credit programs not run up against domestic concerns with the export of technology and jobs? In order to answer these questions, this analysis begins with the goals behind FDI promotion in Japan, and the reasons for the absence of labor opposition to state-supported multinationalization.

Goals of FDI Promotion

In the past, the Japanese state sought to achieve two major objectives with its preferential credit program for FDI: raw materials procurement, and industrial adjustment. Indeed, the initial rationale for initiating FDI loans in 1953 (at a time when no other industrialized nation had yet established such a loan system) was to develop natural resources abroad for import into Japan. Interestingly, very early on the FDI loan system was directed not only to raw materials exploitation projects, but also to industrial sectors perceived to be capable of surviving international competition only by manufacturing in countries with low-cost production, the primary example being textiles.

Table 5.1

Government Foreign Direct Investment Loans, by Industry (percentages)

	Food	Textiles	Lumber, pulp, paper	Chemi- cals	Iron & steel, nonferrous metals	General machi- nery	Elec- trical machi- nery	Trans- port machi- nery
First period (1953–70)	3.8	21.5	29.5	1.9	23.0	4.2	3.5	8.6
Second period (1971–84)	1.3	5.9	5.1	19.1	48.8	1.8	1.9	11.9
Third period (1985–99)	1.0	3.3	1.1	18.4	22.6	2.2	22.2	22.5
Totals	1.1	4.1	2.3	18.3	28.0	2.1	17.7	20.1

Source: Estimated by the author with data provided by JEXIM. Percentages represent the share of each industrial sector over FDI loans for manufacturing. Only FDI loans from the former JEXIM and the international financial operations account were included. Therefore, these FDI loans were targeted almost exclusively at large enterprises, the traditional recipients of JEXIM credit.

The twin goals of FDI promotion were clearly reflected in the industry allocation of public credit over time. Through 1999, agriculture, forestry, fishery and mining received 17 percent of the public FDI loans furnished by the JEXIM. For the manufacturing sector, Table 5.1 reveals a bias in the composition of loans toward raw materials processing sectors (e.g., paper and pulp, steel mills), followed by industries with eroding export competitiveness due to wage increases or currency realignments (e.g., textiles, automobiles, electronics), and heavy industries undergoing structural decline due to rising energy costs (e.g., petrochemicals, nonferrous metals).

In its first twenty years of FDI finance, JEXIM primarily financed natural resource extraction projects abroad to feed processing plants back in Japan (e.g., lumber and pulp received 30 percent of all credit, and iron and steel and nonferrous metals 23 percent). Japan's support for troubled manufacturing sectors began when the textile industry entered a structural process of decline in the mid-1960s, due to wage hikes; accordingly, textiles received 22 percent of manufacturing FDI credit between 1953 and 1970. Next, the Japanese government lent its

Table 5.2

Manufacturing Abroad: Evolution of Japanese Foreign Direct Investment
(U.S.$ million)

	First period (1951–70)	Per- centage of manu- facturing	Second period (1971–84)	Per- centage of manu- facturing	Third period (1985–99)	Per- centage of manu- facturing
Food products	61	6.3	949	4.4	24,813	11.2
Textiles	190	19.7	1,946	9.1	7,381	3.3
Lumber & pulp	212	22.1	973	4.6	5,231	2.4
Chemicals	60	6.2	3,822	17.9	26,330	11.9
Iron & steel, nonferrous metals	138	14.3	4,678	21.9	17,170	7.8
General machinery	67	7.0	1,568	7.3	17,970	8.1
Electrical machinery	71	7.4	3,182	14.9	65,168	29.5
Transportation equipment	103	10.7	2,663	12.5	29,581	13.4
Other manufacturing	61	6.4	1,594	7.5	27,130	12.3
Manufacturing total	963	100.0	21,375	100.0	220,776	100.0

Source: Compiled with Ministry of Finance FDI statistics.

financial muscle to heavy industries dependent on cheap energy (e.g., iron foundries, copper smelting, aluminum refining, petrochemical complexes) when these sectors abruptly lost competitiveness in the wake of the 1973 "oil shock." Chemicals, iron and steel, and nonferrous metals received 68 percent of JEXIM's FDI loans between 1971 and 1984. In the 1980s and 1990s, Japan increasingly financed assembly export industries, such as automobiles and electronics, which were threatened with loss of market share due to the yen appreciation after 1985. The share of electronics and automobiles in JEXIM FDI loans jumped from 2 percent and 12 percent, respectively, in 1985 to 22 percent each in 1999. Not surprisingly, as Table 5.2 shows, the sectoral breakdown of Japanese public credit for overseas investment closely mirrors the evolution of the industrial composition of Japanese FDI flows: from raw materials extraction and light manufacturing, to energy intensive industries, to export assembly sectors.

This close correspondence between the portfolio of public credit and the industrial composition of overseas investment flows underscores the extraordinary reliance by firms in raw materials sectors and structurally depressed industries on government loans to finance their FDI projects. The most extreme case is that of iron, steel, and non-ferrous metals. The share of public FDI loans over total FDI in these industries averaged 55 percent in the postwar period. Likewise, two of the industries that went multinational early on, textiles and lumber-and-pulp, relied heavily on government loans, which represented 32 percent and 42 percent of FDI flows, respectively, between 1953 and 1970. At the peak of its overseas investment drive, the chemical industry (particularly petrochemicals) also depended substantially on government finance. Public loans represented 41 percent of overseas investment expenditure for this industry in the late 1970s. Even those sectors that traditionally self-financed their investment strategies increased their dependence on public finance during troubled times. For example, while the share of public credit over FDI expenditure was only one percent in the electronics industry in the early 1980s, it increased to 15 percent in the 1990s.[1] Thus, throughout the postwar period, the Japanese government used public resources to support private overseas investment selectively, and corporations were willing recipients in their efforts to enhance their global competitiveness.

State FDI Finance and the "Hollowing-Out" Debate

Over time, this active pace of overseas investment across many industries raised fears of de-industrialization, a phenomenon referred to as "hollowing-out" (kūdōka) in Japan. In the mid-1980s, kūdōka became a catchphrase and was widely discussed in the media and in academic circles. Just as in the United States, proponents of the hollowing-out thesis pointed to the possible negative effects on the competitiveness of the domestic economy caused by rapid FDI outflow: curtailment of the technological base, employment loss, and a low-productivity service economy due to industrial migration. In reality, however, the estimates of the negative effect of FDI on employment have varied greatly, as the following studies of the electronics industry illustrate. For example, the Japan Institute of Labor (1984, p. 281) estimated that cumulative FDI until 1979 had produced a net loss of 30,000 to 58,000 jobs in the electronics industry (the range depending on whether the replacement ratio of exports by FDI was one third or 100 percent). A study by the Japan Electrical, Electronic and Information Union (JEIU) (Denki Rengō 1986) concluded that Japanese FDI until 1985 was responsible for 95,000 lost jobs, or 5.3 percent of domestic employment in the electronics industry. Goto (1990, p. 181), on the other hand, calculated the employment loss to be only 31,000 jobs through 1988. In reaction, the JEIU redid its study, and claimed a loss of 95,000 jobs in electronics through 1993 (Denki Rengō 1995, p. 37). A group of Japanese economists concluded that job losses attributable to FDI for the entire manufacturing sector were 172,000, as of 1993 (Minotani 1996, p. 7).

All these analyses estimated the net reduction in employment due to overseas investment. In other words, they considered both negative consequences such as export substitution and reverse imports, and positive effects such as sales of parts and equipment to overseas subsidiaries. However, these studies shared some major shortcomings. First of all, the wide range in the results was caused by an arbitrary selection of the replacement ratio of exports by FDI (30 percent versus 100 percent).[2] Second, these authors implicitly assumed that the same level of exports could be sustained in the absence of FDI. However, industries facing erosion in comparative advantage may resort to foreign production precisely because of the impossibility of maintaining the export drive. In fact, the mainstream view in the FDI field is that foreign direct investment is not detrimental to the home economy. FDI does not substitute for exports; on the contrary, it enhances the international competitiveness of firms and promotes higher value added exports.

Despite this on-going debate about the effects of FDI on the domestic economy, Japanese labor did not oppose preferential finance for the multinationalization of manufacturing industries. The Japanese unions' stance was all the more remarkable considering the serious challenge that organized labor has mounted against much smaller public FDI programs elsewhere in the industrialized world.[3] Three factors explain the benign attitude of Japanese unions toward government FDI finance. First, public FDI credit concentrated on declining sectors that had lost competitiveness due to excess capacity, high production costs, or unfavorable currency realignments. Opponents of state FDI finance would have been hard pressed to accuse the state of promoting de-industrialization when the targeted sectors were characterized by mature technologies, low profitability, and downsizing. In fact, many of these depressed industries also received subsidies for "labor adjustment." For example, Kume (1998, pp. 170–71) showed that labor extracted special legislation to protect laid-off workers in those industries labeled "structurally depressed." To sum up, FDI has not been considered the root cause of decline of these industries, and organized labor in these sectors has benefited from state relief programs.

Second, organized labor did not suffer the brunt of adjustment and, consequently, was less opposed to overseas expansion. For instance, in both textiles and electronics (industries with large workforces that invested actively abroad), job losses were concentrated disproportionately on the nonunionized workforce—small firm employees and part-timers, who were mostly female. For example, in 1965 there were 19,000 men and 88,000 women employed in the cotton spinning industry. As a result of two decades of recession, 69,000 jobs had been lost in this industry by 1985. Women disproportionately suffered the loss of employment opportunities in cotton spinning: As of 1985, there were 63,000 fewer female workers in the industry (Uriu 1996, p. 90). During the so-called *endaka* (high yen) years of 1985–92, which were characterized by a very strong yen vis-à-vis the U.S. dollar, very small establishments in electronics registered the most dramatic job losses. The share of employment in the TV and radio receiver industry for firms with less than 300 employees decreased from roughly 30 to 15 percent in this period (Solís 1998, p. 309). Yet, because workers in these small firms were not unionized, their interests were too fragmented to launch fierce opposition to the relocation of labor-intensive production abroad.

Third, the Japanese government was careful to avoid being accused of fostering hollowing-out. Adjustment assistance packages for industries in structural recession frequently contained clauses on the promotion of both FDI and the maintenance in the homeland of higher value-added activities (for example, in aluminum smelting). Moreover, some public financial institutions were quite explicit about protecting the manufacturing base at home. For example, the Central Bank for Commercial and Industrial Cooperatives (Shōkō Chūkin, discussed in further detail below) extended FDI loans with the condition that the recipient company keep part of its manufacturing operations in Japan (author's interview with Shōkō Chūkin officials, Tokyo [1995]). The thrust of FDI credit policy was, therefore, not to transfer whole manufacturing sectors abroad, but rather to relocate overseas the uncompetitive segments of the industry, while maintaining research-and-development and high value-added activities in Japan.

To sum up, the Japanese government channeled an inordinate amount of public resources to finance private-sector overseas investment without provoking the antagonism of organized labor. For the government, FDI support was an integral part of industrial policy, since it enabled firms with eroding international competitiveness to relocate to low-cost locations and meet the challenge of foreign competitors. The internationalization of production was therefore an effective means of insulating distressed Japanese firms from the rigors of the market. Aware of this, the Japanese government purposely lowered the costs of foreign investment through a huge program for preferential FDI finance. Interestingly, for most of the postwar period, public FDI loans targeted large Japanese enterprises almost exclusively. It was only during the prolonged recession of the late 1980s and 1990s that political pressure built up to extend, and even increase, the subsidization of FDI by small firms.

"Permeable Insulation" and the Promotion of Small-Firm Multinationalization

Japanese FDI has long been distinguished by the active role played by Japanese small and medium-size enterprises (SMEs).[4] In 1977, SMEs represented 40 percent of all new equity investments, and their share peaked in 1988 with a high of 60 percent. During the 1990s, SMEs became highly prominent in FDI flows, as their new equity investments overseas accounted for 45 to 57 percent of the total number of investments.[5] The Asian financial crisis of the late 1990s affected the overseas investment strategies of small Japanese enterprises and, in its wake, annual cases of equity investment dropped from 556 in 1997, to 57 in 1998 (MITI 2000, p. 391). As a result, SME investment in 1998 represented only 11 percent of total Japanese FDI. When the Asian economies stabilized, Japanese SME investment also resumed, with 80 new cases of investment in 1999, but this was still a far cry from the earlier levels.

Japan's Small Firm FDI

Despite the recent cyclical downturn, in comparison with other countries, Japan's small enterprises have shown extraordinary dynamism as multinational investors. For example, from the late 1980s to the early

1990s, Japanese SMEs were responsible for more than half of all new equity foreign investments. In contrast, small enterprises in the United Kingdom accounted for only 25 percent of all foreign affiliates, Swedish SMEs for 23 percent of overseas subsidiaries, and small firms in the United States for a mere 6 percent of foreign affiliates (Fujita 1993, pp. 50, 67–68).

Table 5.3 breaks down small firm FDI between 1971 and 1999 by country and industry. Japanese SMEs traditionally focused on commerce and services in their investments abroad, but during the 1990s, they shifted toward manufacturing in their FDI strategies. Within manufacturing, the machinery sector made up about one-third of small-firm outward investment through the entire period. In the early stages of SME multinationalization, light industry investments were very important. The combined share of the textiles and miscellaneous sectors represented more than half of total FDI accumulated through 1971. From the mid-1970s to the mid-1980s, the processed food sector registered a large share of SME outward investment. More recently, an unprecedented boom in textile FDI enabled this industry to capture a 45 percent share of all SME outward investment between 1991 and 1994, and 36 percent between 1995 and 1999. Machinery, textiles, and miscellaneous manufacturing have, therefore, been the core activities of SMEs in their industrial operations abroad.

Small firm FDI has also shown a distinct pattern of location. For manufacturing, Asia was the dominant destination, followed at a distance by North America and Europe. During the yen appreciation of the 1990s, a renewed concentration of Japanese small firm investment in the Asian continent was evident (with as much as 86 percent of all new equity investments taking place in this region). Within Asia, until 1985 almost all investment occurred in Korea and Taiwan. In the middle of the 1980s, Southeast Asian countries became more attractive to Japanese SMEs seeking to establish and/or expand their production networks abroad. In the 1990s, China emerged as the leading destination for small firm FDI, particularly from the textile industry. In the last decade, close to half of all SME investment cases were located in China. The predilection of Japanese small firms to invest in neighboring developing countries in Asia also sets apart Japanese SME FDI, as small enterprises in other countries predominantly select industrialized nations, given the higher risks associated with emerging markets (Fujita 1998, p. 66).

Table 5.3

Small Firm Foreign Direct Investment, by Industry and Country (number of cases; percentages)

Industrial Profile

	Food products	Lumber & pulp	Textiles	Chemicals	Iron-&-steel, nonferrous metals	Machinery	Manufacturing cases (no.)	Trade	Services	Nonmanufacturing cases (no.)	Total cases (no.)
Up to 1971	6.4	4.3	16.4	6.4	5.9	25.1	439				
1974–80	12.4	4.6	6.0	8.5	8.5	34.8	718	65.5	10.8	1,571	2,289
1981–85	12.4	2.6	7.7	9.4	7.7	33.3	534	63.0	11.7	985	1,519
1986–90	7.5	2.8	11.1	6.8	10.1	37.9	2,388	32.9	16.6	3,294	5,682
1991–94	4.5	2.8	45.3	4.4	6.4	19.2	1,524	36.9	25.4	1,051	2,575
1995–99	4.3	2.9	35.9	7.4	8.8	28.8	1,412	25.1	21.5	657	2,069

Location of Manufacturing Investment

	Korea	Taiwan	Thailand	Philippines	Malaysia	Indonesia	China	Asia total	North America	Europe	Total cases (no.)
Up to 1971	15.9	38.7	n.a.	n.a.	n.a.	n.a.	n.a.	88.2	3.0	0.5	439
1974–80	14.9	17.8	n.a.	n.a.	n.a.	n.a.	n.a.	66.2	20.6	5.2	718
1981–85	12.7	12.9	n.a.	n.a.	n.a.	n.a.	5.4	53.9	35.4	7.7	534
1986–90	12.4	11.2	5.4	1.9	3.7	1.1	8.8	66.1	24.7	6.8	2,388
1991–94	1.8	1.1	5.9	2.8	4.1	5.3	59.0	86.0	8.8	3.9	1,524
1995–99	1.4	2.3	7.9	3.8	3.9	5.4	48.8	80.6	13.3	3.6	1,412

Sources: MITI Small Enterprise Agency, *Chūshō kigyō hakusho*, several issues.

Note: Number of investments by small and medium-size enterprises includes those jointly with large enterprises and individual invest-ments. After April 1984, targeted investment was changed from more than ¥3 million to ¥10 million; and after July 1989, it was changed to ¥30 million. Therefore, the data set is not continuous.

Finally, Table 5.3 shows that the post-1985 yen appreciation marked a watershed in small firm manufacturing FDI. In the second half of the 1980s, industrial investment cases totaled 2,388, far surpassing the previous cumulative postwar record of 1,691 FDI projects. The internationalization of Japanese SMEs continued until the financial crisis of the late 1990s. SME industrial FDI proceeded briskly, with close to 3,000 cases of new equity investments abroad. These high numbers can be explained as attempts by Japanese small enterprises to relocate production abroad in order to avoid the negative effects of yen appreciation on export competitiveness, the possible loss of clients due to the wave of large firm FDI, and sluggish domestic sales due to domestic economic contraction. But the unprecedented dynamism of small firm manufacturing FDI was also a product of substantial government FDI finance. The 1990s witnessed growing FDI subsidization for small firms besieged by the prolonged recession at home and by financial turmoil in Asia in 1997–98.

Public Credit for Small Firm Multinationals: Adjustment or Compensation?

The most remarkable feature in the process of international adjustment by Japanese SMEs in the aftermath of the sharp yen appreciation in the mid-1980s was that for the first time the Japanese state was willing to offer substantial financial support for overseas relocation to troubled small enterprises. Although the Japanese government had inaugurated the FDI loan program through JEXIM in 1953, the bank targeted large enterprises almost exclusively. Before the "high yen" crisis in 1986, the Japan Overseas Development Corporation (JODC) was the only public financial institution that provided FDI loans for SMEs. JODC was established, with the backing of MITI, in 1970 to facilitate imports of natural and energy resources from Asia into Japan. As early as 1973, MITI began to fund pet FDI projects in the developing world through JODC. Overseas investment credits for small businesses were initially offered at very attractive terms: no interest payments except for a 0.75 percent fee charge, and long-term repayment periods of up to 20 years. Eventually, though, these subsidized loans strained JODC's financial resources, and interest rates were charged (Oishi 1994, p. 21). Nevertheless, overall lending remained fairly small: In 24 years, JODC financed a total of 180 overseas projects by SMEs, for a total of $91.2 million.

There were two main reasons why Japanese SMEs resorted to JODC financing rather hesitantly. First, JODC's decision-making structure hampered rapid selection and implementation of projects, since a committee that met only three times a year had to approve each project.[6] Second, until 1984 a fade-out clause discouraged Japanese SMEs from turning to JODC by stipulating that firms were obligated eventually to transfer ownership to the local partner (Oishi 1994, p. 17). These were powerful deterrents for small firms seeking public financial assistance to relocate production abroad.

Consequently, small firms remained dissatisfied with the existing loan programs in support of their overseas investment. Bowing to the demands of their lobby, in 1976 the Diet passed a resolution calling for increased JEXIM support of SME operations. JEXIM complied on the surface by starting an investment consulting service, by attaching preferential conditions to SME loans, and by strengthening institutional connections with banks specializing in SME financing (JEXIM 1983, p. 321). However, because JEXIM was bound by law to adhere to exacting lending requirements (in terms of acceptable collateral and limits on interest rate subsidization), it effectively had little choice but to remain a banker primarily to large firms. Small enterprises were clearly disappointed. In a 1979 survey, SMEs ranked the lack of long-term low-cost financing for FDI projects as one of the main problems in government policy (Takisawa 1982, pp. 69–71).

The Japanese government did not tackle the direct financing of small firm multinationalization until pressed by a severe adjustment crisis during the late 1980s and 1990s. Sharp yen appreciation, rising import competition from developing Asian countries, a prolonged domestic recession, and loss of the client base due to growing foreign sourcing by large assemblers operating overseas, produced a severe environment in which many SMEs struggled to survive (MITI 1994b, pp. 3–7). As part of its broader package to promote industrial restructuring, in 1987 the government opened a special FDI loan program in the three public financial institutions that specialized in small firm credits: the Shōkō Chūkin, the People's Finance Corporation, and the Japan Finance Corporation for Small Businesses (JFS).[7]

The 1993 Small Firm Restructuring Law revised the special lending program for FDI.[8] The goal was to assist SMEs in coping with the deepening process of structural change through diversification and overseas investment. The Restructuring Law limited the supply of preferential

FDI credit to firms in manufacturing, publishing, software, and information services. To qualify for these soft loans, a small firm had to have suffered from a decrease in production of more than 10 percent for three consecutive months within the previous three years; the law made special provisions for exporters and subcontractors, who needed only to prove that their production had decreased more than 5 percent for three months in a row in the last three years (MITI 1993a). Conceivably, these groups were singled out because they suffered the most from the appreciation of the yen and the overseas relocation of large firms.

Access to preferential FDI lending was further eased in May 1995 with reforms to the Small Firm Restructuring Law. From then on, to participate in this program firms needed only to prove that within the past three years they had experienced a 5 percent reduction in production for three consecutive months, and had to submit a plan either to manufacture a slightly different product, renovate part of their equipment, initiate training programs, or conduct a survey on manufacturing conditions in a foreign location (MITI 1995). The most important innovation in the 1995 reform was the introduction of loans from the Association for Small and Medium-Sized Businesses. This institution provided soft loans for the improvement of SMEs with a 15 to 20-year repayment period, a fixed low interest rate, and in special cases no interest at all.[9]

The subsidization of small firm FDI intensified with the Asian financial crisis. In December 1998, in order to assist Japanese SMEs operating in Asia to resist the local credit crunch, the three public financial institutions for SMEs adopted a new FDI financing scheme. Subsidiaries of Japanese SMEs in Asia could now obtain soft loans for working capital (previous FDI loans had been restricted to equipment investments). Moreover, loan applicants with insufficient collateral could instead submit loan guarantees issued by the Association for Credit Guarantees (Shinyō Hoshō Kyōkai) (author's interview with JFS officials [January 2001]).

Through these soft credits, public SME financial institutions played an important role in supporting the overseas expansion of smaller Japanese enterprises. One institution alone, the Japan Finance Corporation for Small Businesses, extended $624 million in FDI loans for 909 projects, which represented close to 10 percent of overseas investment cases of Japanese SMEs between 1987 and 1999. And yet the impact of the special FDI financing program on SME industrial adjustment remained questionable. Far from targeting firms with a high potential to contribute to adjustment, entry conditions were easy enough to result in general access. Due to the economic stagnation of the 1990s, most firms recorded a decrease in production sufficient to qualify for subsidized FDI finance. Revealingly, the government undertook no systematic follow-up on industrial adjustment achievement. Although information on particular cases could be obtained from the prefectural governments or public financial institutions that oversaw the credit process, the government made no effort to gather and analyze data to verify that the stated goal of adjustment had been met.[10]

As the adjustment problem of SMEs proved intractable, the subsidization element in public credit for industrial diversification and international expansion grew. Interest-free loans, and no-collateral loans earmarked for working capital, for SME subsidiaries in Asia were added to the menu of public FDI loans. Further reflecting the politicization of small firm FDI credits was the preference given to projects endorsed by the politically conservative local chambers of commerce. Projects sanctioned by these chambers benefited from lower interest rates than the standard FDI loans offered by the three SME financial institutions (Solís 1998, p. 97).[11] The growing government support for small firm multinationalization was in line with the long-standing practice of using FDI credit to facilitate the industrial adjustment of sectors with eroding competitiveness. Partially reflecting the political clout of the small firm lobby, FDI credit for small enterprises became even more overtly subsidized than the FDI loans furnished to large enterprises through the JEXIM (where collateral was required and interest rates were close to market levels). In this way, public finance of small Japanese transnational corporations is a prime example of Calder's (1988) "politics of compensation" model, whereby politically powerful but inefficient producer groups are generously subsidized at times of crisis. In fact, during the 1990s the politicization of government FDI finance proceeded even further than previous instances of compensation.

Permeable Insulation and FDI Subsidies: Old and New Responses to Globalization

The concept of permeable insulation captures well the dynamics of change in the institutional framework for FDI finance during the 1990s, with its emphasis on overt subsidization of small-firm FDI, and grow-ing politicization of public finance more generally. In the post-develop-mental stage, the Japanese state remained primarily concerned with shielding domestic firms from unrestrained market competition, but its policies were both less cohesive—with more decentralized policy imple-mentation—and less effective, having lost many of its direct levers on industry to deregulation.

The process of change for Japanese state FDI finance reflects both strong continuities with past policy approaches and sharp departures in policy-making structures, especially as the MOF saw its authority over industrial public finance challenged by growing politician activism. The single most important continuity with the past was the core objec-tive of the FDI credit policy: to help Japanese firms weather adverse shifts in comparative advantage, by supporting adjustment in the form of overseas relocation. In other words, the Japanese government con-tinued to respond to the threats of globalization posed by increased competition with foreign producers (experienced both in reduced ex-port competitiveness and growing import penetration) with another form of globalization: the multinationalization of uncompetitive indus-tries and weak firms. Grimes (see Chapter 3) finds a similar logic at work where the Japanese government promoted yen internationaliza-tion to shield firms from the risks of sharp currency realignment. Care-fully supporting internationalization to facilitate Japanese enterprises' adjustment to the vagaries of the world markets seems to have in-formed Japan's foreign economic policy across several issue areas.

Importantly, economic stagnation, intensified inter-party competi-tion, and curtailment of bureaucratic power during the 1990s caused unprecedented changes in Japanese FDI finance as well. For the first time, the Japanese state directly assisted the international adjustment strategies of small firms. While the government had offered substantial financial aid to the small firm sector for its domestic activities in the past, the demand of this lobby group for cheap credit for international-ization went unanswered until the prolonged contraction in demand for SME production that set in during the mid-1980s. Once the road to soft finance for small-firm FDI was paved, SMEs benefited from ever-in-creasing subsidization and the involvement of a larger number of pub-lic financial institutions. Political compensation seems to have overshadowed a genuine concern with economic restructuring.

The proliferation of public financial institutions for heavily subsidizing SMEs' overseas investment is all the more remarkable, given the on-going administrative reform campaign to streamline the bureaucracy and eliminate the inefficient allocation of resources. The movement for administrative reform acquired new life after the collapse of the financial bubble set the stage for a fiscal crisis in the mid-1990s. The Japanese government, pressed to step up its pump-priming efforts and faced with diminishing tax revenues, incurred ever-increasing budgetary deficits financed through bonds. During the 1990s, the calls for administrative reform also intensified due to the public's disenchantment with the government's attempts to rationalize public corporations and agencies, and because of widening mistrust of ministries such as the MOF, after a series of scandals and bankruptcies rocked Japanese financial circles.

Party politics also made their imprint on the evolution of administrative reform during the tumultuous 1990s. In 1994, a new coalition government (LDP-Sakigake-Social Democratic Party) sought to deliver its promise of bureaucratic rationalization by streamlining public financial organizations. Agencies dealing with international finance were deemed an easier target than those extending credit to vocal domestic constituencies, such as the Japan Finance Corporation for Small Businesses or regional development banks.

Therefore, the fate of the JEXIM (a self-sustaining public agency receiving no subsidies from the budget) was the first to be sealed under the banner of administrative reform to eliminate and/or streamline inefficient public corporations. Three options were considered for the reorganization of the JEXIM: (1) its dismemberment by reallocating import finance to the Japan Development Bank (JDB), and "untied" loans and bank loans to the Overseas Economic Cooperation Fund (OECF); (2) integration of the JDB and JEXIM; and (3) a merger between the OECF and JEXIM. In the spring of 1995, the Diet committee in charge of this matter finally decided on the third option—merging Japan's foreign aid agency with the main government bank in charge of large-firm export and FDI lending (*Kokusai Jānaru* 1995, p. 12).

The JEXIM and OECF, in the past at loggerheads over the demarcation of their operations, had to overcome four major challenges as they were forced to integrate.[12] Japan had long been accused of using its aid program to benefit Japanese exporters and investors. To address this international criticism, the first major concern was to keep the official development assistance (ODA) program separate from other official credits (i.e., for export and FDI). The second concern was the impact of the merger on the financial soundness of the new organization. JEXIM was a profit-generating bank, whereas the OECF had frequently incurred losses due to its concessionary loans and grants. Especially worrisome was the negative effect that balance-sheet consolidation could have on bonds issued in the Euromarket. Third, there was concern over the bureaucratic constraints imposed on the new institution's decision-making process. While the JEXIM had enjoyed much autonomy in its daily business operations (consulting only with MOF), the OECF had been much more constrained, since it received tax money and four ministries monitored all of its government loans.[13] A final concern was how the previously separate programs of private sector investment finance could be integrated. Indeed, it is little known that Japan's premier ODA agency—the OECF—also financed private investment in cooperative projects in the developing world.[14]

In the face of these obstacles, it is perhaps not surprising that, as of 2001, the brand-new Japan Bank for International Cooperation (JBIC, Kokusai Kyōryōku Ginkō) showed only minor integration of former JEXIM and OECF operations. The new bank worked with two strictly separate accounts: the international financial activities account (i.e., the former JEXIM activities of export, import, FDI, and untied loans); and the overseas economic cooperation operations account (covering the former ODA and private-sector investment finance programs). In other words, although public international finance was nominally unified under one institutional roof, little real integration took place. In the area of FDI finance, the overlap was glaring, with two separate finance programs for overseas investment and no functional integration in sight. In the end, cynics argued that the major consequence of the merger was political, in that the MOF was deprived of an important position for placing retired high-ranking officials by losing one governorship.

In post-developmental Japan, the LDP and its coalition partners have been more vocal in shaping the institutional framework for FDI finance. The long-term impact of recent political initiatives on public FDI finance is, however, debatable. Politicians promised heavily subsidized FDI loans to small firms and successfully pushed through the JEXIM and OECF merger, despite opposition from the MOF. More importantly, the LDP pushed through structural reform of public finance in one key area: the Fiscal Investment and Loan Program (FILP). In a heated debate between MOF and the LDP, the party prevailed in terminating, as of April 2001, the all-important legal requirement that postal savings and public pension funds be deposited with MOF. These resources had formed the core of Japan's financial industrial policy, whereby MOF allocated the money to the vast network of public financial institutions and corporations (including all FDI financing agencies discussed in this chapter).

Although as of 2001 it was still too early to determine the full implications of this fundamental change for public FDI credit, it did represent a major loss for the MOF of a key lever over industrial credit. Government financial institutions would have to restructure their fund procurement practices once FILP loans were eliminated. After a transition period, the public financial institutions would be expected to finance their activities mostly by issuing agency bonds, and secondarily from FILP bonds and budget subsidies. However, not all public financial institutions seemed equally prepared to raise funds in private markets. For example, while the former JEXIM had ample experience with bond issues, other FDI credit-disbursing agencies did not (such as the JFS and the People's Finance Corporation). The impact of FILP reform on the ability of government FDI agencies to obtain low-cost capital to continue subsidizing overseas investment is, therefore, a key question for future research.[15]

Conclusions

Government support of FDI has been a long-standing feature of Japanese industrial policy. Early on, a developmental state concerned with technological upgrading, export promotion, and the protection of domestic markets from import penetration embraced FDI finance to foster natural resource procurement and industrial restructuring. Indeed, this chapter has shown that public FDI credit disproportionately targeted firms with dwindling international competitiveness, due to high labor or energy costs or unfavorable currency realignments. Through preferential credit, therefore, the government promoted the internationalization of production so that firms could adjust to adverse market trends. Insulating domestic firms from negative shifts in comparative advantage largely motivated the Japanese government FDI finance program.

Significantly, the Japanese government managed to run the largest FDI loan program in the world without antagonizing organized labor. In sharp contrast to the behavior of unions in other industrialized nations, which challenged the legitimacy of much smaller public FDI finance programs, Japanese unions did not oppose public subsidies for foreign investment by Japanese private enterprises. Because the government FDI credit targeted structurally depressed industries for state support in labor adjustment, unions came to consider overseas investment not as the root cause of the decline, but as subsidized adjustment helping to maintain the higher value added segments of the industry within Japan.

The most important features of the FDI finance framework were not affected by organized labor, but by the small firm lobby and by the coalition governments of the 1990s. As the economic condition of Japanese SMEs deteriorated due to sharp yen appreciation in the 1980s, the bursting of the bubble in the early 1990s, and financial turmoil in Asia at the end of the decade, the Japanese government supplied increasingly softer financing for overseas investment by SMEs. Moreover, the activism of the LDP and its coalition partners was evident at two critical junctures: the JEXIM-OECF merger, and the FILP reform. In both instances, the coalition political parties successfully neutralized the MOFs opposition to the proposed changes in public FDI finance.

Therefore, the process of change in Japanese public FDI credit in the last decade exhibits not only strong continuity in the goals behind government preferential finance, but also important changes in the operation of government financial institutions. As suggested by the "permeable insulation" concept, Japan will persevere in its attempts to buffer domestic firms from shifts in comparative advantage through FDI credit, but it seems that the system will be increasingly decentralized with the involvement of more agencies, and more overtly politicized as politician-controlled budget subsidies come to play a larger role in public industrial finance.

Notes

1. Estimated by the author with data provided by MOF and JEXIM. For more detailed analysis and data sources, see Solís (1998). It is important to note that, although the electronics industry's reliance on government FDI credit increased during the 1990s, its dependence on preferential credit did not approach that of structurally depressed industries. The share of public FDI loans over FDI expenditure for precision instruments hovered around only one percent during the postwar period; Nelson (see Chapter 6, this issue) provides a good counterpoint to the argument developed

here, by analyzing the FDI strategies of industries that self-financed their foreign investments.

2. This criticism does not apply to Goto (1990), who estimated the elasticity of exports to FDI to avoid this problem.

3. Labor and management in the United States have often been at odds over the merits of foreign direct investment for the home economy. American labor has argued that outward direct investment results in job losses, reduces the potential for domestic employment creation (since the manufacturing base is relocated overseas), diminishes labor's share of the national income, and weakens the bargaining power of unions given the international immobility of labor versus capital. American labor unions have in the past actively resisted the emigration of U.S. industry. The most ambitious effort to diminish the mobility of U.S. multinational corporations took place in 1971, when the AFL-CIO endorsed the Burke-Hartke bill. The main features of this draft legislation were presidential licensing for all FDI projects with employment effect as the main criterion, corporate disclosure of international activities, and curtailment of offshore manufacturing. Although Congress rejected the Burke-Hartke bill, suspicions about the negative effects of multinational companies on American labor have not died away (see, for instance, Browne and Sims 1993).

4. In manufacturing, SMEs are officially defined as enterprises with fewer than 300 employees and less than ¥100 million in capital; in wholesale trade, as firms with not more than 100 employees and ¥30 million in capital; and in retail trade, as enterprises with less than ¥10 million in capital and fewer than 50 employees (Fujita 1993, p. 55).

5. Undoubtedly, the weight of Japanese SMEs in total FDI is larger when measured by number of investments than when measured by the value of the capital outflow. Unfortunately, the Japanese government does not disclose the financial amount of SME overseas investment, so it is not possible to verify this.

6. Interview with JODC officials (August 1995).

7. MITI conceived of the following adjustment strategies for SMEs: transition to higher value-added production in the same industry or product, minimization of risk through development of supplier relations with several customers, foreign direct investment to avoid losing markets to local suppliers, and entry into new industrial fields (MITI 1994a, pp. 171–72).

8. "Law for Smoothing the Advance of Small and Medium-Size Firms into New Fields" (*Chūshō kigyō shinbunya shinshutsu nado enkatsukahō*).

9. The Association for Small and Medium-Sized Businesses (Chūsho Kigyō Jigyōdan) was established in 1980 under MITI's supervision. Its finance operations were not very large. For example, in the early 1990s the association's annual approved loans ranged between ¥200 and ¥250 billion. Contrast this to JFS's lending volume of ¥2.4–2.8 trillion per year in the early 1990s (Nakagawa et al. 1994, pp. 274, 460).

10. Interview with officials of the Planning Division at MITI's Small Enterprise Agency, Tokyo (June 1995).

11. The control wielded by the local chambers of commerce in approving the softest loans for FDI only ratifies existing practice, since these chambers have since the 1970s authorized the no-collateral loans for SME domestic investment (Calder 1988, p. 346).

12. Interviews with JEXIM and OECF officials, Tokyo (September–October 1995).

13. The ministries supervising OECF were: MITI, MOF, the Economic Planning Agency, and the Ministry of Foreign Affairs.

14. OECF equity finance played a pivotal role in the overseas relocation of heavy industries during the 1970s and 1980s (Solís 1998). OECF's private sector investment finance program totaled $2.5 billion between 1961 and 1999 (OECF 1999).

15. Moreover, reform of Japanese public finance was an on-going process, with heated debate on further reform of the postal savings and major restructuring of the public corporations.

References

Arase, David. 1995. *Buying Power: The Political Economy of Japan's Foreign Aid.* Boulder: Lynne Rienner.

Browne, Harry, and Beth Sims. 1993. *Runaway America: U.S. Jobs and Factories on the Move.* Albuquerque: Resource Center Press.

Calder, Kent E. 1988. *Crisis and Compensation: Public Policy and Political Stability in Japan, 1949–1986.* Princeton: Princeton University Press.

Carlile, Lonny E. 1998. "The Politics of Administrative Reform." In Lonny E. Carlile and Mark C. Tilton, eds., *Is Japan Really Changing Its Ways? Regulatory Reform and the Japanese Economy*, pp. 76–110. Washington, DC: Brookings Institution.

Denki Rengō. 1986. "Denki sangyō no kaigai shinshutsu to koyō e no eikyō suikei" (Estimation of the Effect on Employment of the Overseas Expansion of the Electric Industry). *Seisaku Shiryō Geppō*, no. 131: 1–5.

———. 1995. *Sōzō to kakushi e no chōsen* (The Challenge of Creation and Innovation). Tokyo: Denki rengō.

Fujita, Masataka. 1993. *Small and Medium-Sized Transnational Corporations: Role, Impact and Policy Implications.* New York: UNCTC.

———. 1998. *The Transnational Activities of Small and Medium-Sized Enterprises.* Dordrecht: Kluwer Academic.

Goto, Junichi. 1990. *Labor in International Trade Theory: A New Perspective on Japanese-American Issues.* Baltimore: John Hopkins University Press.

JEXIM (Japan Export-Import Bank). 1983. *Sanjūnen no ayumi* (Thirty-Year History). Tokyo: JEXIM.

———. 1999. *Gyōmu binran* (Operations Manual). Tokyo: JEXIM.

Japan Institute of Labor. 1984. *Kaigai tōshi to koyō mondai* (Overseas Investment and the Employment Problem). Tokyo: Nihon rōdō kyōkai.

Johnson, Chalmers. 1978. *Japan's Public Policy Companies.* Washington, DC: American Enterprise Institute.

Kokusai Jānaru. 1995. "Yūgin to OECF tōgō ni nokoru mujun to sōten" (Remaining Issues and Contradictions in the JEXIM-OECF Merger). *Kokusai Jānaru* 5: 12–13.

Kume, Ikuo. 1998. *Disparaged Success: Labor Politics in Postwar Japan.* Ithaca: Cornell University Press.

MITI (Ministry of International Trade and Industry). 1993. *Chūshō kigyō shinbunya shinshutsu nado enkatsukahō no tebiki* (Guide to the Law for Smoothing the Advance of Small and Medium-Sized Firms into New Fields). Tokyo: MITI.

———. 1994a. *Chūshō kigyō no dōkō ni kansuru nenji hōkoku* (Annual Report on the Trends Among Small and Medium-Sized Enterprises). Tokyo: MITI.

———. 1994b. *Chūshō kigyō shinbunya shinshutsu nado enkatsukahō no gaiyō* (Outline of the Law for Smoothing the Advance of Small and Medium-Sized Firms into New Fields). Tokyo: MITI.

———. 1995. *Kaisei chūshō kigyō shinbunya shinshutsu nado enkatsukahō no tebiki* (Guide to the Revised Law for Smoothing the Advance of Small and Medium-Sized Firms into New Fields). Tokyo: MITI.

———. 2000. *Chūshō kigyō hakusho* (White Paper on Small and Medium-Sized Enterprises). Tokyo: MITI.

MOF (Ministry of Finance). 1992. *Shōwa zaiseishi, 1952–73* (History of Shōwa-Era Public Finance, 1952–73). Tokyo: Tōyō keizai.

Minotani, Chiohiko, ed. 1996. *Sangyō kūdōka: Nihon no makuro keizai* (Industrial Hollowing-Out: Japanese Macroeconomics). Tokyo: Taga shuppan.

Oishi, Takayoshi. 1994. "Kaigaibō 25-nen no kaiko to tenbō" (Recollections and Views of JODC's 25 Years). In Japan Overseas Development Corporation, ed., *25-shūnen tokushu-gō* (25-Year Special Review). Tokyo: JODC.

OECF (Overseas Economic Cooperation Fund). 1999. *Annual Report*. Tokyo: OECF.

Solís, Mireya. 1998. "Exporting Losers: The Political Economy of Japanese Foreign Direct Investment." Ph.D. dissertation, Harvard University.

———. 2003 (forthcoming). "The Politics of Self-Restraint: FDI Subsidies and Japanese Mercantilism." *The World Economy* (forthcoming).

Takisawa, Kikutarō. 1982. *Chūshō kigyō no kaigai shinshutsu* (Overseas Expansion of Small and Medium-Size Firms). Tokyo: Egusa tadamitsu.

Uriu, Robert M. 1996. *Troubled Industries: Confronting Economic Change in Japan*. Ithaca: Cornell University Press.

6

Integrated Production in East Asia

Globalization Without Insulation?

Patricia A. Nelson

Economic integration in East Asia was by 2001 a fact. It was characterized by the strong presence of Japanese multinational corporations
(MNCs) that had expanded their manufacturing facilities to East Asia,
particularly since 1985, and had integrated their production networks
across several countries. It was also directly influenced by the rapid
growth of China as an attractive target for foreign direct investment
(FDI), especially during the 1990s. At the same time, Japanese MNCs
were faced with high prices and continued stagnation at home. Compared with the cost of doing business elsewhere in East Asia, Japan was
simply too expensive. This chapter explores how the globalization of
Japan's multinationals (and their subsequent integration of production
in East Asia) influenced the political economy of Japan, and specifically addresses a problem common to all advanced industrialized nations: the tension between highly globalized firms and the state.

The story that unfolds in this chapter is one of irony and permeable
insulation. I argue that throughout the 1990s and into the early twenty-
first century, Japanese multinationals led the process of change. In
other words, Japan's insulated economy was forced over time to become permeable through the actions of many top firms. How did this
happen? The postwar industrial policy of export promotion stimulated

Japan's highly successful economic growth after World War II, and allowed many firms to become leading world multinationals. Export promotion worked so well that eventually global market conditions forced many firms (notably electronics and automobile firms) to relocate much of their manufacturing overseas—and a good deal of this went to East Asia. Fears grew in Japan of a "hollowed out" industrial structure, as more and more firms moved manufacturing to East Asia and Japan became more dependent on reverse imports—that is, goods produced abroad by a Japanese company or its subsidiary, and imported into Japan. Ironically, all of this was caused by Japan's top firms, the same firms that brought Japan to its postwar peak of industrial strength. Japan's MNCs, the beacons of its twentieth century success, became the nation's twenty-first century headache. Could an economic structure designed to support export promotion be reconciled with a growing dependence on reverse imports?

Set against a backdrop of the historical dynamics within the region, this chapter is structured around three themes: the impact of globalization on Japan's economy and business, FDI patterns of Japanese MNCs in East Asia, and the link between production networks and the rise of reverse imports to Japan. All three of these themes have affected the structure of the Japanese economy and the direction of Japan's economic policy. Throughout the "lost decade" of the 1990s, Japan was confronted with economic recession, government scandals, bureaucratic reorganization, and a revolving door of political leadership. In this climate, government policy toward MNCs was immature but evolving and, by 2001, Japan's multinationals had forced a rethinking of Japan's economic and business policy.

Both automobiles and electronics were key elements of Japan's old export-oriented structure, and both held valuable lessons about the transformation of the Japan's economic structure through the globalization of leading MNCs. It is useful, therefore, to contrast briefly the electronics and automobile industries. The two industries differ in both structure and orientation. Automobile firms that were tied to supply chain networks often encouraged their small and medium-size suppliers to move to East Asia with them, aided by preferential government financing (see Chapter 5). The electronics industry was large and very diverse; some firms pursued the same supply chain strategies as the automobile firms, while others did not. These latter firms chose, for example, to source parts and components from East

Asia and elsewhere based on price and quality, rather than particular historical or business ties. More so than for the automobile industry, electronics manufacturing was highly cost sensitive and technology driven. It was composed of some of Japan's—and the world's—most competitive companies, and many ran on very short product cycles (sometimes only three to six months between new models). During the 1980s, the electronics industry faced few, if any, constraints by local governments during the negotiation of overseas investments, because electronics investments were often welcomed as a part of the local government's development strategy (Doner 2001).

This chapter analyzes firms that are active in optics-based production. As one of Japan's most internationally competitive sectors, optics-based products cross many sectoral boundaries, but are at least partially included in the electronics industry. As an example of the complexity of the sector, in 2001 the Ministry of Economy, Trade and Industry (METI) classified cameras and copiers as precision instruments, facsimiles as telecommunications equipment, and digital cameras as audio-visual equipment. Despite the statistical challenges, these firms served as an excellent example of integrated production, because they led the world in many optics-related technologies, such as optoelectronics and products with optics as their core technology (including cameras, photographic lenses, "steppers" used for semiconductor fabrication, photocopiers, facsimiles, microscopes, and endoscopes). The market leading firms excelled first in consumer products and later expanded their range and depth to include, for example, medical optics, business applications, and a variety of industrial optics.[1] In 2001, fourteen firms led the industry, the most notable of which were Canon, Hoya, Kyocera, Nikon, Minolta, Olympus, Ricoh, and Asahi Optical/Pentax.[2] All of these firms had been highly active participants in East Asian FDI, beginning as early as 1966.

Optics-based firms differed significantly from the computer and related industries (such as the hard disk drive industry) because the competition was primarily among Japanese firms, and it took place mainly in East Asia. Analyses of specific sectors within the electronics industry revealed that Japanese MNCs faced a resurgence of American and/or European MNCs during the 1990s (Borrus 2000; McKendrick, et al. 2000). Something similar was not likely to happen among the optics-based MNCs as of 2001, because Japanese firms dominated the key technologies and appeared set to do so into the near future. Digital products—including cameras, video cameras, multifunction office machines, and the like—have added a new twist to the dominance of these Japanese MNCs, but rather than threatening their position, digital technologies appeared likely to enhance it. This is because digital products required digital optics either to assist inferior components to produce clear images, or to enhance, to the highest degree, the clarity of images produced by top-quality digital components. And in 2001, these technologies were still evolving.

The next section presents a brief account of the background of Japan's export promotion policy. Thereafter follows a discussion of when and how East Asia became the most important target for Japanese manufacturing FDI. The next section analyzes the optics-based firms' production strategies and regional integration in East Asia. The data presented there confirm that integrated production centered on Japanese MNCs meant that Japan was a manufactured goods importer, and could no longer rely on exports as a driver of economic growth. Finally, the implications for Japan of its changed economic structure are considered.

Background

It has been argued that Japan's economic growth was structurally dependent on exports (Vestal 1993; Katz 1998; Sumiya 2000). This meant that Japan depended on the profits from exports to lift economic activity in the domestic economy. The more Japan exported, the better off the economy would be. Export dependence worked very well in Japan for nearly fifty years, but by the 1990s it was no longer viable. Instead, Japanese MNCs (which were the former exporters) began to introduce their products into Japan through reverse imports, mainly from East Asia. Price pressures, including the cost of labor in Japan, negatively affected the international competitiveness of Japan's leading manufacturers (of, for example, home and consumer electronics, motor vehicles, and office equipment). Their expansion into and subsequent growth within the global marketplace necessitated cost cutting for firms to remain competitive and maintain market shares. The result was a "hollowing out" (or de-industrialization) of Japan's basic levels of manufacturing, coupled with a rising demand for reverse imports of many goods. It also meant that to survive, Japanese MNCs had to hold a strong manufacturing position in East Asia's integrated production networks. This section briefly describes how Japan moved from its old economic structure to a new one.

Export-led growth was an outcome of Japan's postwar policy of export promotion, a policy that was actively pursued during the initial stages of Japan's economic recovery. The East Asian security umbrella provided by the United States, and the open U.S. market, also allowed Japan to focus on exportable goods for economic recovery. The logic for export promotion was sound, and the policy was highly suited to Japan's economic recovery after 1945. Japanese firms were restricted to manufacturing civilian (or consumer) products—specifically, necessities or luxuries with positive to high income elasticities of demand, or high value-added goods. Their target markets were the industrialized nations—first the United States, and then Europe—where people could afford expensive, technologically advanced goods.

The industries targeted for early recovery required few imported inputs. This meant that for every item sold overseas, a high percentage of foreign exchange (U.S. dollars) was earned. Japan crucially needed U.S. dollars to pay for imports of raw materials, energy, and technology that were directed to existing and emerging export-oriented sectors of the economy. The government controlled the allocation of foreign exchange by the "link system," which meant that a firm's export performance was linked to the amount of foreign exchange it received (Itoh and Kiyono 1988, pp. 169–73). Thus, the more a firm exported, the more foreign exchange it would receive to pay for costly items such as technology licensing fees or imports. This government policy, among others, promoted higher value-added manufacturing to bring in more foreign exchange and to encourage firms to excel at exporting. Thus, a firm could benefit from government support and move up the technology ladder by producing more and more expensive goods (i.e., higher value-added goods) for export. Japan's old economic structure was therefore a cycle of constantly upgrading the industrial structure of export-oriented goods, for example, from bicycles to motorcycles, trucks, and cars.

Japan's exporters quickly proved to be highly capable and effective. By the mid-1960s, the income elasticity of Japan's exports, measured in terms of growth rates of exports over the period from 1956–57 to 1964–65, was the highest (at 3.55) of all eleven industrialized countries in Itoh and Kiyono's study (1988, p. 157). The lowest were the United Kingdom and the United States (at 0.86 and 0.99, respectively). This meant that Japan exported a higher share of high value-added goods than the United Kingdom or the United States. Notably, however, the income elasticity of Japan's imports was in line with the other industrialized nations in the study. These figures indicated that Japan's exports (not imports) were very different from the other industrialized countries. Japan exported more and more expensive goods over time, just as the policy described above would have predicted.

During the Occupation of Japan, American expectations had been that most of Japan's postwar restrictions on trade and investment would be removed relatively quickly after economic recovery had been achieved (which turned out to be by the 1970s). Up until that time, the U.S. market was largely open to Japanese goods, while the Japanese market remained closed to imports (particularly if they competed with foreign exchange-earning exports) and to inward FDI. The only firms that were allowed to invest directly in Japan were those the government deemed technologically important, and they were allowed in only if they agreed to share some of their technological expertise with Japanese firms (Mason 1992a). The U.S. economy was left open to Japanese imports, because the Japanese economy was perceived as being weak and in need of help. Without the open export markets in the United States from the 1950s, and in Europe from the 1960s, the Japanese economy and the export-oriented industries might never have grown and prospered.

To finance Japan's export promotion, commercial banks (or the city banks), long-term credit banks (e.g., Industrial Bank of Japan), and several government lending institutions such as the Japan Development Bank (JDB), provided both long- and short-term lending. Industries that received loans from the JDB could more easily receive commercial bank financing, since government (or JDB) lending indicated the industries targeted for expansion by the government (Calder 1993). Japan's promotion of high value-added exports (coupled with domestic market protection) allowed Japan to achieve a balance in its merchandise trade in the early 1960s; however, the current account did not begin to show a surplus until the late 1960s (Lincoln 1988).[3]

Tariffs, quotas, foreign exchange controls, export tax credits, and restrictions on inward and outward FDI and corporate ownership were some of the other key policies that allowed Japan's economy to recover quickly after World War II. Military and economic dependence on the United States protected Japan from international pressure (which grew throughout the 1960s) to revalue the yen and to conform to international trading arrangements, at least on paper (see Chapter 4). Japan was allowed to join the "rich countries" after it lowered tariffs, eliminated quota restrictions, and partially opened the market to FDI. By that time, however, many industries were already internationally competitive and the old policies of government protection (many of which still existed) were no longer necessary. Nonetheless, the pattern of exports for growth was continued.

Japan's economy was still largely insulated from the world economy in the early 1980s. Accordingly, Japan's policies led to considerable friction with its trading partners, particularly with the United States. Feeding this friction was the fact that many American firms no longer manufactured consumer goods in the United States, and instead were supplied by, among others, Japanese firms on an original equipment manufacturer (OEM) basis.[4] The larger the U.S.-Japan trade imbalance, the less tolerant the American government grew of Japan's export-dependent policies, particularly during the 1980s (Tyson 1992). By the early 1980s, Japan had become so dependent on exports that over half of its real expansion in gross national product (GNP) in 1980, 1981, and 1984 was directly due to increased exports. In contrast, throughout the 1955–80 period, exports accounted for no more than half of Japan's GNP growth (Vestal 1993, p. 182). The United States pressured Japan throughout the 1980s to open its markets and create a "level playing field" for *all* firms, Japanese and foreign.

In spite of this pressure, the Japanese government continued to encourage exports throughout the 1990s. However, many Japanese multinationals that were exposed to international competition could not wait for the domestic environment in Japan to improve for exporters. Instead, they moved much of their production to East Asia where costs —especially labor costs, a key factor for many competitive products— were much lower.[5]

Optics-Based Industries

To illustrate more fully how Japan's old economic structure worked, the optics-based manufacturers are used as an example.[6] In 2001, the world's leading firms in the optics-based sector were those that had profited from Japan's export promotion and had survived years of intense competition in Japan, the United States, and Europe. They moved up the technological ladder by constantly upgrading and improving the mechanics and components of cameras and lenses, and by expanding and innovating in related products (such as facsimiles, copiers, microscopes, endoscopes, and other medical equipment). While cameras and lenses did not physically look like they had changed significantly, firms were constantly upgrading them technologically. The latest of these upgrades has been digitization. What follows is a very brief account of how Japan's insulated export promotion policies came under threat specifically from the optics-based MNCs.

In the late 1940s and early 1950s, cameras and lenses made in Japan were "exported" to American troops stationed in Japan through the U.S. military post exchanges (PXs). When American military personnel returned to the United States, they took their Japanese cameras and lenses with them, creating a foundation from which additional demand could grow and from which exports to the United States could take off. Over time (although not at first) exporters were also helped by a very favorable exchange rate, which was crucial to maintaining Japan's export demand and economic growth.[7]

By 1960, many of Japan's highly successful exporters of cameras and lenses were still virtually unknown in their home market. One reason was that most consumer goods were luxuries for the average Japanese household in 1950, and as such were subject to import protection and excise taxes of up to 50 to 60 percent in the case of cameras and lenses. High excise taxes significantly dampened domestic demand, while export promotion encouraged the largest and most technologically advanced firms to concentrate solely on exports. Domestic demand quickly grew, however, once excise taxes had been lowered to 15 percent by the mid-1960s, and then removed altogether over the following two decades (Nelson 1998, p. 110). Because the domestic market was protected from imports, firms were able to charge high prices at home, and thereby retain a profit at the expense of the Japanese consumer. Schaede's (2000) "sanctuary strategy," or the successful use of the domestic market as a sanctuary for profit, is an apt description of this practice. These profits were used to expand the firms' dominance in the world market. Export-oriented firms gained the most from Japan's postwar economic policies because exports were given priority over all else, and a protected domestic market brought significant profits.

The exporters also benefited from government-sponsored initiatives to raise both quality and technological standards. They were also encouraged to cooperate through, among others, technological development and information sharing, although this did not always work.

Significantly, the export-oriented firms were given help in developing overseas marketing channels, first through Occupation-era PX sales in Japan, then in the United States and later in Europe. As noted above, Japan's stable exchange rate until 1971 was important in helping many Japanese firms build dominant market shares in the United States by the early 1960s, and in Europe a decade later.

All of these activities improved knowledge flows (and a degree of camaraderie) among the exporters, but competition and the drive for greater market share defined the optics-based industry. By the early 1970s, economic expansion in the developed countries meant rising incomes, more leisure time, and the emergence of a consumer society. Because consumers had more money and free time than in the past, goods that had previously been perceived as luxury items, such as cameras, were demanded by a larger proportion of the population—the mass market. Expanded supply and demand translated into growth and increased competition for the Japanese exporters. This, in turn, led to increased production and saturated markets; MNCs then turned to building new markets in East Asia.

Interfirm rivalry is especially keen in mature, oligopolistic industries where market shares have been established, and where there are a few large firms in specific sectors. In response, many of the leading optics-based firms diversified into other related products (including photocopiers, facsimile machines, steppers, and endoscopes). Intense rivalry in national and global markets fed pressures to achieve economies of scale to keep prices low.[8] Since cameras and lenses (and later office equipment, medical products, and similar items) came to be more technologically complex and more expensive to develop, markets had to be large enough to justify very large production of parts, components, and finished goods.

Canon, for example, developed the Canon AE-1, the world's first computerized camera, in 1976. A central processing unit was put into each camera, reducing the number of camera parts from around 1,300 to roughly 300 (Sandoz 1997, p. 110). Thereafter, cameras were modularized (i.e., built from a limited number of integrated components), and became more reliable and cheaper to produce. The retail price of computerized single-lens-reflex (SLR) cameras, such as the AE-1, fell by between $100 and $150, due in part to economies of scale in component manufacturing and to the reduced cost of component assembly. Canon led the market with its integrated-circuit (IC) cameras, and sales grew quickly. Component-based manufacturing was a central feature of integrated production, especially in East Asia (see below).

The average price of a mass-market camera remained relatively stable over the years, but the camera's technology became increasingly complex and firms were forced to cut production costs. Technological change also stimulated economies of scope. Firms cut costs by developing new precision machinery and complementary products that could absorb the same or highly similar components. Canon and Nikon, for example, developed "stepper" technology through the Very Large-Scale Integration (VLSI) project sponsored by the Ministry of International Trade and Industry (MITI) in the late 1970s. Through this project, Canon and Nikon together gained control of global stepper manufacturing. Canon later developed large-scale integration (LSI) to supply the firm's various high-technology optics-based products, and to continue to raise their technological level. Competition crossed traditional electronics/optics industry lines in 1981 when Sony launched the *Mavica*, the world's first digital still/video camera.[9] In the early twenty-first century, technological change such as digital technology stimulated new production solutions and, given the cost of doing business in Japan (due to high labor costs, stagnant growth, and weak domestic demand), firms entered into new manufacturing arrangements, deepening and expanding their previous investments in East Asia. Japanese MNCs thus began to effect change in Japan's economic structure.

The very effective export promotion policies that were originally meant to help Japan deal with the challenges of the early postwar years eventually came to serve as instruments to insulate Japan's old economic structure from international competition. During the "bubble" years of the 1980s, land prices and wages levels rose to unprecedented levels and the work week contracted. Subsequently, the cost of doing business in Japan skyrocketed. In short, the old economic structure threatened to suffocate the very firms that had made Japan strong. Multinational firms had no choice but to act. They turned to overseas production to create a new integrated production structure based in East Asia.

FDI in East Asia

In the 1990s, East Asia rose to be one of Japan's—and the world's—top destinations for FDI. Despite a downturn after the East Asian financial crisis, the value of Japan's FDI going into the region exceeded that to all other emerging markets in 1998 (METI 2001a, p. 4). This section briefly traces Japan's involvement in East Asia during the postwar period, in order to highlight its long-term nature and the pattern of investment that had emerged over time.

During the 1950s and 1960s, Asia (mainly Southeast Asia) was the recipient of roughly one-fifth of total Japanese FDI outflows, taking a second place ranking after North America (Mason 1999). By the early 1960s, these Asian markets were the most important markets for many Japanese manufactured products, including steel (35 percent of Japan's exports went to the region), textiles (42 percent), and consumer electronics and home appliances (44 percent) (Yoshino 1976, p. 66). Close proximity to Japan combined with lower Japanese prices, as compared to European or American goods, meant that Japanese manufactures found a natural market in East Asia. At the same time, East Asian nations also attempted to protect themselves from Japanese (as well as American and European) imports in order to foster their own industrialization. Japan depended on the region for imports of a variety of raw materials and semifinished manufactured goods that, in some cases, were managed by Japanese trading companies. Once direct investment to East Asia began to take off in the early 1960s, firms took a "follow-the-leader" strategy, a common investment pattern observed among MNCs in oligopolistic industries dominated by a few large firms. Yoshino (1976, p. 67) explained: "Any decision by a firm to establish a manufacturing subsidiary was seen by its rivals as a threat." This threat could only be met through a similar investment by a competing firm (i.e., a follower). However, all outward FDI was subject to a government approval process prior to the early 1970s, and inward FDI was not completely liberalized for another two decades.

Japanese investment went to East Asia in two distinct waves. The first was characterized by relatively modest investments and ran until the mid-1970s. The second wave began in the mid-1980s and lasted through the 1997 East Asian financial crisis, although investment levels had recovered somewhat by 2001. The first wave of FDI went mainly to Hong Kong, Singapore, South Korea, and Taiwan (the four newly industrializing economies, or NIEs, of Asia), and was generally exploitive (of natural resources, for example) in nature. Japanese firms used their investments as export platforms for simple Japanese manufactures. Because high fixed costs in Japan made it important for firms to expand and defend their export markets, they began to assemble products in East Asia using parts and components exported from Japan. The primary goal of Japanese firms was to profit from economies of scale.

For industries in which economies of scale are important for keeping products competitive, large export volumes were a key feature of a firm's strategy. Between 1951 and 1972, Japanese electronics firms established 224 overseas manufacturing subsidiaries (Yoshino 1976, p. 80). Roughly 60 percent of these investments were made between 1965 and 1972, mainly into Taiwan, South Korea and Hong Kong, three of the NIEs. Data from a 1973 MITI survey of Japanese business activity showed that Japanese textile subsidiaries purchased about half, steel and consumer electronics subsidiaries purchased about two-thirds, and precision instrument and automobile firms bought more than three-quarters of their raw materials from their parent firms (Yoshino 1976, p 68). This meant that Japanese investments and their networks of subsidiaries operating in East Asia were tightly controlled and closed to outsiders (Borrus 2000). Their objective was to assist with manufacturing in Japan, not to replace it.

Japan's FDI policy changed after the dramatic appreciation of the yen in the early 1970s, when relative production costs rose in Japan. By 1971, virtually all outward greenfield[10] direct investments without financial limits were automatically approved by the Ministry of Finance (MOF) (Mason 1992b). Thereafter, FDI to East Asia for more advanced manufacturing looked increasingly attractive to leading Japanese firms. Firms used FDI to sustain and control trade by establishing local distribution networks, much as they had done in the United States and Europe (Encarnation 1992). The expansion of Japanese FDI in East Asia in the 1970s proved only the beginning of a much larger phenomenon.

In the second wave, Japanese firms continued to invest in the NIEs, but they also looked for new opportunities to lower manufacturing costs in the second-tier NIEs (Indonesia, Malaysia, the Philippines, and Thailand), and later in China and Vietnam. The appreciation of the yen after 1985, and the subsequent "bubble" years of the late 1980s, forced MNCs to escape the high cost of manufacturing in Japan by relocating to East Asia. Firms were also quick to develop marketing and distribution in the East Asian markets through FDI in order to protect their market positions. In search of cheap, easily trained labor, firms began to invest in local production in East Asia, often at the invitation and with the protection of local governments. Now, investments took on a new role: *replacing* manufacturing in Japan.

The real growth of Japanese FDI to East Asia occurred in the second wave; it doubled within the decade after 1985. In 1995, the figure for Japanese manufacturing FDI (mainly in electrical machinery, chemicals, and metals) heading to Asia was a startling 43 percent, or more than $33.5 billion (Mason 1999, p. 31). Partly due to the increase in Japanese investments, economic growth in the region took off, and the world's attention was fixed on the new "miracle" economies of East Asia. Growth in the NIEs was particularly dampened after the 1997 East Asian financial crisis, but many nations—particularly China—were still expanding at a rapid pace in 2001. The current trend in East Asia among all MNCs is for mergers and acquisitions, various types of corporate alliances and, if necessary, plant closures (METI 2001a).

Despite the drop in Japanese FDI flows to the region after 1997, the volume of reverse imports arriving in Japan continued to grow unabated. The value of reverse imports flowing into the Japanese market reached nearly ¥5 trillion in 1999 and accounted for more than 13 percent of Japan's overall imports by fiscal year 1999 (METI 2001b).[11] Although it is very difficult to measure, intrafirm trade (i.e., trade within a firm) was also growing. Intrafirm trade occurs when a company sends components from one of its manufacturing facilities in one country to its assembly factory in another. This might be, for example, Canon sending high-technology components from Japan, metal parts from its Thai factory, and mechanical parts from one of its Chinese factories to its assembly site in China. The intrafirm trade in parts and components would be channeled through Canon's parts procurement office in Singapore, and would not all appear in Japanese trade figures because the flows occurred outside Japan, albeit within Canon.

In summary, Japan's investment activity in East Asia broadened and deepened after the mid-1980s, and was dominated by multinationals that integrated their production throughout the region (Bernard and Ravenhill 1995). Firms implemented a long-term investment strategy, in that they did not close their first-wave factories in the NIEs in order to open second-wave plants in the second-tier NIEs (Tachiki 1999). Because Japanese firms increasingly shifted medium and high-technology manufacturing out of Japan, the headquarters of Japanese MNCs were slimmed down. Japanese manufacturing was integrated in East Asia such that parts, components, and finished goods passed through several countries in the region before reaching their final markets.

These complex manufacturing systems operated across many countries with differing factor endowments, and served local and regional markets as well as the United States, Europe, and Japan. Firms responded to the recession of the 1990s in Japan, and to the 1997 East Asian crisis, by relocating more manufacturing to East Asia and by increasing their levels of reverse imports. By 2001, top firms projected that their only operations left in Japan would be marketing, research and development (R&D), product design, corporate strategy, and coordination. In many cases, however, first production runs of new consumer products and very high-technology production (including, for example, high-end digital cameras, high-technology lenses, and high-precision medical and manufacturing equipment) remained in Japan. Thus, by 2001, integrated production had become highly complex.

Integrated Production

To illustrate the importance of integrated production and the increasingly global position of Japanese MNCs, this section is based on a longitudinal study of FDI into East Asia by Japanese optics-based MNCs. The fourteen global manufacturing firms analyzed in this section had optics as their core competence—that is, they manufactured optics-based products ranging from cameras, to steppers (used to make semiconductor chips), to facsimile machines (see Table 6.1). Several of the optics-based firms manufactured their own optical glass, as well as components and parts. In 2001, Japanese firms led the world in optics technology and dominated the highly competitive optics-based sector. The few small specialty firms that had not yet invested in East Asian manufacturing (including Cosina and Tokina) are not included in this analysis.

This section begins with a short introduction of the firms represented in the sector, including a detailed analysis of the waves of the firms' investments in East Asia over time. Then, Japan's reverse imports of three goods, each representing an increasingly complex level of technological sophistication, are analyzed. The section concludes with a discussion of how firms manage technological change and low-cost manufacturing at their overseas investment sites.

138

Table 6.1

Key Statistics on the Leading Optics-Based Manufacturers (¥ billion)

Company	Capital stock	Unconsolidated sales	Consolidated sales	Overseas manufacturing ratio (volume)*	Main business
Asahi Optical/Pentax	6.1	78.4 (3/00)	51.3 (9/00)	93.4	Cameras, medical equipment, information communication equipment
Canon	164.8	1,684.2 (12/00)	2,781.3 (12/00)	30.0	Office equipment, cameras, optical equipment
Fuji Photo Film	40.4	817.1 (3/00)	707.2 (9/00)	54.5	General-use and office-use photography products, magnetic materials products
Fuji Photo Optical	0.5	83.4 (3/00)	112.2 (3/00)	n.d.	Cameras, lenses, photo handling & printing equipment, medical equipment
Fuji Xerox	20.0	645.0 (12/99)	n.d.	n.d.	Xerography products, phototelegraphy equipment, calculator input-output devices
Hoya	6.3	126.7 (3/00)	115.7 (9/00)	n.d.	Optoelectronic devices, corrective eyeglass lenses, etc.
Konica	37.5	340.5 (3/00)	271.1 (9/00)	13.3	Photosensitive materials/machinery, office equipment, cameras, optical goods
Kyocera	115.7	507.8 (3/00)	604.6 (9/00)	33.1	Semiconductor parts, electronic parts, communication equipment, etc.
Minolta	25.8	280.8 (3/00)	222.9 (9/00)	40.0	Copiers and other office equipment, cameras
Nikon	36.7	308.6 (3/00)	210.5 (9/00)	n.d.	Cameras, eyeglasses, microscopes, semiconductor-related products, etc.
Olympus	40.8	279.4 (3/00)	217.7 (9/00)	n.d.	Optical equipment, medical equipment
Ricoh	103.1	777.5 (3/00)	735.3 (9/00)	n.d.	Office automation equipment, precision equipment for cameras, etc.
Sigma Koki	1.0	0.9 (5/00)	3.7 (11/00)	0.8	Optical equipment
Tamron	3.8	24.9 (12/00)	26.9 (12/00)	n.d.	Lenses for video cameras, interchangeable lenses

Source: Tōyō Keizai Databank. 2001. *Kaigai shinshutsu kigyō sōran* (Japanese Multinationals: Facts and Figures) (Tokyo: Tōyō keizai).
*Pentax's overseas manufacturing ratio is calculated based on the number of manufactured camera bodies; Fuji Photo Film's is based on sales; n.d.: No data.

Manufacturing in East Asia

Table 6.1 shows that in 2000 Canon—the largest optics-based manufacturer—had consolidated sales (or the combined accounts of the parent and its partially and wholly owned subsidiaries) of ¥2,781.3 billion ($22.3 billion) and unconsolidated sales (sales of the parent company only) of ¥1,684.2 billion ($13.5 billion).[12] This was up slightly from the 1999 figures of ¥2,622.3 billion ($21 billion) and ¥1,482.4 billion ($11.9 billion), respectively. Canon was the world's largest manufacturer of cameras and lenses, despite the fact that these products represented only 10 percent of Canon's total sales. As a very large volume producer, the firm successfully organized production to provide components for a variety of optics-based products, with its primary emphasis on office equipment, cameras, and optical equipment. Canon began to use this volume production strategy in earnest in the 1970s, when it established its own computer component manufacturing. Canon was also one of the world's largest producers of steppers, manufacturing equipment used for semiconductor fabrication, while Nikon—which had consolidated sales of only ¥210.5 billion ($1.7 billion) in 2000—held the other top market position in steppers.

Of the larger firms, Ricoh, Fuji Photo Film, and Kyocera followed Canon with consolidated sales of ¥735.3 billion ($5.9 billion), ¥707.2 billion ($5.7 billion), and ¥604.6 billion ($4.8 billion), respectively. Ricoh specialized in office and precision equipment and, by 2001, had gained the top market share in multifunction digital office machines (fax/copier/printer), because its machines hooked easily into existing systems. Fuji Photo Film produced photosensitive and magnetic materials and products, while its subsidiary Fuji Photo Optical produced cameras and lenses. Kyocera, a leading maker of semiconductor parts and communications equipment, bought Yashica in 1983, thereby also acquiring the Contax brand name (formerly belonging to the German company Zeiss), since Contax and Yashica were in a technical tie-up at the time of the acquisition. Fuji Xerox, a highly successful joint venture between Fuji Photo Film and Xerox (of the United States), was one of the top five firms in terms of unconsolidated sales, at ¥645 billion ($5.2 billion).[13]

The contrast between the largest and smallest of these fourteen firms was marked. The smallest manufacturers were all specialist manufacturers of optical equipment, and varied dramatically in consolidated sales: Fuji Photo Optical (¥112.2 billion, or roughly $900 million), Tamron (¥26.9 billion, $215 million), and Sigma Koki (¥3.7 billion, $30 million). Asahi Optical/Pentax joined this group of the smallest optics-based firms in 2000 (with consolidated sales of ¥51.3 billion, or $410 million), although it was a comprehensive maker of cameras and lenses, medical equipment, certain office equipment, eyeglass lenses, and precision machinery. The firm's consolidated sales dropped by over half between 1999 and 2000 (and remained weak in 2001) due to increased competition—not only in the optics-based products, but also in the digital arena, where new firms had emerged as competitors.

Using capital stock as a proxy for the size of each firm, three specific groups were identified. In ranking order, the largest firms were Canon, Kyocera, and Ricoh, with capital stock of more than ¥100 billion ($800 million). The next group comprised six firms (Olympus, Fuji Photo Film, Konica, Nikon, Minolta, and Fuji Xerox) with capital stock of ¥20–40 billion ($160–320 million). The smallest firms were Hoya, Pentax, Tamron, Sigma Koki, and Fuji Photo Optical with capital stock ranging from a half-billion yen to just over ¥6 billion ($4–48 million).

Only half of the firms shown in Table 6.1 provide figures for their overseas manufacturing ratio, calculated in volume of production (unless otherwise noted). Pentax had the highest ratio, with 93.4 percent of manufacturing of camera bodies being manufactured outside of Japan, while Sigma Koki had the lowest, at 0.8 percent. Olympus estimates that, like Pentax, nearly 100 percent of its film-based (or analog) cameras were manufactured in East Asia in 2001. The statistics were similar for all the other manufacturers listed in Table 6.1 as camera manufacturers (plus Kyocera).[14] Most of these same firms also manufactured digital cameras. As of August 2001, only very simple "toy" digital cameras were manufactured in East Asia, while the rest were manufactured in Japan (see below). Although it is not the focus of this chapter, many of these firms also had some manufacturing in Europe and/or the United States in photocopier and facsimile equipment and supplies. The optics-based firms manufactured in only a few locations in Japan; their mass-market goods were produced mainly in East Asia (see Table 6.2).

China (not including Hong Kong) received the vast majority of the fourteen firms' investments after 1990, with twenty-three individual investments (see Table 6.2). Nine additional investments went to Hong Kong, the earliest by Kyocera (originally Yashica) in 1967. The very earliest investment, however, was by Ricoh into Taiwan in 1965. Other early entrants were: Fuji Xerox and Canon in Taiwan (in 1969 and 1970, respectively); Ricoh in South Korea (1970); Fuji Xerox in the Philippines (1971); Minolta in Malaysia and Pentax in Hong Kong (1973); Hoya in Thailand and Fuji Xerox in South Korea (1974); and finally, Pentax in Taiwan (1975). The follow-the-leader pattern was clearly visible during this period. Then, after a short three-year break, Hoya invested in Hong Kong and then, two years later, in Taiwan. This first wave (1965–75) resulted in eleven investments mainly to the NIEs, with two additional investments by 1980. In the second wave (1985–98), FDI from the fourteen firms enjoyed explosive growth, to-taling fifty-three investments primarily in the second-tier NIEs, China, and Vietnam, as well as some complementary investments in the NIEs. Over 40 percent of these investments went to China after 1990. Thus, the optics-based firms participated in two waves of FDI to East Asia, and pursued a follow-the-leader investment pattern.

Each firm employed a wide variety of investment strategies, such as investing in several countries to spread risk; but firm size was not a good indicator of the number of its investments. Of the largest firms, Canon and Fuji Xerox had invested in six countries by 2000, but Canon had twice as many investments as Fuji Xerox, with twelve plants. Hoya and Kyocera were two other large investors, each with eight investments in five countries, but in terms of capital stock Kyocera was eighteen times larger than Hoya. Ricoh, another large firm in capital-stock terms, had seven investments in five countries while Asahi Optical/Pentax, a small firm, had five investments in four countries. Sigma Koki and Tamron, the smallest of the fourteen firms, appeared to be among the latecomers to FDI in East Asia and had only one overseas investment apiece, in China.

By 2001, almost all of the firms had invested in China or Hong Kong and at least one other country. Olympus pursued the strategy of investing only in China/Hong Kong and Taiwan, which allowed the firm to exploit the expertise of its Chinese-speaking staff at its head-quarters. Other firms, however, concentrated their investments in the second-tier NIEs—for example, Minolta in Malaysia, Nikon in Thai-land, and Pentax in the Philippines (and later Vietnam).

Some of the FDI listed in Table 6.2 were procurement/coordination

Table 6.2

Japanese Optics-Based (and Related) Manufacturing Facilities in East Asia

Country	Multinational company	Est. year (mo.)	Products/Purpose
China	Canon	1991 (2)	Office machines, consumable supplies
	Canon	1990 (1)	Cameras, office machines
	Canon	n.d.	Office machines & parts, consumable supplies
	Canon	n.d.	Camera parts & products
	Fuji Photo Film	1995 (10)	All types of imaging equipment
	Fuji Photo Film	a	Optical equipment, electronic imaging equipment
	Fuji Photo Optical[b]	1994(11)	Optical lenses
	Fuji Xerox	1995 (6)	Mini-laser printers
	Hoya	1995 (11)	Plastic eyeglass lenses
	Konica[b]	1994 (4)	Lenses for optical equipment
	Kyocera	1996 (7)	Precision optical equipment
	Kyocera	1996 (8)	Electronic parts
	Minolta	1994 (10)	Manual-focus SLRs, inexpensive compact cameras
	Minolta	1994 (10)	Photocopiers
	Nikon	1997 (6)	Cameras
	Olympus	1997 (1)	Camera, various precision machinery
	Olympus[b]	1991 (12)	Camera assembly
	Ricoh	1996 (12)	Office automation equipment
	Ricoh	1995 (12)	Thermo-sensitive and plain paper fax machines
	Ricoh	1993 (3)	Cameras
	Ricoh	1991 (1)	Office equipment
	Sigma Koki	1993 (6)	Laser-beam polishing equipment (for lenses/prisms)
	Tamron[b]	1998 (1)	ILs, lenses for video cameras, other optical equipment
Hong Kong (China)	Asahi Optical/Pentax	1973 (6)	Cameras, optical equipment, import/export
	Canon	1994 (5)	Parts procurement
	Canon	1991 (11)	Office machines
	Fuji Photo Film	n.d.	Parts and raw materials procurement
	Hoya	1978 (8)	Lenses for eyeglasses
	Konica[b]	1988 (8)	Copier parts, etc., procurement
	Kyocera	1967 (5)	Precision optical equipment
	Olympus[b]	1988 (10)	Camera products, camera parts
	Ricoh	1995 (4)	Chemical equipment
Indonesia	Kyocera	1992 (1)	Items for Kyocera products
Malaysia	Canon	1989	Optical lenses, cameras
	Fuji Photo Optical	1996 (5)	Subunits for photo-handling equipment
	Fuji Xerox	1992 (10)	Office equipment import/export
	Hoya	1993	Lenses for eyeglasses, related products
	Kyocera	1998 (6)	Electronic parts

Malaysia	Minolta	1988 (2)	Camera parts, metals manufacturing
	Minolta	1973 (5)	Cameras, camera parts assembly
Philippines	Asahi Optical/Pentax	1992 (4)	Thin, highly refractive plastic eyeglass lenses
	Asahi Optical/Pentax	1990 (9)	Cameras, information equipment
	Fuji Xerox	1971 (7)	Photocopiers, fax machines
	Hoya	1997 (2)	Lenses for eyeglasses, related products
Singapore	Canon	1989 (11)	Parts procurement
	Fuji Photo Film	1989 (5)	Photographic chemicals
	Fuji Xerox	1991 (3)	Office equipment import/export
	Hoya	1995 (6)	Glass magnetic disks
	Kyocera	1990 (1)	Electronic parts
South Korea	Canon	1985 (5)	Photocopiers, photocopier supplies
	Fuji Xerox	1974 (8)	Photocopiers
	Kyocera	1987 (6)	Electronic parts
	Ricoh	1970 (7)	Office equipment, sensitized paper
Taiwan	Asahi Optical/Pentax	1975 (7)	Cameras, lenses
	Canon	1970 (6)	Cameras
	Fuji Xerox	1969 (12)	Photocopiers
	Hoya[b]	1987 (5)	Optical glass semi-finished goods
	Hoya	1980 (5)	Lenses for eyeglasses
	Kyocera	1998 (6)	Electronic parts
	Olympus[b]	1989 (7)	Procurement of compact camera parts
	Ricoh[b]	1965 (3)	Cameras, optical instruments
Thailand	Canon	1991 (11)	Metals manufacturing
	Canon	1990 (8)	Office machines
	Hoya[b]	1974 (1)	Lenses for eyeglasses
	Konica	1996 (7)	Photo-sensitive materials
	Nikon	1990 (10)	ILs, SLRs, compact cameras
Vietnam	Asahi Optical/Pentax	1995 (5)	Popular ILs, inexpensive measuring equipment

Source: Tōyō Keizai Databank. 2001. *Kaigai shinshutsu kigyō sōran* (Japanese Multinationals: Facts and Figures) (Tokyo: Tōyō keizai).

Notes: a. Fuji Photo Film incorporated two companies at the same location.

b. One of the objectives of this investment is reverse imports.

n.d.: No data

ILs: Interchangeable lenses

SLRs: Single-lens reflex cameras

sites for managing the company's intra-firm transactions. The firms used the NIEs—for example, Olympus in Taiwan, and Canon in Hong Kong and Singapore, as central locations for purchasing parts and components and coordinating intra-firm trade. These types of investments and activities became evident in the second wave as firms required more active management of these functions in close proximity to their manufacturing plants in East Asia. Furthermore, as wage levels rose in Japan as well as in the NIEs, firms intensified their efforts to raise the skill levels of their overseas employees. Canon's employees from Malaysia, for example, could be sent to the Canon plant in Taiwan to be taught manufacturing and/or assembly methods. These methods could then be transferred to the Malaysian plant, freeing up the Taiwanese plant to take over advanced operations (such as procurement and coordination) that could be transferred out of Japan. Firms took advantage of the diverse skill levels of their employees throughout East Asia, and also raised their employees' levels of know-how to suit their manufacturing requirements.

Pentax offers a particularly good example of this phenomenon. In May 2001, Pentax announced a reform plan with the following aims: to cut costs and expenses, to sell products at more competitive prices, to exploit new business opportunities, to tighten inventory control, to enhance the sales force, and to strengthen the Pentax brand worldwide.[15] Part of its plan was to close one plant in Japan (at Ogawa) that manufactured interchangeable lenses and medical apparatus. All of its manufacturing was to be transferred to the two plants remaining in Japan (in Mashiko and Miyagi) and to one of its overseas plants, located in Vietnam. The Vietnam plant was to become the firm's main facility for manufacturing interchangeable lenses, which meant that the Taiwanese plant (which manufactured interchangeable lenses at that time) would be reorganized to absorb all other camera products manufacturing from Japan, except for particular special-application cameras. The firm's plan would be made possible by limiting the number of new hires, forcing some employees into early retirement, and cutting executive salaries by over 10 percent in fiscal year 2001. It was estimated that these measures would save the firm ¥2 billion annually in labor costs, beginning in fiscal year 2002.

The Pentax example illustrates how important relative labor costs were to the firm's cost considerations and competitiveness. This was also acknowledged by a senior business leader at Olympus, who estimated that in 2001 the wages for Chinese workers at their plants was about one-twentieth of Japanese wages.[16] Moreover, their Chinese employees were highly productive. Firms kept the average age in the overseas plants low because of a constant turnover of new employees on short-term contracts and the seemingly endless supply of new workers. Despite the high turnover rate, the firm enjoyed high productivity at lower cost than could be achieved in Japan.

Reverse Imports

The effects of the East Asian production networks on the Japanese economy are analyzed in this section through bilateral trade data, in particular through Japan's reverse imports from East Asian countries. The import data is instructive since it reveals a great deal about the value and volume of Japan's reverse imports since 1990 (that is, during the second wave of Japan's FDI to East Asia). The three products discussed come from three levels of technological sophistication: low, medium, and high. They are 35mm roll-film cameras (or "compact," point-and-shoot cameras), 35mm single-lens reflex (SLR) cameras, and photographic lenses. While the import data do not reveal the companies from which Japan imported optics-based goods, Japanese firms were the undisputed world leaders in the three products analyzed in detail here. Thus, it is reasonable to assume that the trade data for Japan's imports from East Asian countries indicated those goods that were manufactured by Japanese optics-based firms and reverse imported into Japan.

The import data were collected from the Japan Tariff Association for three representative years (1990, 1995, and 2000) during Japan's second wave of FDI (see Figures 6.1, 6.2, and 6.3). Digital cameras and equipment were mainly manufactured in Japan, although by 2001, many of the simplest compact digital cameras, or "toy" cameras, were manufactured in East Asia. As of December 2000, the cumulative trade data (i.e., imports into Japan) did not have specific product categories for digital goods (e.g., cameras, camera parts, and office equipment). Looking at the origins of the goods imported into Japan (by value), a picture of Japanese trade emerges that supports the view that Japanese firms had developed a complex network of firms and had integrated production in East Asia.

The bars in Figure 6.1 comprise 100 percent of Japan's total imports of 35mm roll-film cameras, commonly known as "compact" cameras. Countries representing a very small share of imports were grouped together as "other." China's dominant share of Japan's imports in 2000 (at 67 percent, up from zero a decade earlier) is immediately striking in Figure 6.1. The other country showing a major gain was the Philippines (up from zero to 10.3 percent). The countries losing import

Figure 6.1   **Japan's Imports of 35mm Roll-Film Cameras, by Country**
(percent, based on value)

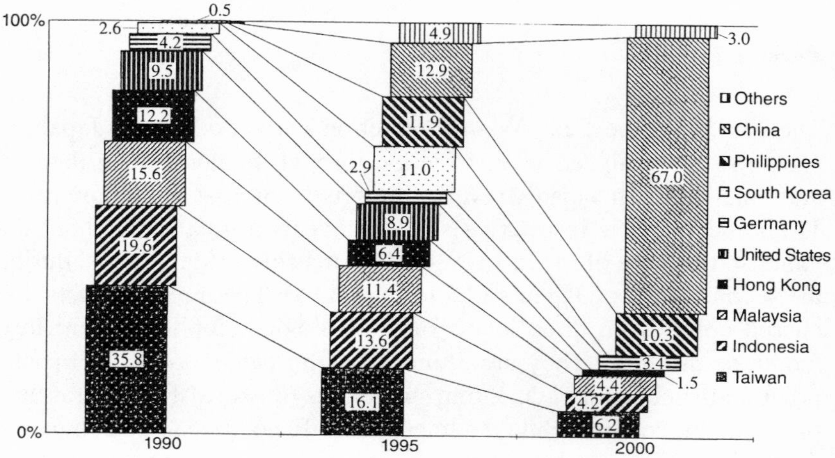

Source: Japan Tariff Association. 2000. *Japan Exports and Imports, Commodity by Country* (Tokyo: JTA). Dec. imports: 841; Dec. 1995 imports: 875; Dec. 1990 imports: 791.

shares over the period were Taiwan, Indonesia, Malaysia, and Hong Kong. Since Japanese firms led the world in compact cameras, we can infer that Japan's increased imports from the Philippines came from Pentax, while the decrease from Malaysia reflected the performance of Minolta and Canon. These import figures were therefore a proxy for Japan's reverse imports from 1990 to 2000.

The value of Japan's total imports of 35mm roll-film cameras nearly tripled between 1990 and 1995 (from ¥12.6 billion to ¥33 billion), but then fell more than 20 percent, to ¥24 billion in 2000. The decline was due to shrinking demand in Japan for analog 35mm "compact" cameras, and was replaced by new demand for compact digital cameras. The Japanese market offered a very wide selection of digital cameras, and mass market sales were estimated to have taken off in early 2000. Between 1999 and 2000, production (mainly in Japan) of all types of digital still cameras by the member firms of the Japan Camera Industry Association (JCIA) more than doubled, from five million to about ten million units, or by value from ¥228 billion to ¥438 billion (JCIA 2001, pp. 35, 37). Due to the high cost of doing business in Japan, however, most of the manufacturers were in the process of moving some digital production to East Asia in 2001. Many firms had already moved "toy" digital camera manufacturing to East Asia to take up slack production capacity, to keep prices competitive, and to build strong product recognition and market share.

Japan's imports of 35mm single-lens reflex cameras, which are technologically more complex than "compact" 35mm cameras, are presented in Figure 6.2. The countries with relatively low imports into Japan are labeled as "other." Because the cameras are high-technology goods, not all of the eight leading camera manufacturers produced SLRs. In fact, Olympus, one of the industry leaders, chose to withdraw from SLR manufacturing in 1998. Perhaps this was why the import data show a remarkable change in the three largest sources of SLRs to the Japanese market over the decade. The countries recording the greatest gains were the Philippines (Pentax), Thailand (Nikon and Canon), and Taiwan (Olympus, until 1998; Pentax and Canon). Because costs were rising and the economy was stagnating in Taiwan, Japan's SLR imports from that country were expected to fall after 2001. The two countries with the highest fluctuations in SLR exports to Japan were China (from zero to 11.4 percent to zero, probably due to the Olympus withdrawal from SLR manufacturing) and Malaysia (from 3.5 to 55.6 to 23.8 percent), thanks to Canon and Minolta, the world's two top SLR makers. The countries from which imports to Japan shrank were Germany (home to Leica and Zeiss) and Hong Kong (Canon, Pentax, and Olympus). Hong Kong's drop was due to the shift to procurement activities as other locations became more suitable for manufacturing. Some of Japan's imports from Germany were also affected by, for example, Leica's relocation in the 1990s of its lower-cost camera production to East Asia, and increased dependence on OEM suppliers.

The value of Japan's imports of 35mm SLRs grew dramatically between 1990 and 1995, from ¥570 million to ¥8 billion, and then stabilized by 2000 at roughly ¥7.5 billion. Again, this indicated that demand in Japan for analog cameras had stagnated, while demand for digital SLRs was growing. By 2001, firms had settled into a pattern of nearly 100 percent production of analog camera bodies in East Asia.

Unlike cameras and camera bodies, the manufacture of lenses—that is, simple plastic and glass lenses for disposable cameras, fixed-mount lenses such as those used on 35mm "compact" cameras, and interchangeable lenses for the more expensive SLR cameras—was still in flux in 2001. Digital camera bodies could easily replace the analog camera bodies, but digital lenses were another story. Analog lenses

Figure 6.2   **Japan's Imports of 35mm SLR Cameras, by Country**
(percent, based on value)

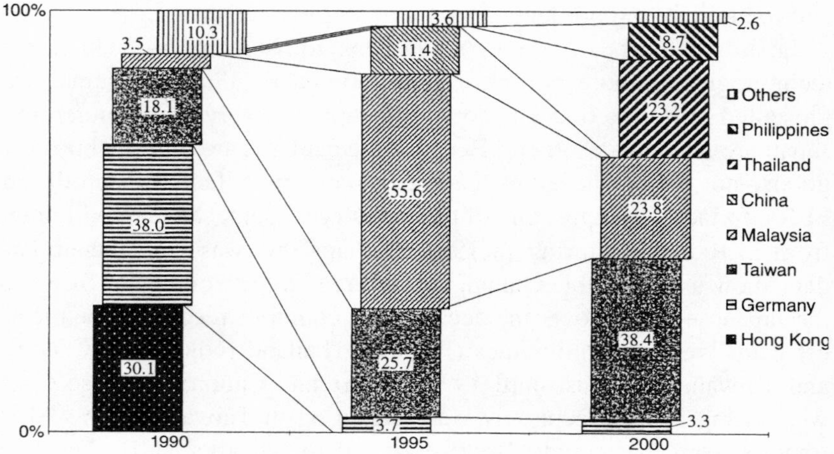

Sources: Japan Tariff Association. 2000. *Japan Exports and Imports, Commodity by Country* (Tokyo: JTA). Dec. imports: 840; Dec. 1995 imports: 875; Dec. 1990 imports: 791.

could be used with either digital or analog cameras, but digital cameras performed best with digital lenses. Whether a firm manufactured lenses in Japan or in East Asia depended on the technological complexity of the lenses, as well as the trade-off between the cost of production and the need to protect its intellectual property.

Japan's imports of analog photographic lenses from 1990 to 2000 are shown in Figure 6.3. During the 1990s, the largest exporting countries to Japan of photographic lenses increased from four to six. The countries supplying very small percentages of Japan's imports were grouped together as "other." The big gainers over the decade were China (up from zero to 32.8 percent), where eight firms manufactured; and Thailand (up from zero to 7.6 percent, with some fluctuation), where Canon, Hoya and Nikon had located manufacturing. The countries recording big declines were Sweden (down from 26.6 to 2.1 percent), the home of the Hasselblad; and Germany (down from 35.7 to 11.6 percent), home to Zeiss, Leica, Schneider, and others. Sweden's exports to Japan may have included lenses for Hasselblad cameras that were originally made elsewhere, for example by Zeiss and Schneider in Germany. The two countries that held steady export shares to Japan were: Malaysia (up from 15.2 to 19.9 percent), home to manufacturing operations of Canon,

Figure 6.3 **Japan's Imports of Photographic Lenses, by Country**
(percent, based on value)

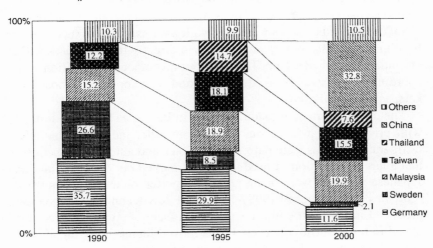

Sources: Japan Tariff Association. 2000. *Japan Exports and Imports, Commodity by Country* (Tokyo: JTA). Dec. imports: 837–38; Dec. 1995 imports: 872; Dec. 1990 imports: 787.

Hoya, Minolta, and Fuji Photo Optical; and Taiwan (up from 12.2 to 15.5 percent), home to Pentax, Canon, Hoya, and Ricoh facilities.

Hoya, for example, was an important firm in optical products, as it manufactured and supplied a broad range of lenses of varying techno-logical levels. Firms utilized a combination of manufacturing strategies. Low-cost manufacturing sites were used for simpler photographic lenses (e.g., plastic lenses), while high-cost manufacturing sites were used for higher-quality lenses made of glass. Within a country such as China, where a variety of skill levels were present, firms manufactured both simple and complex optical goods. This accounts for why China was a major exporter of both compact cameras and photographic lenses. Japan's total imports of lenses for cameras grew steadily from ¥2.7 bil-lion in 1990, to ¥5.2 billion in 1995, and reached ¥7 billion by 2000.

Implications

Of the many reasons for actively investing in East Asia, the most impor-tant was cost. The original impetus for investing in East Asia was to service the Japanese market with *lower-cost* goods, *not inferior-quality* goods. As the East Asian markets began to grow, demand for Japanese optics-based goods expanded, enticing firms to expand their FDI to service local markets. Long-term investments were integrated with the supply of components, parts, metals, and various consumables (such as toner for copiers) to assembly plants, and then directly to consumers within the entire East Asian region. Thus, various manufacturing locations were coordinated for specific local markets and for export from those markets, as described above.

The data indicate that manufacturing in East Asia had shifted in line with price/cost considerations. Data from other industries (including refrigerators, radios, calculators, televisions, and automobiles) confirm that a large proportion of production had moved out of Japan, and that Japanese products were being reverse imported on an increasing scale (Ozawa 1999; Ravenhill 1999). In general, low-technology goods were produced in low-cost countries, and high-technology goods were produced in higher-cost countries. Firms moved increasingly higher technology into plants located mainly in the NIEs. They shifted lower technologies to plants in the newer FDI locations (the second-tier NIEs, China, and Vietnam). Because manufacturing low-technology goods required lower skill levels, the parent firm had time to train new staff, and then to prepare them for the next technological shift upward. Skills such as problem solving were transferred to locals through on-the-job training (Urata 1999). Integrated production throughout East Asia, therefore, allowed each plant within the network to specialize in a particular group of skills and to raise skill levels continuously. Component manufacturing was suited to integrated production in East Asia, because production could more easily be adapted to local skill levels and coordinated among several manufacturing locations.

Olympus was a good example of coordinated manufacturing. The firm manufactured simpler items in East Asia, but complex and sensitive goods in Japan. It reasoned that if a camera, lens, copier, or fax machine had a fault, it could be easily repaired or replaced. However, if an endoscope, a highly precise medical instrument, had a fault that jeopardized a person's life due to malfunction during an operation, then there would be serious consequences for Olympus. For this reason, the firm manufactured its highly sensitive medical instruments such as endoscopes in Japan, which cost much more, but allowed the firm to keep strict control over manufacturing quality. It also allowed firms to make larger profit margins from each endoscope produced, whereas inexpensive consumer goods such as cameras (including digital) do not allow for high margins. Because reliability was all-important, firms had to be careful to protect their global image as manufacturers of reliable, high-quality precision instruments. At some point, if conditions in Japan become too expensive, Olympus may have to relocate even these sensitive manufactures out of Japan.

While this process was still evolving in the early twenty-first century, emerging patterns of trade and manufacturing investment offered the potential for new opportunities for firms exporting from East Asia into Japan, such as the Chinese computer maker Legend (*Economist* 2001). Ozawa (1999) may have been correct in asserting that Japanese firms, and their transplants in East Asia, were at a competitive disadvantage in components and assembly in the electronics and automobile industries, because there were firms in the region that could produce at lower cost than the Japanese firms. The threat to Japanese firms was that they would lose their technological and brand advantages to new East Asian competitors.

The increasingly inter-connected trading relationships in the region offered both positive and negative opportunities for Japanese firms. Firms that managed their new business relationships in East Asia well (and had luck on their side) would succeed in the long run. Innovation in digital optics and components, and the coordination challenges implicit in regional production networks, were expected to raise the level of competition. Digital technologies could potentially trigger consolidation among the traditional electronics firms and the optics-based firms. This may reduce the number of global competitors, while at the same time offering opportunities for smaller local or regional players. It may well be that skillful management of the opportunities and threats in the changing business and financial context of East Asia is what will separate the winners from the losers among Japan's MNCs.

Conclusion and Policy Implications

By 2001, East Asia had grown to become the primary target of Japanese FDI in the manufacturing sectors, and major Japanese multinational firms had integrated production in the region. This analysis points to a number of conclusions. First, the Japanese multinationals that brought Japan to its postwar economic peak had changed the rules of the game, and were reverse importing their goods to Japan. To do this, Japanese firms employed integrated production across the East Asian region. Second, the data highlight the strategic use of long-term FDI in various East Asian nations, complementing the larger trend toward regional economic integration. Third, Japan's reverse imports from East Asia rose steadily during the 1990s, driven by the multinational firms' need to manufacture in low-cost areas, and permeated Japan's previously insulated home market.

The rise of Japan's multinationals and their expansion into integrated production networks tells a universal story of the globalization of business. The Japanese optics-based firms, discussed in detail above, are exceptionally useful for analyzing integrated production because they have led the world in that sector. Thus, the Japanese import data provide a useful tool that gives a strong indication of Japanese firms' exports from East Asia into the Japanese market. Although the firms became active investors in East Asia in the 1970s, it was not until after the mid-1980s that a large number of linked manufacturing plants became operational in the region. The major optics-based firms invested in more than one East Asian nation, and coordinated their East Asian plants across national borders to produce top-quality consumer goods. Intra-firm trade within the region was nearly impossible to trace, since it took place within one firm, and therefore did not show up in the Japanese trade data.

Plants in high-cost countries (e.g., the NIEs), where the firms had been active over a longer period, were in 2001 being used as high-technology manufacturing locations requiring highly skilled employees. A few of these East Asian manufacturing plants were at or near the leading edge in, for example, photographic lens manufacturing and digital cameras. Newer investments (mainly in the second-tier NIEs) were in low-technology manufacturing with skill requirements that suited the local labor supply. China was the exception, with both low- and high-technology manufacturing investments. Firms exploited these long-term manufacturing investments in this way because their products were highly sensitive to price/cost considerations, due to the high level of competition in the industry.

By August 2001, Taiwan had (like Japan) become very expensive for manufacturing, and the government announced that much of Taiwan's manufacturing capacity would move to mainland China. The global semiconductor chip slowdown in early 2001 hit Taiwan especially hard. Both Taiwan and China would benefit from Taiwan's manufacturing move to China, especially since their applications to join the World Trade Organization were approved in September 2001.

As the cost of doing business rose in Japan, especially during the 1990s, the optics-based firms moved more business activities out of Japan, increased their reverse imports into Japan, and opened up new opportunities for other firms. The insulated Japanese market was in the process of being opened to imports through reverse imports in 2001, causing an important shift in Japan's industrial structure. Meanwhile, Japanese MNCs located at home were being emptied of all but their most important functions. Leading firms projected in 2001 that the only operations left in Japan would be marketing, R&D, product design, corporate strategy, and coordination. In short, Japanese multinationals had caused a policy "re-think."

Japan faced numerous problems at the beginning of the twenty-first century. Among those that affected Japanese multinationals most were Japan's strict labor laws and the high production costs in Japan. Strict labor laws meant that Japanese MNCs could not bring inexpensive labor into Japan, and instead had to move manufacturing to where the workers lived. Another problem for manufacturing firms was the lack of desire among young Japanese to work in production, but this was offset by an abundant supply of eager and very efficient workers in East Asia. High business costs in Japan meant that firms were unable to hire new workers domestically (thus raising the average age in the firms) and that they had to find ways to reduce current staff. In this vein, integrated production highlighted synergies among the countries in East Asia. As an advanced industrialized country, Japan had a complementary economic relationship with the NIEs, and with the emerging market economies of the second-tier NIEs, China, and Vietnam. The complementarity was in skills, labor costs, and technological levels.

The East Asian investments of the Japanese optics-based firms provide an excellent example of the sector-specific nature of permeable insulation. Firms in the optics sector clearly preferred noninterference in their affairs, and were no longer dependent on government-led insulation. Instead, they were mapping out a new regional division of labor. If the lessons of the optics industry can be generalized, we may expect to see rapid structural transformation, and perhaps de-industrialization, in those sectors that opt against insulation. In such sectors, the role of the government may run increasingly toward some of the support features that Elder (see Chapter 7) highlights.

While rapid globalization of production will be an attractive strategy for some leading industries and firms, many firms will continue to seek insulation from global competition. However, even those firms that make full use of private and public-led insulation strategies will be unable to ignore the effects of "hollowing out" in the leading sectors, and will need to improve their competitiveness in the face of the increasingly unavoidable globalization of competition. As the experience of the 1990s shows, it was impossible for the government to prevent MNCs from leaving the country. Instead, the government was challenged to create a good environment for competitive firms to stay in Japan; but this would be difficult to accomplish while simultaneously providing insulation for weaker firms. Thus, while MNCs moved ahead, the Japanese state was confronted with the difficulty of maintaining permeable insulation in the economy.

Notes

I would like to gratefully acknowledge the helpful comments of John Ravenhill, the editors and contributors to this issue, the participants of the Japanese Politics Colloquium, and the participants of the Research Institute of Economy Trade and Industry (RIETI) research seminar. I would also like to express my thanks to the Japan Foundation Endowment Committee for its financial support (Grant No. 171). All errors are my own.

1. Industrial optics in materials other than glass or plastics were also developing at a very fast pace, sometimes by specialized firms not considered in this analysis.

2. Hereinafter, Asahi Optical is referred to as Pentax, which is the brand name of the firm's world-renowned camera line and was expected to be adopted as the parent company's name.

3. The current account is net exports of goods and services, minus net imports of goods and services, including invisible trade such as royalties paid on patents.

4. If Company A supplies a finished product to Company B and it carries Company B's brand name, then Company A supplies Company B on an OEM basis.

5. For a discussion of business needs and interests regarding Japan's future international trade policy, see Keidanren (2001).

6. For a more detailed analysis, see Nelson (1998).

7. The exchange rate was originally set at ¥360 to the U.S. dollar in April 1949, in the hope that it would help halt hyperinflation (Tsuru 1996). But from the mid-1950s, and for the next fifteen years, Japanese exports came to have a substantial price advantage over their competitors in the U.S. market and in European markets.

8. The aim of economies of scale, or volume production, is to spread the cost of the initial (and further) investment across more units through large-scale manufacturing.

9. Sony did not manufacture optics as of 2001.

10. "Greenfield" refers to the building of new facilities, as opposed to taking over existing ones.

11. The Japanese fiscal year runs from April 1 to March 31.

12. Each firm's data are reported according to accounting standards based on either the Japanese fiscal year (ending in March) or the calendar year (ending in December).

13. The more important consolidated sales data were not available.

14. Information from Olympus, August 2001.

15. Information from Asahi Optical/Pentax, August 2001.

16. Interview with Toshiro Shimoyama, director and supreme adviser, Olympus Optical, August 2001.

References

Bernard, Mitchell, and John Ravenhill. 1995. "Beyond Product Cycles and Flying Geese: Regionalization, Hierarchy, and the Industrialization of East Asia." *World Politics* 47 (2): 171–209.

Borrus, Michael. 2000. "The Resurgence of U.S. Electronics." In Michael Borrus, Dieter Ernst, and Stephan Haggard, eds., *International Production Networks in Asia: Rivalry or Riches?*, pp. 57–79. London: Routledge.

Calder, Kent. 1993. *Strategic Capitalism: Private Business and Public Purpose in Japanese Industrial Finance.* Princeton: Princeton University Press.

Doner, Richard F. 2001. "Regionalization and Regionalism in Southeast Asia: Implications of the Disk Drive and Auto Industries." Paper presented at the annual meeting of the Association for Asian Studies, Chicago, March 22–25.

Economist. 2001. "Face Value: Legend in the Making. Can Liu Chuanzhi Turn China's Biggest Computer Maker into Its First Global Brand?" *The Economist* (September 15): 74.

Encarnation, Dennis J. 1992. *Rivals Beyond Trade: America Versus Japan in the Global Competition.* Ithaca: Cornell University Press.

Itoh, Motoshige, and Kazuharu Kiyono. 1988. "Foreign Trade and Direct Investment." In Ryutaro Komiya, Masahiro Okuno, and Kotaro Suzumura, eds., *Industrial Policy of Japan*, pp. 155–81. London: Academic Press.

JCIA (Japan Camera Industry Association). 2001. *JCIA Report 2001: Photographic Industry in Japan.* Tokyo: JCIA.

Japan Tariff Association. 1990; 1995; 2000. *Japan Exports and Imports, Commodity by Country* (December). Tokyo: JTA.

Katz, Richard. 1998. *Japan: The System That Soured. The Rise and Fall of the Japanese Economic Miracle.* Armonk, NY: M.E. Sharpe.

Keidanren. 2001. "Towards the Implementation of Strategic Trade Policies: A Grand Design of Japan's Policy as a Nation Built on Trade." June. Accessed March 13, 2002. Available at www.keidanren.or.jp/english/policy/2001/029.html.

Lincoln, Edward J. 1988. *Japan: Facing Economic Maturity.* Washington, DC: Brookings Institution.

Mason, Mark. 1992a. *American Multinationals and Japan: The Political Economy of Japanese Capital Controls, 1899–1980*. Cambridge: Council on East Asian Studies, Harvard University.

———. 1992b. "The Origins and Evolution of Japanese Direct Investment in Europe." *Business History Review* 66 (Summer): 435–74.

———. 1999. "The Origins and Evolution of Japanese Direct Investment in East Asia." In Dennis J. Encarnation, ed., *Japanese Multinationals in Asia: Regional Operations in Comparative Perspective*, pp. 17–45. Oxford: Oxford University Press.

McKendrick, David G., Richard F. Doner, and Stephan Haggard. 2000. *From Silicon Valley to Singapore: Location and Competitive Advantage in the Hard Disk Drive Industry*. Stanford: Stanford University Press.

METI (Ministry of Economy, Trade, and Industry). 2001a. *White Paper on International Trade: External Economic Policy Challenges in the 21st Century*. Tokyo: METI.

———. 2001b. "Value of Reverse Imports and Ratio in Overall Value of Japanese Imports." Mimeo.

Nelson, Patricia A. 1998. "Rivalry and Cooperation: How the Japanese Photography Industry Went Global." Ph.D. dissertation, University of Warwick.

Ozawa, Terutomo. 1999. "Pacific Economic Integration and the Flying Geese Paradigm." In Alan M. Rugman and Gavin Boyd, eds., *Deepening Integration in the Pacific Economies*, pp. 55–91. Cheltenham, UK: Elgar.

Ravenhill, John. 1999. "Japanese and U.S. Subsidiaries in East Asia." In Dennis Encarnation, ed., *Japanese Multinationals in Asia: Regional Operations in Comparative Perspective*, pp. 261–84. Oxford: Oxford University Press.

Sandoz, Philip. 1997. *Canon: Global Responsibilities and Local Decisions*. London: Penguin.

Schaede, Ulrike. 2000. *Cooperative Capitalism: Self-Regulation, Trade Associations, and the Antimonopoly Law in Japan*. Oxford: Oxford University Press.

Sumiya, Mikio, ed. 2000. *A History of Japanese Trade and Industry Policy*. Oxford: Oxford University Press.

Tachiki, Dennis. 1999. "The Business Strategies of Japanese Production Networks in Asia." In Dennis J. Encarnation, ed., *Japanese Multinationals in Asia: Regional Operations in Comparative Perspective*, pp. 183–212. Oxford: Oxford University Press.

Tōyō Keizai Databank. 2001. *Kaigai shinshutsu kigyō sōran 2001* (Japanese Multinationals: Facts and Figures). Tokyo: Tōyō keizai.

Tsuru, Shigeto. 1996. *Japan's Capitalism: Creative Defeat and Beyond*. Cambridge: Cambridge University Press/Canto.

Tyson, Laura D'Andrea. 1992. *Who's Bashing Whom? Trade Conflict in High-Technology Industries*. Washington, DC: Institute for International Economics.

Urata, Shujiro. 1999. "Intrafirm Technology Transfer by Japanese Multinationals in Asia." In Dennis J. Encarnation, ed., *Japanese Multinationals in Asia: Regional Operations in Comparative Perspective*, pp. 143–62. Oxford: Oxford University Press.

Vestal, James. 1993. *Planning for Change: Industrial Policy and Japanese Economic Development, 1945–1990*. Oxford: Oxford University Press.

Yoshino, Michael Y. 1976. *Japan's Multinational Enterprises*. Cambridge: Harvard University Press.

Part III

Domestic Political Economy and Permeable Insulation

7

METI and Industrial Policy in Japan

Change and Continuity

Mark Elder

This chapter takes up the question of how Japan's industrial policy evolved in the 1990s in response to a changing domestic and global environment. In particular, it focuses on the policies of the Ministry of Economy, Trade, and Industry (METI), formerly the Ministry of International Trade and Industry (MITI). This chapter argues that there were elements of both continuity and change, and that these can be understood in terms of a strategy of permeable insulation similar to the other areas discussed in this book. On the one hand, METI branched out in new directions in the direction of greater permeability. On the other hand, many "insulative" policies remained.

In the 1980s, there was a fierce debate over the role of MITI in Japan's economic miracle, and whether other countries could improve their economic performance by adopting all or parts of the Japanese model. Chalmers Johnson, in his classic study *MITI and the Japanese Miracle* (1982), argued that MITI was the pilot agency that steered Japan Inc. to spectacular economic success through the use of industrial policy, which constituted a range of policies used to implement state-led development. Johnson associated industrial policies mainly, though not exclusively, with MITI, though others pointed out that the term could be applied more generally to almost any kind of

microeconomic interventionist policies, including less successful policies of more domestically oriented ministries (Okimoto 1989). Others
argued that many of these policies were not successful or were subject
to interest group politics (Calder 1993; Callon 1995; Samuels 1987;
Zinsmeister 1993).

By the late 1990s, however, MITI was out of the spotlight, and it
came to be viewed as largely irrelevant, a relic of the past, with little to
do besides collect statistics. American Enterprise Institute scholar Karl
Zinsmeister declared that "the Japanese now are discarding industrial
policy and government management of their economy—a widely
underreported fact in the West" (1993). MITI had, after all, lost many
of its formal powers as far back as the 1960s, and to implement its
policies it relied mostly on extralegal verbal persuasion known as "administrative guidance," which was not enforceable by the courts
(Johnson 1982; also see discussion in Schaede 2000, pp. 11–14).
Moreover, many of the "infant" manufacturing industries like autos,
electronics, and steel that MITI tried to promote eventually "grew up"
and produced strong, global companies by the 1980s. Regardless of
whether one believes that the success of these industries was because
of MITI's help or in spite of it, these industries no longer appeared to
need government assistance by the late 1980s. Companies could generate their own technology and finance internally, or obtain them overseas. By the 1990s, the intensification of globalization and the
acceleration of the rate of technological change, particularly the rapid
growth of the internet and related fields, reinforced the idea that traditional industrial policy was dead. Four decades of trade and capital liberalization, however gradual and reluctant, had greatly narrowed the
scope for formal protection, and increased foreign scrutiny had made
informal protection and administrative guidance more difficult (though
not impossible) to hide. And how could a government agency like
MITI ever dream of keeping far enough ahead of the rapidly evolving
internet technology to help Japanese companies compete with their
foreign rivals?

The East Asian financial crisis, which struck a number of countries
that had adopted variants of the Japanese model of development, so-
lidified the view that the era of industrial policy was (or should be)
over (Cumings 1999; Wolf 1998). Even many analyses that emphasized the role of the international dimensions of financial panic and
contagion in causing the crisis were careful to acknowledge the con-

tributing role of various domestic "weaknesses" (Goldstein 1998; Krugman 1999; Noble and Ravenhill 2000; Radelet and Sachs 1998). By the 1990s, it often took a great deal of detective work to uncover and explain MITI's policies and administrative guidance (see, for example, Tilton 1996); and among specialists knowledgeable about MITI, the prevailing consensus was that it was mired in the past, offering tired old solutions, such as tacit encouragement of collusion and subsidies to small business, that would become increasingly irrelevant and ineffective in the age of globalization and the internet (Katz 1998; Lincoln 1999).

When asked directly in interviews in 2000, MITI officials claimed "we do not do industrial policy anymore," and some had difficulty explaining just what their ministry was doing. To be sure, MITI has always been good at saying what the United States wants to hear, and it has been guarded in publicizing its activities in order to avoid fanning the flames of trade disputes. However, at least as of summer 2000, its officials appeared to work as hard as ever, toiling late into the night. For a ministry that supposedly had nothing to do, why were its officials still working so hard, and what were they doing?

The large-scale government reorganization in January 2001 provides further evidence that MITI was still a major player. As part of this reorganization, MITI was given a new, grander sounding name, the Ministry of Economy, Trade, and Industry (Keizai Sangyōshō) (METI). (In the rest of this chapter, METI should be read to include its previous existence as MITI, where relevant.) This change went largely unnoticed in the United States.

This chapter argues that, at the beginning of the twenty-first century, METI still played an important role in Japanese economic policy making, and it outlines the key features of METI's policies. The main point is that METI's industrial policy—defined, very broadly, as microeconomic policies aimed at affecting the allocation of resources—has branched out into important new directions. However, elements of more traditional, industry-specific policies also remained, but even here, the nature of these policies has changed in some respects. Concretely, METI tried to shift toward an emphasis on economy-wide reforms in many areas outside its jurisdiction, which required greater efforts to cooperate with other ministries. METI still tried to promote specific industries, but it used different methods than in the past. It tried to move away from "insulative" and sector-specific protectionist policies, and increasingly toward more "permeable" general policies that could benefit a range of industries. These more general policies included promoting and diffusing information technology, stimulating the development of environmentally friendly products and production techniques, and establishing policies to encourage new venture businesses. Nevertheless, in a number of areas, such as energy and chemicals, more traditional policies were still implemented, including tolerance of collusion to avoid excessive competition and restrain imports.

Rather than providing a comprehensive survey of METI policies, this chapter discusses a selection of cases that illustrate the different policy directions. Cases were selected on the basis of how they clarified the issues at hand. The main focus of this analysis is domestically oriented policy rather than trade policy, even though trade policy continues to be one of METI's critical responsibilities, including important negotiations in the World Trade Organization (WTO), the Asia Pacific Economic Cooperation (APEC) forum, and many more (on the WTO, see Chapter 4). Moreover, this chapter does not aim to evaluate the effectiveness of METI's new policy directions, because as of 2001 it was too early to attempt such a judgment. While these policies had been insufficient to revive the economy by 2001, this did not necessarily mean that they had no effect, or would not have any effects in the future.

This chapter suggests several hypotheses that may explain why METI's policy has shifted, although a full explanation will have to await further research. One conclusion that can be drawn is that as of 2001, the pressures of globalization had by no means forced METI to abandon its efforts to promote the competitiveness of Japanese companies, including the use of more interventionist policies, or converge on the Anglo-Saxon model of minimal, regulatory-style business government relations. However, it is more difficult to pin down the reasons for the shift in policies, including why particular policy directions were chosen instead of others, and why more traditional industrial policies were maintained in some areas rather than others. On the one hand, the broad outline of policy change and continuity appeared to reflect a METI strategy to enhance its own bureaucratic status and promote the interests of manufacturing industries under its jurisdiction, taking into account the increased diversity of these interests. On the other hand, in the late 1990s, Liberal Democratic Party (LDP) politicians appeared to take a more visible role in the formal decision-making process, for example, by establishing a series of blue ribbon economic advisory committees to deal with issues such as competitiveness, technology, and information technology. More research is needed to better assess the relative contributions of bureaucrats and politicians to these policies.

A National Strategy

One important, unchanging element of METI's policy is the overall emphasis on national strategy and the need to promote national competitiveness. The view that competitiveness is too important to be left entirely to the whims of market forces was still strong within METI as of 2001. Although METI officials claimed they did not "do industrial policy" any more, they readily acknowledged that they were working to improve Japan's competitiveness (interviews with various METI officials in Tokyo, June 2000). This view was not limited to METI. A number of high-level advisory committees had been formed in the late 1990s that had pushed strongly for a national strategy, including the Economic Strategy Council, the Information Technology (IT) Strategy Council, and the National Industrial Technology Strategy Development Committee. Regardless of the extent to which their reports were implemented or effective, they underscored the Japanese government's belief that a national strategy was important and desirable, and signaled a willingness to exert effort to formulate such a strategy.

The emphasis on a national strategy to enhance competitiveness was, somewhat surprisingly, also clearly articulated in English. This represented a significant shift from the late 1980s and early 1990s, when METI generally avoided explicit language discussing industrial promotion policies, especially in English, so as not to provide ammunition to "revisionist" scholars who might use it against Japan in debates over trade friction.[1] For example, according to the "Basic IT Strategy," a report of the IT Strategy Council, "Europe and Asia, not to mention the United States, are aggressively developing their IT infrastructures as part of their national strategies in recognition of the importance of creating a knowledge-emergent environment to secure world competitive leadership in the twenty-first century" (IT Strategy Council 2000). The IT Strategy Council, headed by Sony chairman Nobuyuki Idei, specifically set the goal of catching up to the United States: "Japan should aim to surpass the United States in high-speed internet infrastructure within five years" (Guth 2000). In 2000, the Minister's Secretariat wrote in *Tsūsan Jānaru*, METI's in-house journal, that along with the globalization of markets comes "an intensification of the competition between national systems," and in this environment Japan should take the opportunity to create a "Japan-like" value structure (MITI 2000c). Sometimes these reports reflected a desire to lessen Japan's dependence on the United States. Hiroyuki Yoshikawa, chairman of the National Industrial Technology Strategy Development Committee, in the preface to the (provisional) English translation of the committee's report, said that the Science and Technology Basic Law of 1995 intended to "transform Japan into a truly independent nation capable of making an original international contribution instead of following the policies of other countries" (NITS 1999). Clearly, Japan—like other countries—has not accepted Paul Krugman's notion that competitiveness is a "dangerous obsession" and that countries do not compete with each other like firms do (Krugman 1994).

The point here is not to engage in the competitiveness debate or elaborate a new "Japan Inc." conspiracy, but rather to emphasize that Japan has by no means abandoned the idea that nations are in some fundamental sense in competition with each other, however much this may contravene economic theory. Japan's government still believed in 2001 that it was the government's responsibility to do what it could to help domestic firms compete in the global economy. In fact, the Japanese government continued to benchmark Japan's performance against other countries and study their microeconomic promotional policies, for example in the area of government sponsorship of research and development (STA 1999). Public justification of new initiatives often included references to parallel U.S. initiatives in part to ward off criticism (see, for example, Ostrom 1999).

METI's Evolving Policy Orientation

METI's general policy orientation in the late 1990s can be divided into three main parts. The first part, which represents a new policy direction, was a strong effort to emphasize economy-wide reforms, in contrast with the more traditional focus on promoting specific sectors like steel or supercomputers. Examples include areas such as: e-commerce standards and regulation; revision of the Commercial Code; facilitation of corporate reorganization; reform of the tax structure, pensions, and labor standards; promotion of research and development; and improvement of access to financing for new businesses. In terms of technology, METI's goal was to shift the focus from "catch up" efforts to improve existing technology, to promoting innovation and new technology. The ministry planned a big push to support basic research, and tried to break down barriers to research cooperation between universities, industry, and government. This emphasis on economy-wide reforms was fundamentally a move in the direction of permeability, since these measures were not necessarily aimed at shielding domestic firms from competition, protecting domestic markets, or excluding foreign firms, even though they could be used in such a way.

The second part of METI's policy orientation involved promotion of new industries and firms. Many of these promotion policies were of a different character than in the past. Traditional policies, which had focused on infant industry protection, allocation of capital, licensing of entry and restriction of competition, and export incentives, were often no longer feasible due to the cumulative effects of formal trade liberalization, deregulation, and the maturing of Japanese industry. The new policies took on a more general character, and were even more market-conforming than those in the early postwar period. They emphasized goals such as developing technology, improving human capital, increasing information, reducing transaction costs, and in general helping with public goods and coordination problems. Thus, METI claimed to be moving away from the industry-specific promotional policies of the past (MITI 2000c, p. 22; interviews with MITI officials, Tokyo, June 2000). These policies represented a significant shift in METI's policy stance, especially when considered in combination with the new economy-wide policies. Still, despite the differences between the old and new policies, there remained a definite concern with promoting specific sectors, even though many were more broadly defined than in the past (for example, promoting information technology instead of computers, or biotechnology instead of petrochemicals).

Continued support for existing industries, both strong and declining ones, was the third part of METI's policy orientation. Through this support, METI tried to help industries to improve their international competitiveness. Many of these industries enjoyed a certain amount of privatized protection that worked through the distribution system, which in turn was related to lax enforcement of the antimonopoly law, and there appeared to be little effort to change this (Elder 1998; Katz 1998; Tilton 1996; Wolff and Howell 1992; Schaede 2000; Schaede, this volume, Chapter 8). In other words, despite the absence of formal protection, these industries were able to restrain imports through anticompetitive business practices. Thus, despite METI's efforts to shift the policy in new directions, older and newer versions of insulation-type policies continued to be implemented in some areas.

METI's Political Strategy

METI's increasing emphasis on economy-wide measures was also part of a political strategy to expand the ministry's mandate to achieve a more economy-wide jurisdiction, instead of being in charge of just manufacturing. To be sure, many areas where METI hoped to have an impact, such as reforming education, health, or pensions, were of vital importance to METI's core constituency, the manufacturing sector. It goes without saying that METI had little or no policy-making authority in these newly targeted areas, and so in many cases there is little it could do other than lobby Diet members or other ministries on behalf of manufacturing, or use a public relations strategy.

One big opportunity to do this arose with the establishment of fifteen interministerial coordination committees (*kankei shōchō renkei kaigi*) charged with implementing the "Program for Improvement of the Environment for the Creation of New Industries."[2] This program was part of the "Action Plan for the Change and Creation of Economic Structure (First Follow-up)," which was approved by the Cabinet in December 1997 (Cabinet 1997, appendix). These fifteen committees corresponded to industry areas listed in the plan (see Table 7.2, below). METI and several other ministries belonged to all committees, while the Ministry of Finance (MOF) was involved in only three.

MITI's past efforts to expand its jurisdiction had led to fierce turf wars with other ministries (Callon 1995; Johnson 1989), and it could be expected that further efforts would likely yield the same result. Yet, as of 2001, METI efforts to influence policies of other ministries had met with some success. For example, cooperation with the Ministry of Justice (MOJ) on efforts to reform the Commercial Code and with the MOF on related tax law changes achieved concrete results in the form of new laws (interviews with METI officials, summer 2000). METI did not get everything it wanted in these changes, but important progress was made. In contrast, METI's turf war with the Ministry of Posts and Telecommunications (now part of the Ministry of Public Management, Home Affairs, Posts and Telecommunications) over telecommunications policy and the future of Nippon Telegraph and Telephone (NTT) certainly continued. Thus, while turf battles continued to be fierce in areas with more overlap in jurisdiction such as telecommunications, policy differences with strong mainline ministries such as Justice—where METI had no hope of gaining turf—were muted. For these reasons, negotiations with the Ministries of Labor or Health and Welfare could be expected to be more policy-oriented than turf-oriented, and may have a greater chance of success.

Paradoxically, METI's lack of formal policy tools, and even a lack of formal jurisdiction in some cases, could be an asset rather than a liability in its efforts to expand its sphere of influence to include economy-wide reform. In areas where it does not have primary jurisdiction, METI's main tools are limited to public relations and quiet lobbying. A lack of formal jurisdiction may make it easier to use the bully pulpit to cajole other conservative, recalcitrant ministries into considering substantial reforms more seriously, since advocating a policy in an area where it did not have jurisdiction would be less likely to create conflicts among its own industry constituents. For example, METI might be less inhibited about taking a strong public stance on health care reform than the Ministry of Health and Welfare, which has to appease a range of powerful constituencies. In contrast to METI, most other ministries retained substantial regulatory powers and jurisdictional authority, including Health, Labor and Welfare; Land, Infrastructure and Transport; Education, Culture, Sports, Science and Technology; and Public Management, Home Affairs, Posts and Telecommunications.

In order for METI to negotiate successfully with these ministries, a public relations strategy is important. The case of reform of the Commercial Code showed that a quiet strategy of constructive engagement, in which credit is shared with other ministries, can also yield results (see also Chapter 9). Thus emerged a win-win proposition for METI: If its lobbying of other ministries did not succeed in effecting reform, at least METI would be seen by the public as a progressive "ministry of reform" or "ministry of deregulation", with the blame falling on the other ministries. Makoto Kuroda, a former MITI vice minister for international affairs, remarked: "The world has

changed. Now it's MITI's job to tell other ministries to improve competitiveness through deregulation" (quoted in Landers 1997). If the
pushing succeeded, however, METI could receive a share of the credit.

In the twenty-first century, METI will have many opportunities to
try out this strategy. A variety of advisory councils, cabinet-level committees, interagency committees and other groups have been trying to
address many of the broad-ranging policy issues discussed here, and
METI has been involved through the provision of information, and in
many cases staff support. These bodies included the IT Strategy Head-
quarters, IT Strategy Council, National Industrial Technology Strategy
Development Committee, and the Economic Strategy Council.

METI and Administrative Reorganization

The effort to expand METI's purview is reflected in MITI's metamor-
phosis into METI as part of the government's large-scale reorganization
implemented in January 2001. Some suggest that MITI may have influenced the final form of the administrative reform proposals (Ito 1997;
Vogel 1997), though not everyone agrees with this interpretation
(Mishima 1998). Either way, MITI definitely fared much better than
most of the other economy-related ministries, especially in comparison
with the MOF (which had its regulatory bureaus spun off), the Ministries of Construction and Transportation (which were forced to merge),
and the Ministry of Posts and Telecommunications (which was folded
into the Ministry of Public Management, Home Affairs, Posts and Telecommunications). Not only did METI retain its overall powers and jurisdiction, but it also expanded somewhat, absorbing parts of the
Economic Planning Agency. Moreover, its name was changed from the
narrower Ministry of International Trade and Industry to the more en-
compassing Ministry of Economy, Trade, and Industry.

The government reorganization of January 2001 also resulted in a
number of changes in METI's internal structure that reflect the new
overall policy orientation described above (see Table 7.1). There are
four significant points to be made about this internal reorganization.
First, with electronics as a key exception, almost all manufacturing bureaus were consolidated into a single bureau. This reorganization
would facilitate the resolution of conflicts of interest between manufacturing industries, by reducing the need for coordination at the bureau level. The old Basic Industries Bureau was renamed the

Table 7.1

METI's New Organizational Structure

Old MITI Bureaus	New METI Bureaus
• Minister's Secretariat	• Minister's Secretariat
• Trade Policy	• Trade Policy
• Trade Administration	• Trade and Economic Cooperation
• Industrial Policy	• Economic and Industrial Policy
• Basic Industries	• Manufacturing Industries
• Machinery and Information Industries	• Commerce and Information Policy
• Environment and Industrial Location	• Industrial Science and Technology Policy and Environment
• Daily Life Industries	

Manufacturing Industries Bureau (Seizō sangyō kyoku), and it received the auto and machinery sections, in addition to steel, chemicals, and other metals and materials. It was now also in charge of textiles, paper, construction materials, and other sectors previously belonging to the Daily Life Industries Bureau, which was eliminated.

Second, the new structure implied an increased focus on information technology and electronics, and in particular their connection with the distribution system. The old Machinery and Information Industries Bureau was renamed the Commerce and Information Policy Bureau (Shōmu jōhō seisaku kyoku), and it acquired several sections from the former Industrial Policy Bureau dealing with distribution. This bureau is now in charge of the electronics industry. Presumably, the intent was to make it easier to promote the modernization of Japan's distribution sector using information technology.

Third, the new structure allowed a much stronger emphasis on technology. A new Industrial Science and Technology Policy and Environment Bureau (Sangyō gijutsu kankyō kyoku) replaced the old Environment and Industrial Location Bureau. Much of this new bureau came from the Agency of Industrial Science and Technology (Kōgyō gijutsu in), which had always been affiliated with MITI; now, the agency's functions were transferred to the ministry proper. The new bureau also retained the Environmental Policy and Recycling Promotion Sections. The industrial location sections were transferred to the new Economic and Industrial Policy Bureau, which replaced the old Industrial Policy Bureau.

Fourth, the old Industrial Policy Bureau received a name upgrade to the Economic and Industrial Policy Bureau (Keizai sangyō seisaku kyoku). The Industrial Policy Bureau had long been regarded as MITI's flagship bureau, and its chief was typically next in line to become administrative vice minister, the highest career official in the ministry. The renamed bureau retained its overall planning and coordination sections, and presumably its strategic functions. As mentioned above, some sections relating to the distribution industry were moved to the new Commerce and Information Policy Bureau. In return, it received sections relating to regional policy and industrial location.

It is evident that this reorganization was more of a streamlining, not a wholesale restructuring. The original MITI functions remained essentially intact, but were reorganized in a somewhat more rational fashion. The reorganization seemed to strengthen METI's horizontal functions (ranging across industries, not tied to a specific industry), especially the new emphasis on technology. Importantly, however, METI did not abandon its vertical functions (relating to specific industries) and jurisdiction. If anything, the industry-specific functions appeared to have been consolidated and more focused in the two new vertical bureaus, Manufacturing, and Commerce and Information Policy (Kokusei Jōhō Sentā 2000).

Of course, the name change did not really come with increased legal powers, so in one sense it may be symbolic. Clearly, in order to effect economy-wide reforms, it would be necessary for METI to negotiate with other ministries. This is precisely what METI has done, and future policy making would be even more dependent than before on negotiations with other ministries.

Economy-Wide Structural Policies

METI's increased emphasis on economy-wide reforms was a key new policy direction. One central element of this policy was to make progress on general structural issues, often relating to human capital, finance, or corporate law, that were outside METI's jurisdiction but very important to its key constituents, the manufacturing industries. Other elements of this policy included issues where METI had jurisdiction, but not exclusively so, such as the promotion of e-commerce and information technology, technology policy, and policies to promote new business formation and small business.

General Structural Issues

Among the structural policy issues outside METI's jurisdiction were pensions, health insurance, labor deregulation, university reform, tax policy, and reform of numerous elements of the Commercial Code. All of these immediately affected the manufacturing industries, and thus were of concern to METI. The ministry was especially keen to develop a 401(k)-style pension system. In the late 1990s, this issue was discussed in the Industrial Structure Council, one of METI's key advisory bodies, demonstrating a high level of concern (ISC 1997). Serious discussions about reform of the Japanese university system were also launched at the turn of the century. New measures to improve labor market flexibility, such as relaxation of regulations on temporary workers, have been instituted. Many of these measures were also designed to promote flexibility and reduce transaction and information costs. While other ministries and agencies were not necessarily opposed to reform, these issues were very complex and interrelated, and the interests of many different groups other than METI were at stake, so the scope, shape, and pace of changes needed to be negotiated.

The revision of several provisions of the Commercial Code in 1999, in order to facilitate corporate reorganization, is an important example of a case in which METI succeeded in beginning the process of reform in an area outside its jurisdiction. The MOJ and METI negotiated revisions as part of the 1999 Industrial Revitalization Law (*Sangyō saisei hō*). These revisions were accompanied by a number of related changes in the tax law that required negotiation with the MOF. Previously, the Commercial Code contained many provisions that made corporate restructuring difficult, expensive, and time consuming. Under the basic philosophy of traditional Japanese law, courts were seen as having a responsibility to protect the public interest and exercised a significant amount of oversight over proposals for corporate reorganization. This oversight involved long delays and high transaction costs (such as requiring certifications and audits by independent lawyers, who in turn hired accountants), and as a result corporate reorganization was rarely attempted.

MITI engaged in lengthy negotiations with the Ministries of Justice and Finance to try to streamline this aspect of the Commercial Code. MOF was reluctant because of possible revenue implications. Both MOF and MOJ had a difficult time understanding the implications of the changed economic conditions on the competitiveness of Japanese companies and the role of the proposed changes in helping companies cope with these conditions. MOJ was also reluctant to drastically change the fundamental basis of Japanese commercial law, especially given the enormous effort it would take, including convening various advisory committees and persuading retired MOJ officials and law professors at the University of Tokyo and elsewhere of the necessity of change. Finally, MITI convinced the other ministries of the merits of relaxing some of these restrictions.

The resulting reforms made it easier to implement mergers and acquisitions, spin-offs, and management or employee buyouts. Stock options were legalized. There were also related tax measures to make it easier for companies to take advantage of the new provisions of the Commercial Code. The Commercial Code is still not fully modernized, but participants felt that significant progress was made (Nakahara 1999a, 1999b). Other related legal changes included the legalization of holding companies, and various measures to improve corporate governance (see Chapter 9). While the ultimate effectiveness of these measures will only show over time, this kind of policy initiative represents a significant change compared to the policies of the past.

Measures to Promote E-Commerce and Information Technology

At the turn of the century, METI also intended to play a leading role in the promotion of e-commerce and information technology industries. Rather than using traditional policies, such as promoting coordination by firms, the new approach seemed to do so mainly through economy-wide measures, including some that involved reducing transaction and information costs. Among METI's high priorities were measures to facilitate e-commerce, for example legalizing electronic contracts and digital signatures, and establishing other related rules (JECC 2000, pp. 62–64). METI also pushed laws to promote privacy on the internet. Total IT-related budget requests for fiscal 2001 totaled about $7 billion (Dewey Ballantine 2001).

Moreover, demand promotion became an important part of the government's internet strategy. The 2000 "e-government" initiative could be seen in this light. Measures included digitization of public administration within central and local governments, as well as of public services to the private sector, publication of administrative information via the internet, central government support for local governments, reform of regulations to increase the number of documents that could be submitted electronically, and digitization of procurement procedures. There were also plans to upgrade the technological capability of schools (IT Strategy Council 2000). The economic stimulus package drawn up in October 2000 provided for ¥200 billion (roughly $1.5 billion) to promote computer literacy, including basic internet training for seven million people (Suzuki 2000).

These measures, when fully implemented, promised to yield large efficiency savings. Yet, as anyone who had visited Japanese central government offices in 2001 could plainly see, implementation of this vision would require very large investments. This could provide a large demand stimulus for the relevant industries. Industry experts estimated that the central government was likely to spend more than ¥500 billion (about $4 billion) by March 2004, and that total expenditures for both central and local governments on creating government networks would reach ¥1 trillion ($8 billion) by fiscal year 2003 (Suzuki 2000). Of course, this demand stimulus would not necessarily benefit only Japanese firms. Yet, given the presence of Japanese firms in internet-related industries, domestic benefits from a large increase in demand would be expected to be large.

Last but not least, the 2000 IT Strategy Council report called for the establishment of an ultra-high-speed network infrastructure and enhanced competition in the telecommunications market. The report did not specify whether the network was to be built publicly or by the private sector, but either way the result would be a significant improvement in infrastructure as well as a demand stimulus. The report also called for the promotion of research and development in this area. Interestingly, the report advocated increased competition in the telecommunications industry. This was aimed at reducing NTT's dominance over this market, which was viewed as having created formidable obstacles to the spread of the internet and e-commerce in Japan (IT Strategy Council 2000). An economic package was drawn up in October 2000, providing for ¥800 billion (about

$6.4 billion) to build fiber-optic networks and other infrastructure (Suzuki 2000).

The IT Strategy Council's report did not just call for the promotion of IT for its own sake or as part of a competition among nations. It also viewed IT as a way to help Japan solve pressing social problems. These included coping with the aging society, medical and nursing care, improving transportation and traffic, environmental protection, improving education, and promoting art and science. Nevertheless, IT promotion was clearly an example of national targeting. Japan was afraid of falling behind, and a feeling of national crisis could be sensed. But the way in which the Japanese government planned to promote this agenda appeared to respond to past criticism of industrial policy. Thus, IT promotion was launched as an economy-wide promotion effort, with a focus on reducing information and transaction costs, stimulating demand, and upgrading technology, and not a traditional policy of using infant industry protection and reducing excess competition.

Technology Policy

Traditionally, Japanese industrial policy placed a large emphasis on technology promotion, and that has not changed. In 1999, Japanese government expenditures on science and technology amounted to ¥3.2 trillion (about $26 billion), of which MITI's share was about ¥493 billion ($4 billion), or about 15 percent. In 1997, Japanese government research and development (R&D) expenditures accounted for 0.63 percent of GDP (in contrast with 0.8 percent for the United States), and 19.1 percent of all national nondefense R&D expenditures (in contrast with 15.7 percent for the United States) (STA 1999, pp. 106–7, 215).

However, at the turn of the century, the composition of R&D spending began to change. In the past, Japan's technology policy had focused mainly on promoting applied technology, rather than on basic research (Anchordoguy 1997). But METI was trying to shift gears and push the nation's technology establishment to increase the amount of basic research. In the early postwar period, Japan could license technology based on basic research done elsewhere, but as Japan reached the technological frontier, increased basic research would be necessary to maintain Japan's competitive position. To be sure, this was not going to happen overnight, and significant resources continued to be devoted to applied technology, to enable Japan to catch up with the

United States in key areas of new technology. So, even though a recent report by the National Industrial Technology Strategy Development Committee called for transforming the technological innovation system from a "catch-up" type to a "frontier-creation" type (NITS 2000), the transition may take considerable time.

Another new element was an emphasis on systemic improvements in the R&D system. These included expanding and improving training of researchers, making more use of foreign researchers, and long-term structural reform of the university research system. In particular, METI worked to create a better system of coordinating research between business, government, and universities. Again, change would not occur overnight, and would probably require extensive negotiations with the Ministry of Education, Culture, Sports, Science and Technology. Nevertheless, these goals were promoted in a variety of government reports (including IT Strategy Council 2000, MITI 2000a, NITS 1999, STA 1999). Of course, just because these policies were stated in a wide range of government reports did not say much about the speed or degree to which they would be implemented. Still, it was official government policy to work toward these goals.

In addition to this attempt to formulate technology policy in a more systemic fashion, there continued to be a significant amount of government-sponsored or coordinated research designed to promote specific industries, including key industries in METI's jurisdiction such as automobiles, steel, and chemicals. The 2000 Japanese version of *Japan's National Technology Strategy* (*Kokka sangyō gijutsu senryaku*) was 408 pages long, and most of it was organized by economic sector (NITS 2000).

In automobiles, for example, the government plan for the year 2000 promoted a myriad of projects including fuel cells, electronic toll collection, and other "intelligent transportation" systems, building on the strength of Japan's auto industry. Many of these were related to making autos more environmentally friendly. Funds earmarked by METI for various "Clean Energy Vehicle"-related projects exceeded ¥21 billion (about $170 million) (MITI 2000b).

The semiconductor industry was another example where insulative-type technology policy seemed to make a comeback, through METI's sponsoring of research projects. Semiconductors, previously a high-profile Japanese industry, had largely been forgotten in terms of industrial policy. After becoming a highly successful industry no longer in need of government help, Japanese semiconductor manufacturers were challenged by Korean firms in the 1980s and 1990s, using Japanese-style industrial policy. Some Japanese producers dropped out, and the ones remaining seemed competitive on the basis of their own efforts. Moreover, some have argued that even in the heyday of Japanese government-sponsored cooperative research projects in high technology, there were many problems, including coordination difficulties and reluctance of companies to be involved (Callon 1995). However, since the 1990s, the Japanese semiconductor industry had been largely depressed, as U.S. companies like Intel took the lead in key areas like microprocessors, and as competition from South Korean and other East Asian firms intensified.

In this environment, MITI launched a new joint research project in 1999 to help develop basic technology for the next generation of semiconductors using 0.1 micron technology. The participants were ten Japanese semiconductor producers (NEC, Toshiba, Hitachi, Fujitsu, Mitsubishi, Matsushita, Sony, Sharp, Sanyo, and Oki), and they committed a total of 100 researchers to the project (*Nikkei*, October 25, 1999). Apparently, the Japanese electronics companies had shed their earlier aversion to these cooperative projects. The participation of Sony was particularly ironic, since some of its officials, shortly after the project was launched, had criticized the tendency of other companies to look to METI for help and suggested that METI was no longer able to be of much use to the industry (interviews, Tokyo, June 2000). Thus, it is evident that industry-specific technology promotion policies have not disappeared, and that some of the more traditional technology promotion policies, such as government-sponsored research consortia, may in fact be reinstated.

New Business Formation and Small Business Promotion Policy

Another of METI's new priorities was to promote the formation of new businesses, and this job fell mainly to METI's Small and Medium Enterprises Agency. Some U.S. researchers have argued that one of the keys of U.S. success in the internet economy in the 1990s was what they call the "Silicon Valley System," which fostered the creation of new companies that were the source of rapid innovation and adaptation to new economic environments (see, for example, Cohen et al. 2000, p. 26). Smaller companies can commercialize new technology rapidly through access to venture capital, experienced management, and contract manufacturing. METI agreed with this view, and began to promote venture businesses in the 1990s. METI was very concerned that Japan had fallen behind in terms of new business formation, and was therefore losing out on the innovation and technology that smaller entrepreneurial companies generate. It was said to be very difficult to start these kinds of companies in Japan, because it was difficult for them to obtain access to finance, human resources, and management support. METI began to use various small business programs to try to address these problems.

This was a significant change in METI's attitude towards small and medium-size enterprises. The old view, developed in the 1960s, was that small firms were less productive than large ones, and the policy objective was to improve their productivity through modernization and pursuit of economies of scale through mergers. The new view was that small firms were a source of dynamism, flexibility, mobility, and creativity, and therefore the ministry should develop a more positive stance towards them (SMEA 2000a, 2000b; interviews with officials of METI's Small and Medium Enterprises Agency, Tokyo, June 2000). This change in the basic policy stance was reflected in a 1999 revision to the Small and Medium Enterprises Basic Law (*Chūshō kigyō kihon hō*).

This is not to say that the old policy gave small and medium-size enterprises little attention or help; in fact METI's Small and Medium Enterprises Agency has long provided substantial assistance. What has changed is the overall direction of METI policy, and the rationale behind it. Thus, instead of trying to turn small enterprises into large ones (or improve their complementarities with large ones), METI shifted its policy to try to harness the special advantages smaller companies may have in adapting to the rapidly changing environment of the internet economy. One priority was to promote start-ups and new venture businesses through finance and credit guarantees. There was even a measure to allow limited equity participation by the government in some small start-ups. Other policies included encouraging small companies to improve their management structure and make better use of information technology, and strengthening the ability of small companies to generate new technology. Management consulting services for small business were initiated. These were funded by central government and provided through the Japan Small and Medium Enterprises Corporation (Chūshō Kigyō Sōgō Jigyōdan) and local governments (JASMEC 2001). Much of the consulting is subcontracted out to private consultants, who are required to register with METI and pass an exam or take a training course. There were 15,491 registered consultants as of April 1999 (SMEA 1999, pp. 34–37; interviews, Small and Medium Enterprises Agency, Tokyo, June 2000). The main objective of consulting was to improve basic management skills and help with common problems like upgrading information technology systems. Still, one wonders whether a government-sponsored consulting system could be used to bolster hidden traditional industrial policies of reducing excess competition by tacitly promoting cooperation and collusion, though historically it has been difficult to do this in industries with many small companies.

Despite these efforts to promote small businesses through nontraditional policies, small business policies still involve a large amount of subsidies. The Small and Medium Enterprises Agency has a large budget for loans and various subsidies to small businesses, and this is supplemented by a number of other public and quasi-public funding agencies. METI's total budget in FY 2001 for small and medium-size enterprises was ¥134 billion (over $1 billion) and the total government budget for small and medium-size enterprises was ¥195 billion (about $1.6 billion). While this may not seem like a lot, much more is available through various quasi-public funding agencies. Three of the biggest ones, Small Business Finance Corporation (Chūshō Kigyō Kin'yū Kōko), National Life Finance Corporation (Kokumin Seikatsu Kin'yū Kōko), and the Central Cooperative Bank for Commerce and Industry (Shōkō Chūkin) requested a total of ¥8.5 trillion (about $68 billion) in new lending authority for FY 2001 (SMEA 2001). As of March 31, 1999, loans outstanding provided by these three agencies totaled almost ¥30 trillion (about $240 billion) (SMEA 1999). Even though these agencies are legally separate from METI, they are affiliated with the ministry and play an important role in small business policy implementation. METI's Small and Medium Enterprises Agency is at the center of the policy-making process. Moreover, the Small Business Finance Corporation and the Central Cooperative Bank for Commerce and Industry were both headed by former MITI administrative vice ministers as of 1999 (Tōyō Keizai 2000).

METI has attempted to distribute benefits from these programs according to objective criteria, and hold the recipients to performance standards. For at least some new programs involving subsidies, firms are required to submit business plans that are evaluated by panels of independent experts, and METI itself is not supposed to intervene in the decisions. Many loans are also distributed by private banks. METI was well aware that Diet members might try to influence the distribution of benefits to particular firms, so it took steps to try to insulate these programs, including removing itself from the individual decisions (SMEA 1999, p. 8; interviews with METI officials, Tokyo, June 2000). Objective criteria and performance requirements are definitely official policy, but given the large number of complex programs relating to small business, it is impossible to know whether objective criteria were indeed widely used or consistently implemented.

Of course, small business promotion policy was neither new nor apolitical. Lincoln (1999) has criticized this system as a kind of welfare for small business, and given the large budget involved this may be the ultimate effect of the policy, even if METI used it to promote structural reform and even if some or most of the benefits were distributed according to objective criteria. Still, when challenged about small business policy and the significant sums of money spent, METI has been quick to point out that the U.S. Small Business Administration has also spent a great deal of money promoting similar goals with similar policies. In fact, in designing its new policies to promote small business, METI looked to the U.S. Small Business Administration as a guide (interviews with METI officials, summer 2000). True, there is no guarantee that these policies will make even a small step towards creating a "silicon valley" of small, entrepreneurial high-tech companies in Japan, and certainly METI was under no such illusions that these policies would produce quick success. Still, it would be a mistake to characterize these policies as no different from those in the past, and METI does seem to be trying to adapt to changing conditions by experimenting with new policies.

Policies to Promote Specific Industries

Efforts to promote specific industries have not stopped, despite METI's increasing emphasis on more general, economy-wide policies. In fact, a wide range of industries continues to be targeted. One important change is that in many cases there has been a shift in emphasis away from more traditional policies of protection and curbing "excess competition," and toward policies that are aimed more at reducing costs, upgrading technology, and stimulating demand. Included here are measures such as developing infrastructure, upgrading human resources, deregulation, and promoting the diffusion of information technology (Cabinet 1997). Nevertheless, many of METI's traditional client industries still benefit from a policy that tacitly allows competition to be restrained through lax enforcement of the antimonopoly law, including steel, chemicals, paper, and other basic goods industries (Beeman 1999; Elder 1998; Tilton 1996). Schaede (Chapter 8) argues that because of a pronounced shift to "self regulation" in these industries, protectionist and anticompetitive effects remain strong.

It is impractical here to try to discuss every industry in which MITI/ METI has been involved; but it is possible to get a sense of overall priorities, particularly in terms of the promotion of new industries. Interestingly, MITI's annual document, *Priority Trade and Industry Policies*, typically focused on more economy-wide measures and did not clearly indicate priorities in terms of specific industries. Nevertheless, the Cabinet's *Action Plan for the Reform and Creation of Economic Structure* indicated fifteen broadly defined industry areas for promotion (Cabinet 1997), and it listed METI as a member of all of the interministerial committees formed to implement the plan.[3] This plan represents policy that METI is obligated to implement. The fifteen industry areas are listed in Table 7.2, along with illustrative examples.

At first glance, this list looked like a comprehensive laundry list, prompting the question of what industries were left out, especially when the designated industries ranged from babysitting to supersonic aircraft. Some items seemed overtly political, like ocean industries (possibly intended to benefit the politically powerful fishing industry) and industries relating to urban environment (perhaps an attempt to appeal to urban voters). Some more narrowly specified industries appeared to have been singled out for special treatment, such as biotechnology, and air and space. Moreover, even industries that did not appear directly on the list, like construction, steel, chemicals, or autos, were likely to benefit indirectly, either through increased sales or cost reductions.

The selected industries were all thought to have potential for high growth, and to form a base for future employment. These industries also fit well with other government efforts to address important social problems (such as the aging society, environment, and urban life). Moreover, it was probably hoped that promoting these industries would improve the competitiveness of a wide range of other industries.

Another way of thinking about the rationale for focusing on these industries was suggested by the analytical framework of Michael Porter's

Table 7.2

Industry Areas Targeted for Promotion

Industry area	Examples
1. Medical and welfare	Home health care service, medical equipment
2. Daily life and culture	Education service, tourism, fashion, babysitting, textiles, household goods
3. Information and telecommunications	Software and system integration, intelligent transport systems (ITS)
4. New manufacturing technology	Integration of IT, new chemical processes; micromachines, robots, lasers, new materials, minaturization, fine ceramics
5. Distribution and logistics	Improve efficiency through new technology, information technology
6. Environment	Eco-materials, low-pollution manufacturing, recycling industry
7. Business support	Outsourcing of business support functions, office and network security, advertising, design industry
8. Ocean	Develop industries near coastal areas
9. Biotechnology	Use of genetic technology for medicine, agriculture, chemicals, energy
10. Urban environment	New, environmentally friendly materials for urban construction, building ventilation systems, new transportation, environment and safety systems
11. Air and space	Next-generation supersonic plane, avionics, global positioning system (GPS)
12. New energy and energy conservation	Refuse-derived fuel, clean-energy vehicle, solar power
13. Human resources-related industries	Temporary staffing, training, internships
14. Internationalization-related industries	Ports, airports, roads, consulting, and information for foreign companies in Japan
15. Housing-related industries	Housing construction, building materials

Source: Cabinet, 1997.

Competitive Advantage of Nations (1990). In a way, Porter's argument can be interpreted to support strategies of permeability rather than insulation. Porter argued that governments should not try to improve competitiveness through protection, short-term cost reduction, or other traditional targeting measures. Rather, policy should focus on: (1) firm strategy and structure, particularly promoting competition; (2) development of advanced factors of production; (3) promotion of sophisticated demand; and (4) promoting "clusters" of related industries that can build on each other's strengths. Many of the industries on Japan's priority list do coincide with these objectives, whether or not Japanese officials were consciously considering Porter's arguments. The list of industries built on Japan's strengths in existing industries, such as manufacturing and electronics, and promised to strengthen Japan's "clusters" in these areas. It dealt with some of Japan's key "selective factor disadvantages" such as energy and human resources. All industries on the list can be seen as tapping into or aiming to develop sophisticated demand, particularly in areas of high social priority, such as dealing with problems relating to the environment and aging society. The list also emphasized what appear to be key emerging technologies, including information technology, manufacturing technology, biotechnology, new energy, and new materials. Of Porter's four factors, the only one that is not emphasized in METI's policy is promoting competition, although the more general policies referred to earlier do address issues of firm strategy and structure. The coincidence of this list of "targeted" industries with Porter's policy guidelines is somewhat ironic, given that Porter specifically argued that targeting is not likely to be effective.

In sum, METI has not given up targeting specific industries, but there has been a shift in the rationale for which industries are emphasized, as well as a shift in the content of the policies. Yet, in some industries there have been important continuities with past policies. Industrial policy is not dead. It is very much alive, but it is constantly changing. These issues will be illustrated by looking in more detail at three industry examples below.

Environment-Related Industries

In recent years, METI has taken an active leadership role in the area of environmental protection and recycling. For example, it has sponsored laws to mandate recycling in areas such as automobiles and electronic appliances. In political terms, the promotion of industry and environmental protection are often seen as conflicting goals, as was clearly illustrated in the United States by President George W. Bush's decision to withdraw from the Kyoto Protocol on global warming, on the grounds that it would be harmful to business. In contrast, in Japan, METI adopted more of a pro-environment stance. Furthermore, METI seemed to view environmental protection as an increasingly important facet of industrial policy. METI appeared to have adopted Michael Porter's (1990) view that strong environmental regulations can serve as a demand stimulus to develop environmental protection and recycling industries and related new technologies.

This emphasis on environmental protection had clear political implications. First, it made METI appear progressive and "green," strengthening its public image. Second, the environmental focus would make it easier to obtain government research and promotion funds for industry. Third, any research and promotion funds would appear to foreigners as part of environment policy rather than as a return to the old industrial policy, thereby perhaps heading off some future potential trade friction. Fourth, mandated recycling could develop into a WTO-legal nontariff barrier, affording Japanese firms an advantage through advanced knowledge of design-in recycling requirements. Finally, the manufacturing industries under METI's jurisdiction would benefit most from these policies, particularly important struggling industries like steel and chemicals, but also electronics and automobiles.

Air and Space Industries

Critics of industrial policy have often labeled this industry as one of the more dramatic cases of failure (see, for example, Porter et al. 2000, pp. 31–32). Despite decades of heavy promotion, as of 2001 Japan had yet to build a complete civilian aircraft, and a series of rocket failures had put the future of the space program in doubt. Nevertheless, others have argued that Japan has made a number of achievements in this field, particularly in the field of new materials as well as in aircraft parts (Friedman and Samuels 1993). Now, Boeing airplanes are made with an ever-increasing share of Japanese-made parts.

Far from writing its aircraft and space industries off as failures, Japan was aggressively strengthening them even more. In 2002, Japan planned to begin full-scale development of a new mach-2 supersonic transport plane, possibly in cooperation with foreign partners, which was hoped to go into commercial service in 2020 (Kyodo News Service, February 19, 2001; *Daily Yomiuri*, February 10, 2001). Japan was also developing two next-generation military aircraft to be made in Japan, including an antisubmarine patrol plane to replace the P-3C, and a cargo transport plane to replace the C-1. The Finance Ministry proposed ¥5.3 billion (about $42 million) for ongoing development of these planes in fiscal 2001 (Kyodo News Service, December 20, 2000). Again, it is by no means certain that these programs will be successful or without problems, but it is clear that industrial policy is still active in air and space industries.

Energy and Chemical Industries

Energy and chemicals are two industries where METI has in the past exercised fairly extensive oversight, and it clearly continued to do so at the turn of the century. The energy industry still had substantial bureaucratic resources devoted to it, and was represented at the agency level in the Energy and Natural Resources Agency. The agency remained a part of the new METI even after the government reorganization of 2001. While deregulation has proceeded in a slow but steady fashion over the last few years, and although METI seemed committed to a thorough restructuring of the industry, this restructuring remained incomplete and METI guidance remained strong.

Similarly, METI's guidance remained strong in the chemical industry, which was undergoing restructuring and slow deregulation. As of 2001, Japanese chemical industry publications continued to describe government policy (including recommendations of advisory councils appointed by the prime minister, such as the Economic Strategy Council and the Industrial Competitiveness Council) as calling for traditional industrial policy measures such as reductions in excess capacity and employment countermeasures (Kagaku Kōgyō Nippōsha, various years). Moreover, as of the mid-1990s, many widely used petrochemicals were still subject to formal tariffs with effective rates ranging from 4 to 24 percent (Masuda 1995, pp. 65–70). Clearly, old-style industrial policies have not been completely abandoned in all industries.

Explaining Change and Continuity in METI Policy

As of 2001, any claim of a conclusive explanation of the pattern of change and continuity in METI policy would have been premature. However, we can explore some preliminary hypotheses based on the four categories that political scientists often use to classify explanations for policy change: international factors, institutions, interest groups, and ideas.

One conclusion that could be reached as of 2001 was that globalization had not caused Japan to abandon industrial policy and converge on the Anglo-Saxon model of minimally regulated markets. To be sure, international pressure, particularly from the United States, by the late 1990s had constrained many overt policies of insulation that Japan had used in the past. Yet Japan, and in particular METI, found ways to continue some of these policies.

The main contending perspectives that bear on explaining METI policy are institutions and interest groups. Concretely, the question is the relative influence in the policy-making process of the METI bureaucrats, the politicians, and business interests. Much of the evidence presented in this chapter suggests that METI was shifting into the role of a policy entrepreneur, trying to advance its own power and prestige through finding creative ways to advance the interests of its key constituents, the manufacturing industries. METI certainly did well in the administrative reorganization of 2001. Many of the policies adopted by the Cabinet referred to in this chapter were prepared by METI's main advisory committee, the Industrial Structure Council. This means that METI had significant influence over the development of these policies, since METI chose the council members, provided its staff, and formed its agenda. METI definitely had incentives to try to stake out a role in a rapidly changing policy environment in which industrial policy seemed to be less and less relevant.

But it is also important to consider how much politicians influenced policy. In the late 1990s, it became clear that politicians were playing an increasing role in policies relating to METI (see Chapter 2). The strongest evidence consisted of the fact that former prime ministers Hashimoto, Obuchi, and Mori played an increasingly visible role in articulating economic policy, and in particular appointing several blue ribbon advisory panels on issues such as information technology strategy, technology strategy, and industrial revitalization. Moreover, the members of these committees seemed less dependent on bureaucratic influence than their predecessors, since they included powerful critics of traditional economic policies like Sony chairman Idei Nobuyuki (IT Strategy Council) and economists Nakatani Iwao and Takenaka Heizō (Economic Strategy Council). As noted earlier, some saw the 2001 administrative reorganization of the ministries as evidence of increased influence of politicians (Mishima 1998), while others believe bureaucrats may have influenced the final form of the reorganization plan (Ito 1997; Vogel 1997).

An argument can also be made for an increased influence of business on METI policy. The presence of prominent businessmen on key prime ministerial advisory committees could be seen as an example of this. Moreover, there was evidence of lobbying by Keidanren on many issues discussed in this chapter (interviews with Keidanren and METI officials, summer 2000). Nevertheless, more detailed research on the decision-making process in specific policy cases is needed before the relative influence on policy of bureaucrats, politicians, and business can be fully assessed.

Finally, it is possible to argue that Western ideas may have had some influence on the policy. In the 1980s and 1990s, large numbers of Japanese elite bureaucrats and business people studied in foreign graduate programs in business, government, and international relations, often in the United States. By 2000, many of these former students had reached decision-making positions in their organizations in Japan. Most of the graduate programs they attended included a heavy dose of neoclassical economics, and those who studied Japan's economic and political relations in the United States were exposed to debate and criticism of Japan's economic and political systems. While these Japanese overseas students may not have found the critiques very persuasive, they were exposed to outside ideas that may have played a role in motivating changes in METI policy.

Conclusion

In conclusion, the combination of change and continuity in Japan's industrial policy described in this chapter illustrates the combination of permeability and insulation with which Japan has responded to changes in the domestic and international political and economic environment. On the one hand, in terms of permeability, there has been a clear effort to move away from some of the protectionist and anticompetitive policies of the past, and a desire to try to reap the benefits from global trends and new technologies. On the other hand, in terms of insulation, some protection remained, particularly informal protection fostered by the trend towards self-regulation (see Schaede, Chapter 8). And even in the cases where industrial policy had moved away from protection, there was still a clear sense that the government must help Japanese industry in the transition, even if that meant turning to promotional measures that might also benefit foreign firms (e.g., promotion of human capital, facilitation of corporate restructuring). In some cases, like the development of the supersonic transport, cooperation with foreign firms will be necessary, even though the goal is to promote Japanese aerospace companies. So even while implementing measures to promote Japanese firms, there is a definite trend away from the idea that foreign firms should be actively excluded from the Japanese market. (In fact METI's official policy is to encourage foreign investment in Japan.) For industrial policy, permeable insulation means that while Japan's strategy is moving in a new direction, but there are still important elements of continuity.

Notes

1. Johnson (1999) argued that in the 1980s and 1990s MITI tried to play down the extent to which it was engaged in industrial policy to avoid giving the impression that Japan's economic system was fundamentally different.
2. *Shinki sangyō sōshutsu kankyō seibi purogrammu.*
3. Other (pre-2001) ministries involved in all committees include the Economic Planning Agency, Science and Technology Agency, Ministry of Construction, Ministry of Posts and Telecommunications, Ministry of Transportation, and Ministry of Labor.

References

Anchordoguy, Marie. 1997. "Japan at a Technological Crossroads: Does Change Support Convergence Theory?" *Journal of Japanese Studies* 23, no. 2 : 363–97.
Beeman, Michael. 1999. "Japan's Flawed Antitrust Regime." *Japan Information Access Project Working Paper* (October 28).
Cabinet. 1997. "Keizai kōzō no henkaku to sōzō no tame no kōdō keikaku: Dai ikkai fuoroappu" (Action Plan for the Change and Creation of Economic Structure: First Follow-up). *Naikaku kettei* (Cabinet Decision, December 24).
Calder, Kent. 1993. *Strategic Capitalism: Private Business and Public Purpose in Japanese Industrial Finance*. Princeton: Princeton University Press.
Callon, Scott. 1995. *Divided Sun: MITI and the Breakdown of Japanese High-Tech Industrial Policy, 1975–1993*. Stanford: Stanford University Press.
Cohen, Stephen S., J. Bradford DeLong, and John Zysman. 2000. "Tools for Thought: What Is New and Important About the 'E-conomy.'" BRIE Working Paper 138 (February 22). Berkeley: Berkeley Roundtable on the International Economy.
Cumings, Bruce. 1999. "The Asian Crisis, Democracy, and the End of 'Late' Development." In T. J. Pempel, ed., *The Politics of the Asian Economic Crisis*, pp. 17–44. Ithaca: Cornell University Press.
Daily Yomiuri. 2001. "Ministry Unveils Prototype of Mach-2 Plane." *Daily Yomiuri* (February 10).
Dewey Ballantine. 2001. "The Internet in Japan: Catalyst for Change? (Extended Summary)" (February). Online at www.dbtrade.com/ecommerce/extended_summary.html (accessed March 14, 2001).
Elder, Mark. 1998. "Why Buy High? The Political Economy of Protection for Inter-

mediate Goods Industries in Japan." Ph.D. dissertation, Department of Government, Harvard University.

Friedman, David, and Richard J. Samuels. 1993. "How to Succeed Without Really Flying: The Japanese Aircraft Industry and Japan's Technology Ideology." In M. Kahler and J. Frankel, eds., *Regionalism and Rivalry: Japan and the United States in Pacific Asia*. Chicago: University of Chicago Press.

Goldstein, Morris. 1998. *The Asian Financial Crisis: Causes, Cures, and Systemic Implications*. Washington, DC: Institute for International Economics.

Guth, Robert. 2000. "Japanese Aim to Outspeed U.S. Internet—Ambitious Five-Year Goal Reflects Belief Nation Can Take the Lead." *Wall Street Journal* (August 31), p. A17.

ISC (Industrial Structure Council, Sangyō Kōzō Shingikai). 1997. "Kinkyō teigen" (Emergency Proposal) (November). Mimeo.

Ito, Hiro. 1997. "For Real Deregulation, MITI Must Go." *Daily Yomiuri* (September 11).

IT Strategy Council. 2000. "Basic IT Strategy" (November 27). Online at www.kantei.go.jp/foreign/it/council/basic_it.html (accessed June 15, 2001).

JASMEC (Japan Small and Medium Enterprises Corporation). 2001. "Benchaa kigyō shien" (Venture Business Support). Online at www.jasmec.go.jp/venture/index.html (accessed August 31, 2001).

JECC (Japan Electronic Computer Company). 2000. *JECC konpyūta nōto* (JECC Computer Notes). Tokyo: JECC.

Johnson, Chalmers. 1982. *MITI and the Japanese Miracle: The Growth of Industrial Policy, 1925–1975*. Stanford: Stanford University Press.

———. 1989. "MITI, MPT, and the Telecom Wars: How Japan Makes Policy for High Technology." In C. Johnson, L. Tyson, and J. Zysman, eds., *Politics and Productivity: The Real Story of Why Japan Works*. New York: Harper Business.

———. 1999. "The Developmental State: Odyssey of a Concept." In M. Woo-Cumings, ed., *The Developmental State*. Ithaca: Cornell University Press.

Kagaku Kōgyō Nippōsha. 1999. *Kagaku kōgyō nenkan, 1999-nenpan* (Chemical Industry Yearbook, 1999 Edition). Tokyo: Kagaku kōgyō nippōsha.

Katz, Richard. 1998. *Japan, the System That Soured: The Rise and Fall of the Japanese Economic Miracle*. Armonk, NY: M. E. Sharpe.

Kokusei Jōhō Sentā. 2000. *Shōchō saihen gaidobukku: Seifu an hen* (Ministries and Agencies Reorganization Guidebook: Government Proposal Edition). Tokyo: Kokusei jōhō sentā.

Krugman, Paul. 1994. "Competitiveness: A Dangerous Obsession." *Foreign Affairs* 73, no. 2: 28–44.

———. 1999. *The Return of Depression Economics*. New York: W.W. Norton.

Kyodo News Service. 2000. "Finance Ministry Proposes Record 4,995 billion-yen Defense Budget." *Kyodo News Service* (December 20).

———. 2001. "Japan to Develop Supersonic Aircraft in March 2002." *Kyodo News Service* (February 19).

Landers, Peter. 1997. "MITI No More: Even Diluted, Japan's Reform Plans Promise Real Change." *Far Eastern Economic Review* (September 4).

Lincoln, Edward. 1999. *Troubled Times: U.S.-Japan Trade Relations in the 1990s*. Washington, DC: Brookings Institution.

Masuda, Masao. 1995. "Problems Concerning the International Competitiveness of the Petrochemical Industry," no. 51 (October). Tokyo: Japan Development Bank.

METI (Ministry of Economy Trade and Industry). 2001. "Heisei 14 nendo ni muketa keizai sangyō seisaku no jūten: Maemuki no kōzō kaikaku o tsūjita jiritsuteki seichō no jitsugen" (Key Points of Economy and Industry Policy for Fiscal Year 2002: Realization of Independent Growth through Forward-Looking Structural Reform) (August). Online at www.meti.go.jp/topic/data/e10829aj.html (accessed August 31, 2001).

Mishima, Ko. 1998. "The Changing Relationship Between Japan's LDP and the Bureaucracy: Hashimoto's Administrative Reform Efforts and the Bureaucracy." *Asian Survey* 38, no. 10: 968–85.

MITI (Ministry of International Trade and Industry). 2000a. "Fiscal 2001 Priority Trade and Industry Policies." Government report (August).

———. 2000b. "Tsushō sangyō shō no jidōsha bunya ni okeru kanren yosan, zeisei, zaitō" (MITI's Budget, Tax, and FILP in the Automotive Area). Online at www.meti.go.jp/kohosys/topics/10000092/kanren.html (accessed August 15, 2001).

———. 2000c. "Nijūisseiki keizai sangyō seisaku no kadai to tenbō" (Twenty-First Century Economic and Industrial Policy Issues and Prospects). *Tsūsan Jānaru* (June): 18–27.

Nakahara, Hirohiko. 1999a. "Jigyō saikōchiku ni kakawaru sho seido no seibi to sangyō saisei e no michi" (Improvements in Various Systems Relating to Enterprise Restructuring and the Road to Industrial Revitalization). *Saiken Kanri*, no. 87 (January 5): 82–86.

Nakahara, Hirohiko. 1999b. "Sangyō katsuryoku saisei hō dō tsukawarete iru ka: genjō to kadai" (How the Industrial Revitalization Law Can Be Used: Current Conditions and Topics). *Kinyū Hōmu Jijō*, no. 1555 (August 25).

Nikkei (Nihon Keizai Shimbun). 1999. "Kanmin de kaihatsu handōtai shin gijutsu: Tsūsanshō to ōte 10 sha" (New Semiconductor Technology to Be Developed Through Bureaucratic-Private Sector Cooperation: MITI and Ten Large Companies). *Nihon Keizai Shimbun* (October 25).

NITS (National Industrial Technology Strategy Development Committee). 1999. *National Industrial Technology Strategies in Japan* (December).

———. 2000. *Kokka sangyō gijutsu senryaku* (National Industrial Technology Strategy) (April 10).

Noble, Gregory W., and John Ravenhill. 2000. "Causes and Consequences of the Asian Financial Crisis." In Gregory W. Noble and John Ravenhill, eds., *The Asian Financial Crisis and the Architecture of Global Finance*, pp. 1–35. Cambridge: Cambridge University Press.

Okimoto, Daniel I. 1989. *Between MITI and the Market: Japanese Industrial Policy for High Technology*. Stanford: Stanford University Press.

Ostrom, Douglas. 1999. "The Competitiveness Debate Comes to Japan." *JEI Report* 24 (June 25).

Porter, Michael E. 1990. *The Competitive Advantage of Nations*. New York: Free Press.

Porter, Michael E., Hirotaka Takeuchi, and Mariko Sakakibara. 2000. *Can Japan Compete?* Cambridge, MA: Basic Books/Perseus.

Radelet, Steven, and Jeffrey Sachs. 1998. "The Onset of the East Asian Financial Crisis." CAER II Discussion Paper 27 (March 30). Cambridge: Harvard Institute for International Development.

Samuels, Richard J. 1987. *The Business of the Japanese State: Energy Markets in Comparative and Historical Perspective*. Ithaca: Cornell University Press.

Schaede, Ulrike. 2000. *Cooperative Capitalism: Self-Regulation, Trade Associations, and the Antimonopoly Law in Japan*. Oxford: Oxford University Press.

SMEA (Small and Medium Enterprises Agency), MITI. 1999. *Reference Materials for Japanese SME Measures* (November 11). Unpublished document.

———. 2000a. "Chūshō kigyō hakusho" (Small and Medium Enterprises White Paper). Tokyo: Ministry of Finance.

———. 2000b. "Outline of Japan's New SME Policies" (February 7).

———. 2001. "Heisei 13 nendo chūshō kigyō taisaku zaitō yōkyū nado no gaiyō" (Summary of Fiscal Year 2001 Small and Medium Enterprises Policy Fiscal Investment and Loan Program Request). Online at www.chusho.meti.go.jp/taisaku/_yosan/000901zaitou.html (accessed August 9, 2001).

STA (Science and Technology Agency). 1999. "Kagaku gijutsu hakusho" (Science and Technology White Paper). Tokyo: Ministry of Finance.

Suzuki, Yumiko. 2000. "Plans for E-Government Inspire Spending Spree." *Nikkei Weekly* (October 23), p. 1.

Tilton, Mark. 1996. *Restrained Trade: Cartels in Japan's Basic Materials Industries*. Ithaca: Cornell University Press.

Tōyō Keizai. 2000. *Seikai kanchō jinjiroku 2000-nenpan* (Personnel Reference of the Political World and the Bureaucracy, 2000 Edition). Tokyo: Tōyō keizai shimpōsha.

Vogel, Steven K. 1997. "Can Japan Disengage? Winners and Losers in Japan's Political Economy, and the Ties That Bind Them." BRIE Working Paper 111 (December). Berkeley: Berkeley Roundtable on the International Economy.

Wolf, Charles. 1998. "Too Much Government Control." *Wall Street Journal* (February 4).

Wolff, Alan William, and Thomas R. Howell. 1992. "Japan." In Thomas R. Howell, Alan W. Wolff, Brent L. Bartlett, and R. Michael Gadbaw, eds., *Conflict Among Nations: Trade Policies in the 1990s*, pp. 45–144. Boulder: Westview Press.

Zinsmeister, Karl. 1993. "MITI Mouse: Japan's Industrial Policy Doesn't Work." *Policy Review* (Spring): 28–35.

8

Industry Rules

From Deregulation to Self-Regulation

Ulrike Schaede

A major point of contention between Japan and its trading partners has long been the issue of market access and competition. For decades, foreign companies have complained about an "uneven" playing field and limited access to Japan's large, affluent market due to industrial policy, implemented by the Ministry of Economy, Trade, and Industry (METI) and other ministries to uphold vast regulations and protect domestic producers. Foreign governments, in particular that of the United States, backed their domestic corporate interests by initiating a series of trade negotiations intended to increase market access, beginning with agriculture and then progressing to manufacturing, transportation, telecommunication, and the service and financial industries.[1] The Japanese government responded to these pressures with a process of seemingly never-ending "regulatory reforms." This chapter argues that the result of this extended process is a prime example of permeable insulation.

Over the last two decades, Japan has announced almost too many deregulation programs to count. To mention just a few of these, the 1983 Japan-U.S. Yen/Dollar Committee proposed interest rate deregulation and a sequence of financial reforms, many of which were accomplished by 1994 (KZJK 1985). The 1986 Maekawa Report contained a laundry list of deregulation proposals, although it was not obvious what this program really achieved in the end. A March 1995 deregulation initiative across all ministries was aimed at reducing the number of ministerial rules and regulations pertaining to all industries (see, for example, MITI 1995). Following on its heels, the five-year "Big Bang" financial reform program was announced with great fanfare in 1996, as a move finally to make Japan's financial markets "free, fair and global" by 2001, implicitly admitting that the 1983 initiative had been insufficient to achieve this. A 1999 "Three-Year Deregulation Program" was supposed to reduce further the regulatory grip of Japan's ministries over their industries. In the process of these various deregulation programs, some of Japan's major trade and industry laws were revised and restrictions on cross-border transactions lifted. Perhaps the most important impact of these reforms was how they changed the competitive landscape in Japan's financial industry (Hoshi and Kashyap 2001).

Curiously, though, after twenty years of deregulation we find that, while a few Japanese product markets have in fact opened up, the majority continue to be dominated by Japanese firms. True, some notoriously protected industries suddenly began to change; for example, within just a few years in the 1990s, the finance and automobile industries opened up significantly. Yet, market share data for the 1990s revealed that the average foreign market share ("import penetration") across a wide range of intermediate and end products was less than 5 percent (see, for example, JFTC 1993; Nikkei 1998). Although on paper deregulation had pertained to all industries, in reality it had affected product markets differently. Apparently, deregulation and the numerous legal revisions and regulatory amendments resulted in some markets breaking open and others remaining closed.

The explanation for this puzzle is that while deregulation has indeed proceeded, in the process official regulation has been replaced with private regulation by the industries themselves. Left largely to their own devices, industries could decide on the openness of their own markets; given this choice, some industries opted to be permeated by more competition, while others chose to insulate. Deregulation has resulted in a choice between open and closed markets, because it reduced the ministries' ability to guide industries, and no new mechanisms of oversight were introduced in its stead. Reforms have rewritten many of the laws that previously allowed ministries to employ the intricate and often subtle carrot-and-stick mechanisms of "administrative guidance" (i.e., extra-legal regulation). Because the informal processes of admin-

istrative guidance were not replaced by more formal means of commerce oversight, deregulation of entry requirements created a regulatory void. Many industries realized an opportunity to step into this void
and structure their own market rules. Just how these rules were structured differed across industries: Some opted to open up to competition,
while others strove to replicate the protectionist setting previously provided by the regulators. Thus, firms in many industries began to structure their own restrictive rules of market entry, limits to competition,
and other means to deter entry by new competitors. While this was a
major shift for Japan—as private rules were substituted for regulation
by ministries, and power shifted away from ministries and toward industries—for foreign competitors, the result looked very much like
"more of the same," as many product markets remained insulated from
foreign competition.

Self-regulation by industry also meant that official government deregulation programs were rendered largely meaningless in those industries that chose to self-regulate with the goals of substituting and
upholding previous protectionist regulation. The only serious challenge to such protective self-regulation could be provided by a reorganization of Japan's antitrust law and its enforcement. As of 2001, the
Japanese antitrust authority was ineffective in containing self-regulation, and no powerful constituency within Japan was pushing for a revision of antitrust enforcement. Thus, as long as Japan's deregulation
and reform program focused on the reduction of industry-specific
rules, rather than the creation of new mechanisms of oversight and a
fundamentally new approach to antitrust enforcement, deregulation
mainly served to make Japanese regulators less important, but did not
lead to more open markets across all industries in which deregulation
occurred.

The outcome of official deregulation, in combination with the concurrent increase in industry self-regulation, has been permeable insulation. By not monitoring market behavior and enforcing antitrust
statutes against private trade barriers, Japan's government allowed industries to structure their own markets, so that they could either self-
promote (by inviting competition) or self-protect (by closing up their
market). Allowing government regulation to be replaced by self-regulation meant that the Japanese state withdrew—only to enable some
firms to insulate, and other firms to break out. It is highly unlikely that
the government designed its deregulation policies with this outcome in

mind; however, when confronted with the increase in self-regulation, it chose not to stop it.

Japan's Regulatory System and Change

An analysis of the logic of deregulation in Japan is greatly helped by the important differentiation between two fundamental types of regulation: "entry regulation" and "process regulation." Entry regulation refers to a government's rules on who is allowed to compete, as determined by certain minimum requirements (e.g., on capital or expertise); it is implemented through the issuance of licenses, permits, and other official stamps of approval. In contrast, "process regulation" refers to the monitoring of firms once they have entered the market, such as through reporting and disclosure requirements, or on-site inspections. In most industrialized countries, entry regulation is typically spelled out in laws and regulations, and process regulation is conducted based on formal rules by separate supervisory agencies. In the United States, examples of such agencies are the Federal Communications Commission, the Securities and Exchange Commission, or the Commodities and Futures Trading Commission (Greer 1993; Weidenbaum 1990). In general, the regulatory process consists of a combination of these two types of regulation, and emphasis typically differs by industry. For example, banking regulation in most countries consists of both minimum capital requirements for licensing and regular inspections, whereas some service industries may be based on licenses only (e.g., hairdressers, carpenters), and others may have free entry but regular process supervision (e.g., investment banking, restaurants).

Countries and their legal systems differ as to where the emphasis is placed and how the actual regulation is conducted. Japan's regulatory focus has long been almost exclusively on entry regulation. Entry approval came in a large array of different legal types of licenses, permits, or authorizations, all of which were issued by the cognizant ministry (all referred to as "licenses" in the remainder of this chapter). In contrast, after a company had received permission to enter a market, subsequent process regulation was highly informal, if it occurred at all. With the exception of the financial industry, where the Financial Services Agency was created only in 1998, there were no specific supervisory agencies in Japan in 2001. Instead, process monitoring was also placed in the hands of the cognizant ministries, which were thus in charge of both nurturing and supervising the industries. For example, during the 1950s and 1960s, the Ministry of Finance (MOF) had to ensure a stable financial system with no bankruptcies while also making sure that banks obeyed the rules; because economic growth was the overriding priority, supervision was sometimes compromised for the sake of expansion. Other ministries faced similar regulatory conflicts of interests; for example, the Ministry of Health and Welfare was in charge of fostering a strong pharmaceutical industry and of securing public safety (the HIV-tainted blood scandal of the 1990s was only the most egregious example of the ministry's bias toward growth). The easiest way to solve this conflict of interest, inherent in giving a ministry the two tasks of industry promotion and supervision, was to rely on informal contacts with the regulated firms that allowed for early problem detection and backroom deals for quiet solutions.

Process regulation by the ministries occurred through various informal, albeit institutionalized routes. The first route was through constant interaction between the ministry and the regulated company. This was implemented via a designated company employee, whose task was to contact the bureaucrat in charge at the cognizant ministry on a regular and frequent basis, and to exchange information on company specifics and new regulation. This employee was the so-called *-tan*, as in "MOF-*tan*" in a bank—that is, the employee in charge of contacts with the MOF. The second route of informal exchange was the "Old Boy" network created through a process called *amakudari* (descent from heaven), whereby retired bureaucrats were hired by private firms with the explicit task of smoothing the information flow between company and ministry. A third route of Japan's informal process supervision was through the industry's trade association, which was often in charge of collecting industry data for the ministry and discussing upcoming regulatory changes with the ministry (Schaede 1995, 2000).

Between the 1950s and 1990s, Japan's ministries thought of process regulation primarily as a means to solve problems quickly and informally, while the regulatory emphasis was squarely placed on entry regulation. This had two important implications. First, it gave rise to the phenomenon of administrative guidance, whereby without a specific legal basis ministries enticed certain behavior by regulated companies in return for preferential regulatory treatment. For instance, a ministry could promise easier access to a license, or threaten to deny a future license application. The more licenses to be issued, the more powerful the ministry. Administrative guidance also had (and continues to have) a strong situational character, as licenses could be granted or revoked in discretionary fashion and without easy legal recourse for the licensee. Yet, by the 1990s the continuing process of deregulation began slowly to undermine the ability of ministries to induce particular corporate behavior. The financial "Big Bang" program that began in the late 1990s included amendments of some of the basic laws that had previously afforded ministries leverage. While administrative guidance continued to exist, ministries had lost many of their powerful tools and increasingly had to formulate guidance based on negotiations with the regulated industries. This further undermined the strength and relevance of process regulation.

A second implication of Japan's emphasis on entry regulation was how it shaped U.S.-Japan negotiations of market opening and the results of deregulation in Japan. In contrast to Japan, regulatory focus in the United States has traditionally been on process regulation. True, requirements for entry licenses were numerous in the United States as well, but they were typically based on a clearly formulated set of requirements, and in principle anyone who fulfilled the specified requirements would receive a license. Regardless of whether or not an industry was subject to licensing requirements, incumbent companies in many industries were formally monitored or inspected on a regular basis (Weidenbaum 1990). In the United States, this focus on process regulation was considered to be "fairer," as it allowed firms to compete as long as they complied with the rules.

Given this way of thinking, U.S. companies objected to Japan's less-than-transparent, informal, and occasionally discriminatory regulatory process. Supporting domestic corporate interests, the U.S. government began to push for "deregulation" in the early 1980s—meaning primarily the removal of entry licenses. And even the complaints regarding "reregulation" (the introduction of new rules with the abolition of old ones) referred to the introduction of new entry rules.[2] However, what was really necessary for Japan to open its markets was, in fact, an increase in process regulation—that is, more monitoring and supervising market rule compliance by all firms.

However, because Japan relied almost exclusively on informal monitoring, it lacked the institutions and rules for process supervision. Therefore, by the 1990s the process of deregulation began to cause a regulatory void, by reducing entry rules without placing more emphasis on supervision. The decline in ministerial leverage, exacerbated by post-bubble period scandals in the late 1990s, greatly diminished the bureaucrats' authority in informal supervision. For example, in reaction to scandals about inappropriate dinner outings by MOF officials at the expense of their regulatees, the position of the MOF-*tan* was abolished in most banks, and bureaucrats were asked not to converse regularly with bank employees. Further, following public outrage at government spending in general, and perks for bureaucrats in particular, reforms were suggested to restrict, or even bring to an end, the institutionalized processes of *amakudari*, in which the government negotiated with private firms the post-retirement placement of high-ranking bureaucrats.

Meanwhile, business did not sit still. Rather, realizing that deregulation of entry rules without an increase in monitoring could cause confusion in their markets, many industries set out to fill the regulatory void through increased self-regulation. Implemented through the industries' trade associations and formulated to fit their needs, self-regulation was used for different purposes by different industries, but in all cases resulted in an increase of private rules over official ones. Japan's markets remained insulated in many respects, although the element of choice contained in self-regulation allowed breakouts from insulation by those industries operating at the cutting edge of global competition.

Self-Regulation

The term "self-regulation" (*jishu kisei*) describes a process by which a trade association, comprised of the leading firms in an industry, designs rules of trade for that industry and enforces those rules through self-designed sanctions. While self-regulation is certainly not unique to Japan's trade associations, the increased scope and depth with which Japanese associations pursued it beginning in the 1990s made its role in the regulatory system much more significant than in other countries. This was possible because of the confluence of a lenient antitrust system, the particular evolution of Japan's political economy, and deregulation.[3]

Types and Examples of Self-Regulation

Self-regulation encompasses a broad spectrum of activities, which can be grouped into two main categories:

a. *Administrative self-regulation.* This category includes activities that aim to structure the rules and regulations of the industry, with the primary motive to facilitate or enhance trade. Activities include: setting standards or minimum quality requirements, conducting quality inspections, setting rules on advertising and ethical standards, controlling mutual trade credit financing, or providing mutual management support. Often, these activities increase the overall quality reputation of the industry and advance economic growth. While some of these activities may have anticompetitive effects, most types of administrative self-regulation are trade-enhancing, and are therefore legal in many countries.

b. *Protective self-regulation.* This category refers to all activities ultimately aimed at shielding the industry from competition by creating defensive barriers to trade. Examples include: agreements on prices, entry barriers, exclusive trade tie-ups, boycotts, and refusals to deal with nonmembers of the association. The legal interpretation of these activities differs across countries: While price-fixing is usually considered illegal, countries diverge in how they consider, for example, restrictions in the distribution system. Thus, whereas from the U.S. perspective much of protective self-regulation looks like "unfair trade practices," which are restricted by law, not all of it is interpreted as such in Japan.

The boundaries between administrative and protective self-regulation are blurred. Sometimes administrative self-regulation may evolve into protective self-regulation over time, or companies may choose actions that contain both aspects of self-regulation. For instance, an association might set industry standards—either on minimum quality requirements or certain product characteristics—such that only incumbent firms can meet these standards; whereas setting standards is generally considered a trade-enhancing activity, setting them at the disadvantage of potential competitors is not. One, somewhat curious, example of this strategy comes from Japan's flat glass industry, where standards were actually set too low for full competition. Window glass manufacturing is based on a large number of standards, including safety provisions. In the mid-1990s, U.S. glass manufacturers claimed superior safety properties of their products, given stricter safety standards in many U.S. states than in Japan. Still, it was difficult for these manufacturers to export glass to Japan because safety standards for

Japanese public buildings were lower and different, so that windows could be produced more cheaply by Japanese companies. Although safety requirements for windows sounded like a reasonable standard, setting them such that they gave an advantage to domestic firms resulted in a trade restriction.[4]

Another outstanding example of blurred legal boundaries concerns the "trade habits" (*shōkankō*) that are common practice in the Japanese distribution system. Consisting of a complicated system of rebates, returns, exclusive wholesaler relations, and retail price maintenance—each of which by itself is not necessarily a powerful barrier to entry—these "trade habits" have developed over years into an intricate, interwoven system that often results in insurmountable obstacles for outsiders seeking to compete. Examples abound of product markets where these mechanisms were in place in the 1990s, including the beer industry, electronics, books, cosmetics, paper, pens, and many other consumer products.

Perhaps the best-chronicled case is that of the photographic film industry. Japan's market leader, Fujifilm, had over time constructed a distribution system for its product that lined up a series of regional and local exclusive wholesalers who assured regular and constant supply of film to outlets all around Japan, from specialized photo stores to subway kiosks and tourist park vendors. This distribution network was expensive, and to maximize sales, Fujifilm introduced a variety of rebate schemes, including one whereby a retailer would earn a higher margin per roll of film, the more rolls he sold. Moreover, for exclusive outlets, Fujifilm promised to take back unsold and expired film at no cost, thus limiting the retailer's risk in losing capital through overstocking; as retailers rarely ran out of stock, availability to film anywhere at any time was assured. This was strategically important because, from the consumer's perspective (except for professionals, perhaps), switching costs in film were low, making availability the primary purchase variable. Therefore, in competing against Kodak, Fujifilm would win if its product was more readily available. For Kodak, the fact that Fujifilm had tied a majority of film wholesalers and retailers into its distribution network meant that it faced insurmountable barriers to providing wide access to its product.[5]

Moreover, price rules in the distribution system are often related to price agreements among the product manufacturers, who then use restrictions on their exclusive retailers to enforce their price-fixing through the retail system. A typical example is the consumer electronics industry. Matsushita Electric Industries, the world's largest electronics manufacturer in the 1990s, sold its various brands (National, Panasonic, Technics, JVC) through vertically aligned, exclusive retail outlets. In 1995, the company controlled more than 25,000 such stores all over Japan. Sony, Toshiba, and Hitachi likewise sold through exclusive retail outlets. The companies printed a reference price on the cardboard boxes in which products were shipped, and stores were forced to follow reference prices through a threat of discontinuation of shipments. Once in a while, retailers seemingly offered discounts from this reference price to lure customers into their shops. Suspicious of recurring patterns in these discounts, Japan's Fair Trade Commission (JFTC) (Kōsei Torihiki Iinkai) had looked into these practices for many years until, in 1992, the four largest firms were found to have agreed not only on the product price, but more deceptively on a specific percentage discount off their reference price; the manufacturers then required their exclusive retailers to follow this predetermined "discount." In this way, the four companies had fixed prices and yet created the impression of competition, while in fact also controlling the occasional discount, thus fully controlling the retail price structure (JFTC 1994, pp. 86–94).[6]

Finally, protective self-regulation can simply be an attempt by an association to raise the price for a good or service, and then monitor all members. In addition to the simple motive to increase profits, such arrangements often serve more complicated objectives. A fitting example is the case of a northern Tokyo association of mahjong club owners in 1996. Mahjong is originally a Chinese game based on small pictograph stones and dice, which in many ways assumes the social and functional equivalent role of poker in the United States. Mahjong clubs match groups of four players who bet on their luck. These clubs were regulated by a special law that set the maximum hourly fee at ¥620, as of 1996. Partially as a result of the recession, however, in the mid-1990s the clubs in northern Tokyo charged only about 70 percent of this maximum price and, with dwindling clientele, many club owners found themselves in dire straits. The local mahjong club owners convened in their association and decided that, rather than let some of their members go bankrupt, they would all raise their fees to the legal limit of ¥620; the association printed out a price schedule that all members posted in their clubs (JFTC 1996, p. 28).

This case highlights several important aspects of self-regulation. First, even in industries that are normally competitive, recession can trigger efforts at cooperation and price agreements. Second, the logic with the price hike in the mahjong case was that even with below-average attendance, all owners could stay in business. One wonders why at least one of the club owners would not try to attract all players by charging lesser fees, and then take over the entire market after everyone else failed. Why did everyone comply with the price hike? Two explanations stand out for this seemingly odd behavior. First, the legal fee limit of ¥620 per hour put an upper bound on the profits that an aspiring monopolist could earn if he was successful in breaking the cartel. This was too small a future payoff to risk alienating all other club owners, since in normal times everyone could charge ¥620 even with all clubs open. Second, precisely because there was more than enough demand during boom years, taking over the local industry and then rigging prices would inevitably have caused a great loss in reputation, which was an important asset to a club owner; thus, all club owners were better off by going along with the price hike.

Why Companies Self-Regulate

Frequent interactions with industry competitors come at immense costs for a company, of which employee time expenses and constraints to individual corporate strategy are only the most visible. While exact data on trade association memberships are difficult to come by, interviews and data analysis conducted in 1995 revealed that most firms in Japan—even small ones—were members of at least one trade association, and large firms typically belonged to several. Moreover, in interviews with thirty-seven major trade associations conducted in 1995, I found that these associations had, on average, nineteen committees with seventeen members, as well as seventy-five subcommittees with ten members each (Schaede 2000). Committees met monthly, and therefore the average number of employees attending committee meetings exceeded 1,000 per month for just these thirty-seven associations. Although many trade associations in Japan were smaller than those surveyed, if we visualize the traffic related to committee meetings of just the 3,000 largest industry associations, we get an idea of how much time, effort, and money companies were willing to expend for the purpose of self-regulation.

What, then, are the benefits from self-regulation? In general, there are four primary reasons why companies find self-regulation beneficial over time:

1. As for administrative self-regulation, companies may have three prime objectives: first, to replace or augment existing official regulation in fast-changing markets (e.g., in high-technology industries such as biotechnology or investment banking); second, to create a reputation of fairness and sound business by self-enforcing ethical standards and launching social responsibility campaigns, as in many medical or other professional associations; and third, to increase the bargaining power of the association's members vis-à-vis large customers, especially in intermediate product markets. These types of activities are common to trade associations in many countries, and they are typically considered legal, unless adherence is coerced or rules are used to limit competition in the industry.

2. In combining practices of administrative and protective self-regulation, the predominant motive is for companies to reduce uncertainty through extensive exchange of information, including investment plans and costs. The goal is to lower variance in profits. The means to achieve this goal are plentiful, including agreements to reduce capacity, to keep dividend payments low, to allocate customers and markets, or to require exclusive trade rules in the distribution system (e.g., boycotting discount stores) and other "trade habits," as previously mentioned.

   Related to the objective of stabilizing profits over time is the use of self-regulation to construct a "sanctuary strategy." This strategy aims to build a profit cushion in the home market that allows companies to compete forcefully through price discounts abroad. Lower profits in export markets are counterbalanced by higher profits in the domestic market. To implement this strategy, self-regulation may include price fixing, retail price maintenance in the domestic market, and other means to restrain competition in the home market.[7]

3. As for purely protective self-regulation, companies may aim to increase profits through collusion with their competitors; this objective is typically achieved through price fixing. One challenge for price cartels is the monitoring of cartel members to insure adherence with the price limits. Self-regulation through constant meetings and through distribution rules is the ideal tool for carrying out

price agreements. Yet, while price fixing may be the most obvious motive of self-regulation and the one practice that is easiest to observe, it is not typically the dominant objective.

4. A particularly important reason to participate in self-regulation in Japan is group pressure. Because self-regulation often pertains to access to the distribution system, sometimes companies have no choice but to participate in the cooperative agreements of the industry, lest they be excluded from business. Examples abound of how self-regulation can be structured such that undermining the agreement becomes bad corporate strategy. Moreover, promotion systems in Japanese companies set incentives for individuals not to stand out, thus limiting the efforts of individuals to resist industry pressure to self-regulate.

Whatever the motivation, in the early twenty-first century most Japanese firms were members of one or more trade associations, and all trade associations engaged in some form of self-regulation—be it to self-promote or self-protect.

Why Self-Regulation Is Stable

This chapter argues that self-regulation introduces permeable insulation to Japan because it affords industries choice where previously there was official regulation. Self-regulation is becoming increasingly important in Japan because it fills the regulatory void caused by entry deregulation in the 1980s and 1990s and a lack of concurrent increase in process regulation. Given that regulatory reform is a process, one might think of self-regulation as just a temporary "filler" that could soon be replaced by market mechanisms or further reforms and new state regulation. However, there are several reasons why the relevance of self-regulation in Japan is unlikely to diminish in the medium run, and why self-regulation—and the permeable insulation it entails—are bound to be important features of Japan's political economy for many years into the twenty-first century.

First, self-regulation as an activity of trade associations is inherently stable, because it is couched in repeated interactions of various kinds. Moreover, foreign participation in self-regulation may in some cases change the thrust of self-regulation and lead to more open markets, but it will not undermine the actual process or the viability of self-regulation as an activity pursued by all trade associations. And finally, as will be argued in the next section, to curb self-regulation Japan will have to revise its antitrust system fundamentally; however, there are no indications that this is at all likely or even possible.

To argue these points in order, first, it may look as if self-regulation might be unstable, because cooperation among firms to restrict prices or close markets is basically a cartel and, like other cartels, invites cheating (i.e., the exploitation of an opportunity to increase market share by at least one company in the industry). However, protective self-regulation differs importantly from a cartel by being a continuous process nested in the trade association and connected to other, long-term industry activities, such as lobbying. Self-regulation is an institutionalized, ongoing process, and it is thus inherently much more stable than a cartel, where companies get together with the singular purpose of fixing prices. While cartels in Japan typically build on self-regulation and are often organized through trade associations, self-regulation is not based on a cartel, and it may not constitute a cartel. Self-regulation is therefore more perpetual and predictable than a cartel.

Structuring and enforcing protective self-regulation is much easier if the number of participating firms is small (because it is easier to agree), and the industry is stable (because sudden shifts in technology or demand require renegotiation). Many Japanese trade associations have addressed this problem by breaking into small chapters, either geographically or by product specification. For example, there are regional chapters of *tatami* (rice straw mat) makers, and the writing utensil industry is broken up into more than five separate associations by product—those for pencils, ball pens, fountain pens, highlighters, erasers, and white-out ink. As a result of this approach, with 15,426 associations (as of 1999), Japan had more than twice as many trade associations as the United States, adjusted by size of the two economies (JFTC 1999, p. 287; Schaede 2000, chap. 2). Moreover, data analysis has supported the notion that protective self-regulation is more likely to occur in industries with less technological change, more homogeneous products, and where the association has adopted special organizational measures, such as a representation of all member firm executives on the association's board (Schaede 2000, chap. 6). Thus, while there are industry characteristics that facilitate self-regulation, Japan's trade associations have also been very astute in structuring their associations such that self-regulation is possible and sustainable in the long run, even where those characteristics are not present.

Self-regulation is further stabilized because it also includes self-enforcement—that is, the association is in charge of supervising compliance. Regular and frequent meetings ensure constant interaction and mutual monitoring. Having outlined the competitive behavior for their industry, companies often negotiate business plans or divide markets either by territory or product category. Companies may agree to refuse to deal with companies that are not association members, and monitor their members' behavior by requesting detailed trade statistics from each. An industry may create a fund that everyone has to pay into, and a company that deviates from the agreed-upon plan may find its contribution confiscated as a penalty. Adherence to agreements is often enforced in the marketplace, through the association's watching prices charged by their competitors.

Moreover, many industries use standardized rate schedules and control the books of their members to insure compliance. One industry repeatedly investigated over the years for this practice is propane gas. Various local chapters of the Propane Gas Wholesalers Association had issued "management guidance" to their members by way of suggesting a standard cost-accounting table. Whereas the claim was to help small entrepreneurs, effectively the table prescribed that all members charge the same percentage over the purchase price, and thus resulted in a price cartel (JFTC 1995). The staff of the association's local chapters was also seen monitoring adherence by contacting customers and inspecting members' profit reports. Interestingly, in the thirty-two years between 1963 and 1995, JFTC issued no less than thirty-four informal and formal notices to the various local chapters of this association (see below for why there were no effective legal deterrents).[8]

Therefore, because self-regulation is tied into the larger activities of trade associations, and because it includes institutionalized mechanisms of self-sanctioning, it is stable internally even without being reinforced by the government. Administrative self-regulation, being trade-enhancing, is naturally in the interest of all members. In terms of protective self-regulation, in those instances where it has failed, product markets may have become more open; however, the threat of retaliation by incumbent firms and of new competition from the outside has often been sufficient incentive for firms to agree with and to abide by the restrictive market rules.

Next, one might think that foreign entry could undermine the stability of self-regulation, either by way of foreign companies opening up subsidiaries in Japan or by their acquiring Japanese firms. The revision of the Foreign Exchange Law in 1998 removed all remaining legal constraints to capital inflow and outflow, and the extended recession reduced the stock price of many Japanese firms, triggering a sharp increase in foreign direct investments into Japan, especially in wholesale finance and automobiles. While self-regulation in these two global industries may well have been boiled down to administrative rules only, there are several reasons why increased foreign participation is unlikely to affect the overall logic of self-regulation, at least in the medium term.

First, a foreign firm that begins operations in Japan will either be excluded from the association due to restrictive self-regulation, or it will become a member. It will be excluded only if it is small and unlikely to undermine industry rules on its own; if so, it will not pose a threat to the system. If included, the firm can shape the association's self-regulation, but there is no obvious reason why it would want to disturb even protective self-regulation (other than perhaps if it entails price fixing). In a regulatory void such as that experienced in Japan in the early twenty-first century, rules by the trade association are often preferable to no rules. What is more, as long as a foreign firm is part of the "in" group, it will welcome entry barriers and other restrictions just as much as the domestic incumbents. An example of this scenario was provided by the insurance industry. Throughout the 1980s and early 1990s, U.S. insurance companies had lobbied hard for government support in prying open Japan's insurance markets. When the breakthrough was finally accomplished in 1995 and a few U.S. insurance companies were allowed to open subsidiaries in Japan, these companies suddenly changed their tune and asked the U.S. government to prevent more deregulation in Japan as that would "destabilize" the market.[9] Companies around the world like to self-regulate.

Even in situations where a foreign firm finds self-regulation disadvantageous and too restrictive, it may have no choice but to go along. For the same reason that Japanese companies feel group pressure to participate in trade association activities, foreigners that refuse to do so are likely to find themselves without access to the distribution system. Finally, even if an influential, large foreign firm could disrupt some of the protective practices in its industry, the result would be that this one industry would move toward more administrative, rather than protective self-regulation—that is, the industry would open up. However, one industry moving from protective to administrative self-regulation does not change the overall market situation in Japan, and it certainly does not undermine the entire logic of self-regulation.

Thus, in the long run the biggest impact of foreign participation in self-regulation in Japan will be how it affects permeable insulation—that is, the balance between those sectors that choose to self-promote and those that self-protect. If it turns out that, over time, foreign firms indeed effect self-regulation by shifting it toward more open markets, more sectors of Japan's economy may become more permeable. This process will take time, however, and in any event the system of self-regulation is bound to continue.

Self-Regulation and Antitrust

Besides its embeddedness and the likelihood of cooperation even by foreign firms, the third and most fundamental reason why self-regulation is stable in the medium term is political. At the turn of the century, there were no powerful constituents in Japan that found self-regulation to be objectionable. There were thus few voices calling on the authorities to contain it, either through more formal process regulation in each industry or through a stricter application of antitrust statutes for all industries. As long as this was so, there were few official limitations to the rule making by trade associations.

Antitrust enters the picture in the following way. The substitution of deregulation by industry self-regulation means that industries can structure their own markets. As we have seen, some industries have used this opportunity to open up; but not many industries were so competitive as to reach this outcome, and in many industries the outcome of self-regulation was a replacement, or even an increase, in restrictive measures. The only regulatory tool available to stop these trade-restricting measures was antitrust enforcement.

In general, throughout the postwar period the JFTC has been less than effective in curbing self-regulation. Given that the demarcation between administrative and protective self-regulation is not clear, it is not always easy to see, let alone prove, measures of protective self-regulation. Moreover, throughout the postwar period, as part of their administrative guidance many ministries encouraged companies to engage in protective self-regulation as a way to implement industrial policies. In the process, even competitive industries such as automobiles or electronics learned that it paid to cooperate, especially in times of recession or when faced with a foreign competitive threat. Since this often occurred under the umbrella of the Ministry of International Trade and Industry's (MITI's) industrial policy, there was little the JFTC could do. Even in cases where self-regulation was obviously protective to an extent that violated Japan's antitrust statute, the JFTC faced tremendous difficulties in containing this behavior because of the tradition, structure, and logic of Japanese antitrust enforcement. As of 2001, in spite of repeated announcements that it would increase its enforcement activities, the JFTC remained weak when faced with instances of protective self-regulation.

The JFTC's difficulties stemmed from two interrelated factors, both grounded in the letter of the antitrust law and the legal doctrine developed over time. When the JFTC identified a potential violation, it had a choice among four possible ways to proceed: (1) bring a criminal case; (2) launch a formal, administrative case; (3) treat the case informally; or (4) do nothing, due to insufficient evidence. In the United States, roughly 50 percent of all cases brought by the Federal Trade Commission and the Department of Justice between the 1950s and 1990s were brought as criminal cases (i.e., with the possibility of resulting in fines and imprisonment), whereas the other half were brought as formal administrative proceedings (Kawagoe 1997, pp. 459–60). In contrast, the JFTC prosecuted a total of only ten criminal cases in the fifty years between 1947 and 1997; this equaled less than one percent of all 1,007 formal cases of that period. Instead, most cases were settled informally in Japan, through the issuance by the JFTC of a written "warning" or oral "caution" (Schaede 2000, chap. 5). Neither of these measures carried any penalties.

Moreover, Japan's antitrust law[10] differentiates between outright cartels such as through price fixing (prohibited under Section 3), and "unfair trade practices" such as boycotts and other barriers to entry (prohibited under Section 19). Traditionally, the law has placed stronger emphasis on cartel prosecution, and Section 3 prescribes a set of penalties, including surcharges and fines, for violations. In contrast, unfair trade practices such as those entailed in protective self-regulation have been covered by the much more lenient Section 19, which allows for no more than a legally inconsequential "cease-and-desist" order, and which offers no provisions against repeat offenders.

An analysis of all postwar antitrust cases brought by the JFTC reveals that the agency used Section 3 for many price-fixing cases, but chose to treat the majority of protective self-regulation either informally or, when applying the law, to do so under Section 19 (Schaede 2000, chap. 5). Moreover, in looking at JFTC prosecution over the years, one finds that on average the JFTC settled more than four times as many cases informally (i.e., without even invoking the law) as it brought formally. This had two important implications. It sent a strong signal to associations that antitrust violations could be settled fairly easily, thus creating few legal deterrents to protective self-regulation. It also meant that no body of legal precedents was created that would have helped to change the legal doctrine over time.

In addition to these legal constraints, the JFTC, possibly more than antitrust authorities in other countries, was subject to political pressure in terms of how strictly to enforce the law and what kind of interpretations to adopt. In the United States, too, antitrust enforcement seems to vary with administration and business sentiment.[11] Japan, of course, was ruled consistently by the pro-business Liberal Democratic Party during the postwar period. What is more, the JFTC was constrained in its activities by the priorities given to industrial policy attempts to support important companies. For the JFTC to adopt a stricter posture on self-regulation in the twenty-first century would require a change in political sentiment. Politicians and the ministries in charge of regulating the various industries would have to agree that a more rigorous interpretation of the antitrust law would be good for Japan. As of 2001, however, this stance was rarely found. In fact, no constituency within Japan—neither Liberal Democratic Party (LDP) politicians, nor bureaucrats, nor business, nor consumers—brought any real pressure onto the JFTC to change its law enforcement practices.

Finally, the JFTC had its own, very straightforward reasons why it was not eager to prosecute protective self-regulation more rigorously. Just like other antitrust agencies, the JFTC faced budget constraints and, like other antitrust authorities, was therefore likely to prosecute those cases that yielded the largest fines and highest visibility (Goshal and Gallo 2001). These were large price-fixing cases, such as construction bid rigging, where surcharges and criminal fines could be levied to retrieve a certain amount of the calculated damage. In contrast, expressing in yen amounts the damage caused by, for example, exclusive deals in the distribution system, was much more difficult because fines were more complicated to assess. Such cases were considered more cumbersome and labor intensive, while having less impact. The JFTC's incentives were to concentrate its activities on cases that would yield high fines and gain the backing and appreciation of the public.

The combination of these factors made real change in self-regulation through different and stricter antitrust enforcement unfeasible. At the turn of the century, self-regulation had assumed a dominant role in Japan's new regulatory system. Self-regulation was achieved without ministerial involvement and official backing, but it was not opposed by the government. While neither the bureaucrats nor the politicians planned for this situation to evolve, once they realized the outcome of permeable insulation brought about by self-regulation, they accepted the practice as an equilibrium outcome in Japan's regulatory system.

Conclusions

Permeable insulation is the policy outcome that allows for sectorally differentiated responses to globalization. The substitution of self-regulation for official regulation in many industries is one important means through which this differentiation by sector is accomplished: By letting industries determine their own rules, the government introduces choice into its system of regulation.

Japan's deregulation programs in the 1980s and 1990s did not yield the expected increases in market access for new competitors, because they were accompanied by an increase in self-regulation that was curtailed neither through new process regulation nor through heightened antitrust enforcement. In the course of deregulation, Japan amended many previous rules relating to a large numbers of issues, and covering many industries. Important basic laws, such as the Foreign Exchange Law, were liberalized. Industry laws, such as that pertaining to the transportation industry, were rewritten. Ministries had fewer means to induce or enforce certain corporate behavior. While entry regulations remained numerous, the Japanese government's efforts to reduce their numbers were real and ultimately resulted in a significant change. Yet, this did not lead to free market access by new competitors across all industries, because many of the previous official regulations were simply replaced by industry self-regulation.

Most protective self-regulation takes the form of entry barriers, boycotts, and price restrictions. Historically, the JFTC has opted to deal with such potential antitrust infractions leniently. As a result, as of 2001 existing legal doctrine did not treat unfair trade practices as cartels, even if they included price restrictions, and did not provide legal ground for repeat offense prosecution. Even if the JFTC admonished a trade association to stop its unfair trade practices, the association could repeat the same practice without having to fear more serious punishment. The law thus placed no real deterrent on protective self-regulation.

At the beginning of the twenty-first century, an equilibrium situation had emerged. Self-regulation was inherently stable because it was embedded in a set of accompanying activities by trade associations. Even foreign firms entering Japan, though they may initially have pushed for more open markets, were neither sufficiently numerous and widely represented, nor had they, as incumbents, for any good reason interested in undermining the practices of self-regulation. Finally, the government showed no signs of attempting to change the practice. As of 2001 there was no prominent constituency within Japan pushing for a different treatment of unfair trade practices, and thus self-regulation. The JFTC was unlikely to change its stance on self-regulation without a political mandate for change; and for such change to be meaningful, it would have to be accompanied by an increase in process regulation —the missing regulation for which industry self-regulation is meant to substitute. As long as there is no evidence that Japan's politicians are planning such a large-scale institutional and regulatory change, industry self-regulation is there to stay.

Probably the main reason why industry self-regulation has emerged as a key feature of Japan's regulatory system at the turn of the century is that its structural outcomes fit Japan's overall policy approach so perfectly. In previous episodes of industrial policy, a ministry designated "strategic industries" and then afforded these industries protection and support, even if that came at the expense of the development of other industries. In contrast, in the twenty-first century, industries more than ever before make their own choices of whether to open up or to remain closed. While many markets remain protected, aggressive industries are allowed to opt out. Deregulation has resulted in permeable insulation.

Notes

1. See Johnson (1982) on the role of MITI in postwar Japanese economic policy; Schoppa (1997) on the logic of "foreign pressure" (*gaiatsu*) and trade negotiations, Yamamura (1990) on the U.S.-Japan trade debate, and Prestowitz (1988) for an example of U.S. opinion in the late 1980s.

2. Vogel (1996) has argued that the process of removing licensing requirements is often combined with the introduction of new requirements, in a process of "re-regulation" staged by the bureaucrats to maintain power over industries. This may be one reason why deregulation in Japan is a never-ending story. However, evidence shows that Japan has indeed either removed or relaxed a large number of entry requirements across many industries. Vogel's concept, therefore, does not fully explain why market restrictions remain in the early twenty-first century.

3. See Schaede (2000) for details on the history and evolution of trade associations, and of antitrust and industrial policy in the immediate postwar period.

4. At the time, U.S. trade negotiators claimed that safety requirements for windows in public buildings were a policy matter, so that the government was behind this standard. While it is true that the Ministry of Construction had to introduce and enforce the standard, it was proposed and specified by the Flat Glass Association of Japan, such that it would benefit its three member firms (interviews, Tokyo, 1995).

5. See Dewey Ballantine (1995) for a detailed account of how Fujifilm structured its distribution system. While this report places too much emphasis on the government's role in structuring what was fundamentally a self-regulatory system, the details of the system itself are accurately described. The Eastman Kodak Company eventually took this case to the U.S. government, which filed a suit with the World Trade Organization (WTO) (see Pekkanen, Chapter 4). Importantly, the WTO did not rule on the existence of barriers in the distribution system, but only determined that there was insufficient evidence of strong government involvement in structuring them. Given that the distribution system was based on self-regulation, this finding seemed appropriate.

6. See Schaede (2000, p. 132) for other examples. The JFTC launched a formal case in this instance, and the four companies accepted the recommendation to stop the practice in 1993. No fines or other penalties were levied.

7. One obvious concern with self-regulation is the danger that it may result in collusive practices that harm the efficiency of the industry and its firms. If firms block market entry and rig prices, over time they face the danger of becoming sloppy and cost-inefficient, and some of Japan's domestic industries have succumbed to this slack. Yet, some of Japan's export-oriented industries have successfully avoided the pitfalls of collusion. There are three major ways in which industries can benefit from self-regulation while escaping potential pitfalls: (1) By focusing on their international competitors, besides their domestic ones, as the measure for competitiveness and benchmarking, companies can avoid being blindsided; (2) by sharing cost and other strategic information for the domestic market, companies can make more informed business decisions and reduce waste of resources; and (3) by limiting self-regulation to those activities that do not harm efficiency, companies can leave room for competition—for example, even under price agreements they can agree to compete on quality. Therefore, while self-protecting industries may suffer a loss in efficiency from increased self-regulation, competitive industries can use self-regulation to self-promote—

that is, to structure the rules of trade so as to enhance competitiveness.

8. See Schaede (2000, p. 137) for sources and more examples, as well as an account of the mechanisms of antitrust enforcement in postwar Japan.

9. Interview with U.S. government official, 1995.

10. The full title of the law is "Law Concerning the Prohibition of Private Monopolies and the Assurance of Fair Trade" (*Shitei dokusen no kinshi oyobi kōsei torihiki no kakuho ni kan suru hōritsu,* shortened to *Dokkinhō*), Law No. 54 of 1947.

11. For evidence of more active antitrust enforcement when the Democratic Party is in office, see Posner (1970) and Weidenbaum (1990). Their insights are challenged by Ghosal and Gallo (2001), who show that antitrust enforcement varies with business cycle and budget constraints, rather than White House administrations.

References

Dewey Ballantine. 1995. "Privatizing Protection: Japanese Market Barriers in Consumer Photographic Film and Consumer Photographic Paper." Report prepared for the Eastman Kodak Company. Rochester, NY, and Washington, DC.

Ghosal, Vivek, and Joseph Gallo. 2001. "The Cyclical Behavior of the Department of Justice's Antitrust Enforcement Activity." *International Journal of Industrial Organization* 19: 27–54.

Greer, Douglas E. 1993. *Business, Government, and Society.* New York: Macmillan.

Hoshi, Takeo and Anil Kashyap. 2001. *Corporate Finance and Governance in Japan: The Road to the Future.* Cambridge: MIT Press.

JFTC (Japan Fair Trade Commission). 1993. "Shuyō sangyō ni okeru ruiseki shukkō shūchūdo, Heisei gannen/ni-nen" (Concentration Ratios for Shipments in Major Industries for 1989 and 1990). Government report. Tokyo: JFTC.

———. 1994. *Kōsei torihiki iinkai nenji hōkoku Heisei 5 nenpan* (JFTC Annual Report 1993). Tokyo: Ministry of Finance.

———. 1995. "Jigyōsha dantai no katsudō ni kan suru dokusen kinshi-hō no shishin" (Antimonopoly Guidelines Concerning the Activities of Trade Associations). Government report. Tokyo: JFTC.

———. 1996. "Jigyōsha dantai no katsudō ni kan suru shuyō sōdan jirei, Heisei 7-nen" (Report on the Most Important Consultation Cases for Trade Associations in 1995). Government report. Tokyo: JFTC.

———. 1999. *Kōsei torihiki iinkai nenji hōkoku Heisei 11 nenpan* (JFTC Annual Report 1999). Tokyo: Ministry of Finance.

Johnson, Chalmers. 1982. *MITI and the Japanese Miracle: The Growth of Industrial Policy, 1925–1975.* Stanford: Stanford University Press.

Kawagoe, Kenji. 1997. *Dokusen kinshi-hō—Kyōsō shakai no feanesu* (The Antimonopoly Law: Fairness in a Competitive Society). Tokyo: Kinzai.

KZJK (Kinyū Zaisei Jijō Kenkyūkai). 1985. *Kin'yū jiyūka to en no kokusaika* (Financial Liberalization and the Internationalization of the Yen). Tokyo: Kinzai.

MITI (Ministry of International Trade and Industry). 1995. "Tsūshō-sangyōshō no shokan-gyōsei ni kakaru kisei-kanwa yōbō oyobi sono kentō jōkyō" (Plans and Current Status Reports for Deregulation of Ministerial Regulations by MITI). Government report (March). Tokyo: MITI.

Nikkei (Nihon Keizai Shimbunsha).1998. *Shijō sen'yūritsu'99* (Market Concentration Data for 1999). Tokyo: Nihon keizai shinbunsha.

Posner, Richard. 1970, "A Statistical Survey of Antitrust Enforcement." *Journal of Law and Economics* 13: 365–419.

Prestowitz, Clyde V., Jr. 1988. *Trading Places: How We Are Giving Our Future to Japan and How to Reclaim It*. New York: Basic Books.

Schaede, Ulrike. 1995. "The 'Old Boy' Network and Government-Business Relationships in Japan." *Journal of Japanese Studies* 21, no. 2: 285–323.

———. 2000. *Cooperative Capitalism: Self-Regulation, Trade Associations, and the Antimonopoly Law in Japan*. Oxford: Oxford University Press.

Schoppa, Leonard. 1997. *Bargaining with Japan: What American Pressure Can and Cannot Do*. New York: Columbia University Press.

Vogel, Steven K. 1996. *Freer Markets, More Rules: Regulatory Reform in Advanced Industrialized Countries*. Ithaca: Cornell University Press.

Weidenbaum, Murray. 1990. *Business, Government, and the Public*. Englewood Cliffs, NJ: Prentice Hall.

Yamamura, Kozo, ed. 1990. *Japan's Economic Structure: Should It Change?* Seattle: Society of Japanese Studies.

9

Changing Japanese Corporate Governance

Christina L. Ahmadjian

As it moved into the new millenium, Japan experienced a corporate governance crisis. Suddenly, the issue of corporate governance was transformed from an obscure concern of financial economists and legal experts into front-page news. The mass media blamed corporate misbehavior and economic doldrums on a lack of concern for shareholders, cozy cross-shareholding relationships between firms and banks, boards of directors that looked more like old boys' clubs than responsible monitors, and executive compensation packages that gave CEOs little incentive to improve the bottom line. Foreign institutional investors traveled to Japan to promote governance reforms. Some managers of large Japanese multinationals complained that existing governance practices hindered efforts to compete globally. Reforms in financial accounting regulations, sales of cross-held shares, increased foreign investment, and ongoing negotiations for a revision of the Japanese Commercial Code all transformed the political and economic institutions that had previously supported a distinctive Japanese system of corporate governance.

These changes in corporate governance are extremely important to understanding the political and economic change in the Japanese economy in the 1990s and the first years of the new millennium. A corporate governance system comprises a wide range of practices and institutions, from accounting standards and laws concerning financial disclosure, to executive compensation, to size and composition of corporate boards. A corporate governance system defines who owns the firm and dictates the rules by which economic returns are distributed between shareholders, employees, managers, and other stakeholders. As such, a nation's corporate governance regime has deep implications for firm organization, employment systems, trading relationships, and capital markets. Thus, changes in Japan's system of corporate governance would have important consequences for the structure and conduct of Japanese business.

As with many aspects of economic and political change in Japan during this period, debate on the prospects of corporate governance reform tended to be framed around two extremes. Those who predicted convergence argued that existing Japanese institutions had failed (see, for example, Katz 1998) and that global capital and product markets would inevitably drive Japanese firms to a "global standard"—or more specifically, American practice (see, for example, *Economist* 2001). Others argued that the pace of change in Japan was much slower than met the eye (Yamamura 1997), and that distinctive elements of the Japanese system were worth preserving (Dore 2000).

This chapter argues that neither perspective fully explained the trajectory of corporate governance reform in Japan. Rather, corporate governance reform in the 1990s reflected the theme of permeable insulation. During this period, on the surface there appeared to be a pronounced trend toward openness and adoption of international standards. Firms increasingly adopted practices long associated with U.S. corporate governance, such as small boards and stock options. Managers, bureaucrats, and the mass media all argued that Japanese firms must adopt a global standard of corporate governance to assure that Japanese firms remained competitive in a global economy.

These changes, however, were of far less consequence than suggested by the amount of publicity they received. Stock option grants were small and boards, though reduced in size, remained insider dominated. During this period, Japanese firms were markedly reluctant to make changes that would increase the influence of outsiders on boards, and true independent directors remained rare. Firms were also reluctant to implement changes that would undermine the authority of the company president to appoint and dismiss directors, approve his own compensation levels, and select his own successor. Thus, while the rhetoric of the global standard became widespread, most firms remained insulated from the market, and transparency and accountability to shareholders remained low.

This chapter examines two pillars of corporate governance: executive compensation and board composition. The introduction of stock options (legalized in 1997) and several aspects of board reform are explored, including the *shikkō yakuin* (corporate executive officer) system, independent directors, and the debate over the future of the *kansayaku* (corporate auditor) system. The material presented is based on my field research and includes information collected from extensive interviews with corporate executives, bureaucrats, academics, investors, and others involved in governance reform. I have also relied considerably on the written documentation on corporate governance, ranging from proposals for reform to opinion surveys, that emerged from various study groups and organizations over this period.

An Overview of Corporate Governance

In its broadest sense, corporate governance refers to a complementary set of legal, economic, and social institutions that protect the interests of a corporation's owners. In the Anglo-American system of corporate governance, these owners are shareholders. The concept of corporate governance presumes a fundamental tension between shareholders and corporate managers or, in more theoretical terms, an agency problem (Berle and Means 1932; Jensen and Meckling 1976). While the objective of a corporation's shareholders is a return on their investment, managers are likely to have other goals, such as the power and prestige of running a large and powerful organization, or entertainment and other perquisites of their position. In this situation, managers' superior access to inside information and the relatively powerless position of the numerous and dispersed shareholders of the American firm, mean that managers are likely to have the upper hand.

Economists have offered a number of solutions to this agency problem between shareholders and managers. In general, these solutions fall under the categories of incentive alignment, monitoring, and discipline. Incentives of managers and shareholders can be aligned through stock options or other market-based compensation. Monitoring by an independent and engaged board of directors ensures that managers behave in the best interests of the shareholders (Fama and Jensen 1983). CEOs who fail to maximize shareholder interests can be removed by concerned boards of directors, and a firm that neglects shareholder value is disciplined by the market through takeover (Jensen and Ruback 1983).

In the late 1980s and early 1990s, researchers' interests moved beyond the boundaries of the United States to consider the distinctly different governance regimes found around the world (Charkham 1994; LaPorta, et al. 1998; Roe 1994). Japan was a particular focus of interest, since Japanese corporate governance diverged so widely from U.S. practice (Schaede 1994). In contrast to the U.S. managers, Japanese managers did not take it for granted that shareholders were the ultimate owners of the firm. Rather, a Japanese firm sought to balance a wide range of stakeholders, including creditors, employees, managers, and business partners (Aoki 1990; Fukao 1995). Specialists on the Japanese economy identified a number of mechanisms that, taken together, constituted an effective system to protect the interests of these stakeholders.

Influential main banks monitored firm performance and provided both discipline and resources to those in financial trouble (Hoshi, Kashyap and Scharfstein 1990, 1991; Sheard 1994). Closely linked business groups, or *keiretsu*, used ownership stakes and interlocking directorships to monitor not only their investments in each other, but also to ensure long-term, mutually beneficial business relationships (Gerlach 1992; Gilson and Roe 1993). "Administrative guidance" (*gyōsei shidō*) and the system of *amakudari*, in which retired government officials assumed post-retirement careers as private-sector managers, ensured that relevant ministries kept close tabs on firm behavior (Schaede 1994).

Until quite recently, experts contrasted the Japanese system of corporate governance favorably with the Anglo-American system (Roe 1994). The Japanese system, they argued, encouraged patient capital and close sharing of information between firms and their shareholders, which in turn promoted innovation, stability in employment, and interfirm cooperation (Gerlach 1992). Conversely, the American system, with its shortsighted shareholders, hostile takeovers, and greedy executives, held back growth and innovation (Porter 1992).

Mounting Pressures for Governance Reform in Japan in the 1990s

The perception of Japanese corporate governance as effective and worthy of imitation around the world changed drastically with the burst of the bubble economy in the early 1990s. As the 1990s progressed, *kōporēto gabanansu* or *kigyō tōchi*, terms virtually unknown previously except in small circles of legal experts, became common vocabulary among managers and the business press. Committees of corporate executives, investors, academics, and bureaucrats published a barrage of reports, proposals, and surveys highlighting Japan's corporate governance crisis and proposing solutions.

There is room for debate over the degree to which inadequate corporate governance was to blame for the bubble economy, as well as the scandals and low growth rates of the 1990s. There is, in fact, wide debate as to the degree to which corporate governance can be clearly linked to better or worse economic performance (Blair 1995). It is clear, however, that changes in the Japanese economy in the 1980s and 1990s rendered the postwar system of governance, as described above, less effective. From the late 1980s, large firms increasingly turned to capital markets rather than banks for funds. As a consequence, the incentive for banks to monitor firms declined (Aoki 2000). Similarly, *keiretsu* ties between firms began to weaken. Large manufacturers began to loosen long-term relationships with some of their suppliers (see, for example, Ahmadjian and Lincoln 2001). Mergers across corporate groups—such as those between Sumitomo Bank and Mitsui Group member Sakura Bank, and between Fuji Bank, Dai-Ichi Kangyo Bank, and Industrial Bank of Japan—suggested further weakening of *keiretsu* identity.

Banks, in response to the banking crisis of the 1990s, sold large portions of their stock portfolios, further weakening the main bank system and loosening *keiretsu* ties. Between 1986 and 1999, banks' holdings of publicly listed shares declined from 16.1 percent to 12.8 percent (see Figure 9.1). Foreign institutional investors purchased many of the divested shares, and foreign participation in the stock market grew sharply, from 4.7 percent to 12.4 percent over the same period.[1] Throughout the 1990s, foreign share purchases represented a large proportion of activity on the Tokyo Stock Exchange, and consequently foreign investors had considerable influence on share prices, and thus on corporate management.

Foreign investors brought their own notions of corporate governance into the Japanese market. During the 1980s, corporate governance became a rallying cry for institutional investors such as the California state employee pension fund (CalPERS). Investor activism, a heated market for corporate takeovers, and an increasingly strong rhetoric of share-

Figure 9.1 **Changing Patterns of Share Ownership in Publicly Listed Firms, 1986–1999** (percent of shares issued)

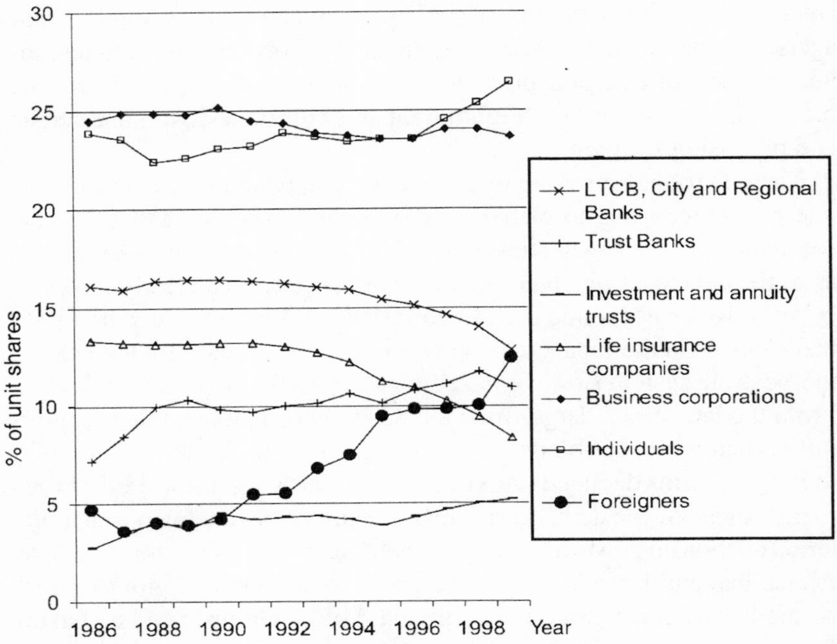

Source: Tokyo Stock Exchange, "2000 Share Ownership Survey" (2001).

holder value—fanned by the business press and academics—led to what Michael Useem (1996) has termed "investor capitalism," in which a firm's leading, and perhaps sole, objective, was deemed to be maximization of shareholder value. Investors promoted better corporate governance through strong, independent boards of directors and properly compensated managers, as a way to promote their interests. With the globalization of financial markets and advances in financial technology, interest in corporate governance soon spread. Institutional investors began to demand that non-U.S. firms adopt corporate governance practices similar to those that had been established in the United States (particularly, those pertaining to board independence and composition).

The burst of the bubble and stagnation of the Japanese economy coincided with an increasing interest in corporate governance in the United States and western Europe. Furthermore, a spate of corporate scandals, including the cover-up of massive stock-trading losses at

Daiwa Bank, the hiding of product liability claims by Mitusbishi Motors, sales of tainted milk by Snow Brand, and various other incidents of corporate negligence or outright corruption, raised concerns about lack of transparency and accountability of Japanese firms.

Globalization and the Rhetoric of Reform

One of the most striking aspects of corporate governance reform in Japan during this period was the widespread acceptance, at least in rhetoric, that Japanese firms needed to adopt a global standard of corporate governance. For example, the Corporate Governance Forum of Japan (CGFJ), a group of business executives, academics, investors, and journalists that was one of the earliest proponents of corporate governance reform, began its "Corporate Governance Principles" with a statement emphasizing global compatibility of corporate governance:

> The globalization of the marketplace has ushered in an era in which the quality of corporate governance has become a crucial component of corporate survival. The compatibility of corporate governance practices in an international context has also become an important element of corporate success. The practice of good corporate governance has been a necessary prerequisite for any corporation to manage effectively in the globalized market. (CGFJ 1998, p. 36)

The group went on to make it clear that its notion of corporate governance revolved around a firm's obligation to its shareholders:

> The legitimacy of the *shachō* [CEO] derives from, and is recognized only by his or her sense of dedication and responsibility to the shareholders and their representatives, the board of directors, through the pursuit of the maximization of corporate value. (CGFJ 1998, p. 38)

A range of statements from widely divergent sources similarly reflected this rhetoric of a global standard of corporate governance. A Liberal Democratic Party (LDP)-endorsed bill proposed to limit director liability for shareholder derivative suits (i.e., lawsuits by shareholders against corporate directors) and to strengthen the existing *kansayaku*, or corporate auditor, system. While this bill was widely criticized for weakening corporate governance, it was couched in language quite similar to that of the CGFJ: "It is time to introduce the

Global Standard of corporate governance, looking to the model of the U.S. firms in strengthening the function of outside directors, and to improve focus on shareholders" (*Shōji Hōmu*, 1998, p. 54).

As the LDP's statement on corporate governance indicates, much of the rhetoric of the global standard clearly associated this standard with U.S. practices. Discussions of corporate governance reform, whether in the mass media or in reports from government, academics, or other groups, featured little discussion of alternative models, such as German or other continental European systems.

Taken at face value, this rhetoric suggests that Japanese corporate governance practices would soon converge with this "global standard." Indeed, throughout the 1990s, a number of reforms intended to align management and shareholder incentives, or to improve monitoring and discipline of top managers, were introduced. Stock options became legal in 1997 and spread rapidly. Firms began to shrink their boards of directors, and many instituted a system of *shikkō yakuin*, or "corporate executive officer," as an attempt to delineate the supervisory function of a board of directors from the operating responsibilities of the top management team. Many firms also announced appointments of independent directors. But how deep and thorough were these changes? And what did they really signify? The next sections explore these questions through a more detailed analysis of reforms in executive compensation and board composition.

Executive Compensation

One pillar of a corporate governance system is a mechanism to align incentives between managers and shareholders (Jensen and Murphy 1990). Stock options are one way to achieve this alignment. The value of a stock option to a corporate executive depends on the stock's market value and, in this way, ties an executive's compensation to the value of a firm's shares.

In 1996, Sony became the first Japanese firm to introduce stock options. Since actual stock options were still prohibited by the Commercial Code at the time, through a bit of financial engineering Sony created a pseudo-stock option. The ban on stock options was lifted shortly thereafter, in 1997, and by 2000 more than 800 firms had adopted stock options (Daiwa 2000). Most firms appeared to limit stock option grants to members of boards of directors (since Japanese boards of directors tend to be operating managers as well, this meant the senior management team).

The process by which the Japanese Commercial Code was revised to allow stock options marked a sharp break from the long-standing procedure for revisions in law. Politicians introduced a bill to revise the Commercial Code directly to the Diet (by a process known as *giin rippō*), without first going through the standard procedure of examination and study by a committee of legal scholars under the auspices of the Ministry of Justice (the Hōsei Shingikai, or Legislative Council). Stock options had wide support, both from the ruling coalition and a number of opposition parties. The bill passed on May 15, 1997, and became law on June 1, just in time for the late-June rush of shareholders' general meetings (a firm was required to receive the approval of shareholders before issuing stock options). Legal scholars accused politicians of blindly serving the interests of big business, and criticized their willingness to circumvent the standard law-making process and forgo the usual process of study and negotiations guided by the Legislative Council. A group of legal scholars wrote in the influential legal journal, *Shōji Hōmu*:

> This bill was put together with the LDP and some people from the business world, and with some ministerial cooperation from the Ministry of Finance and Ministry of Justice. The contents of the bill were unknown to anyone else, until they were finally reported in the newspaper a few days before it was submitted to the Diet. (*Shōji Hōmu* 1997, p. 76)

They further criticized the process as "opaque and secretive."

At first glance, the speedy passage and wide support of stock option reform was consistent with a move toward convergence between Japanese and U.S. practices. A closer look at the details of the reform, however, suggests otherwise. While stock options became legal, numerous provisions ensured that they had limited substance. The Commercial Code limited stock option grants to no more than 10 percent of a firm's outstanding shares, and a firm was required to submit a list of the names of potential grantees for approval by the shareholders' general meeting. Unfavorable tax consequences and unfavorable stock market conditions also decreased their appeal.

Furthermore, the introduction of stock options was not accompanied by fundamental changes in the determination and allocation of executive compensation. Executive compensation continued to be determined by very senior executives and firms rarely disclosed the details to shareholders. Only the boards of a handful of firms established independent compensation committees to set compensation for the CEO and top executives. In most companies, however, the process for setting executive compensation (including that of the president) remained highly secretive. While firms were required to report the total amount of director salaries (i.e., the president and the rest of the top management team), very few firms broke this figure down by individual executive. A survey of 1,310 firms conducted by the Tokyo Stock Exchange in the year 2000 found that only fifteen firms disclosed individual directors' remuneration (Tokyo Stock Exchange 2000, pp. 12, 13, 24). Of the nondisclosing companies, seventeen planned to disclose individual remuneration, while 793 said they would not consider it. An executive responding to the same survey suggested that outside parties (such as shareholders) had no legitimate reason to want this information: "We are urged to disclose individual directors' remuneration, but such a disclosure would have an aspect of only satisfying third parties' curiosity."

In my interviews, several managers noted that disclosure of compensation and independent compensation committees were neither necessary nor desirable in Japanese firms. They argued that Japanese firms did not suffer from the problem of excessive CEO compensation observed in the United States, and thus did not need to concern themselves with compensation issues. While perhaps justified, this view completely missed the fundamental link between compensation and corporate governance. The purpose of disclosure of compensation is not to allow outsiders to evaluate whether an executive is making too much or too little, but rather to disclose to shareholders the degree to which compensation is tied to shareholder interests.

The process by which stock options were introduced, as well as their spread among Japanese firms, reveals evidence consistent with permeable insulation. There was a real change in regulation to allow stock options, and many firms adopted stock options upon their legalization. However, stock option grants remained small, and like other forms of executive compensation, insiders determined the amount and allocation with no input from representatives of shareholders (such as, for example, a compensation committee composed of independent directors). In the vast majority of firms that adopted stock options, there was no concurrent move toward greater disclosure and transparency.

Composition of Boards of Directors

The board of directors represents another pillar of corporate governance. In general, the board of directors represents a firm's owners, and monitors the CEO to assure that he and his management team are operating in the owners' best interests. If the interests of owners and managers diverge (as is assumed by the theory that forms the underpinnings of much corporate governance research), a board of directors will only be an effective monitor if it is independent. Thus, the monitoring capability of a board declines drastically if it consists solely or mostly of insiders.

In 1990, the average U.S. firm had nine outside directors and three inside directors (Ward 1997, p. 99). Although the law does not require a firm to have outside directors, the New York Stock Exchange requires a firm to have a board with an audit committee consisting of at least three "financially literate" independent directors. Interestingly, the dominance of American boards by outsiders is a relatively new phenomenon, historically speaking: In the 1920s to the 1960s, the average big company board had a majority of insiders (Ward 1997, pp. 61, 99).

Independent boards of directors play an important role in other economies as well. Large German firms are required to have a supervisory board, with representation from both shareholders and labor (the proportion depends upon the specific type of company). No member of management can be on the supervisory board, and thus the supervisory board consists of 100 percent outside directors. These play a critical role in monitoring and, if necessary, disciplining the CEO. Duties of the German supervisory board include approving items such as the company's accounts, major capital expenditures and strategic acquisitions, appointments to the management board, and the dividend (Charkham 1994).

In contrast, Japanese boards rarely played a supervisory role during the postwar period. Though the Japanese Commercial Code stipulated that the board of directors represent the shareholders, and required that the board approve a wide range of decisions in the best interests of the shareholders, board meetings were usually little more than a formality. One reason is that Japanese boards were very large. A 1990 study of one-hundred large firms found that board size ranged from eight to fifty-six, and averaged 30.6 (Takeuchi 1991, cited in Schaede 1994). The boards of only 19 percent of the firms surveyed in this study had any outsiders at all. And, many outside directors were retired government officials, bankers, or managers from important trading partners or parent companies, who could not be called independent. Furthermore, board members, both insiders and outsiders, tended to assume operating responsibilities. Top operating executives, as well as heads of important functions and divisions, tended to have seats on the board. Japanese boards of directors did not monitor management because they, themselves, were top management.

While Japanese boards of directors did not play the monitoring role that they did in the United States and Germany, boards nevertheless had an important function in the Japanese corporate system. Board membership was the ultimate achievement for an employee who had slowly ascended the ranks in the age-based promotion system utilized by most large firms. Board membership was thus an important incentive: While not every employee could aspire to be president, the large size of boards made board membership a more reasonable goal. Board membership also played an important ceremonial role—there were certain functions that only a board member could perform. For example, in an interview, a respondent suggested that general contractors in the construction industry deliberately kept their boards large in order to have enough directors to attend numerous ground-breaking and ribbon cutting ceremonies.

Critics of Japanese corporate governance took aim at the lack of independence and unwieldy size of Japanese boards. CalPERS's corporate governance standards for Japan, for example, urged reductions in size and increases in independence of boards. The "Corporate Governance Principles" of the CGFJ, the group of concerned corporate executives and other leaders whose 1998 corporate governance principles for Japan were broadly publicized, similarly focused on these issues of board size and independence. Press reports suggested that Japanese companies actually responded to these criticisms by reducing board size, separating monitoring and operating functions, and increasing numbers of independent directors. But how meaningful were these changes?

Board Size Reductions and the Shikkō Yakuin System

In 1997, Sony, with great fanfare, reduced its board size from 38 to 10. It renamed those directors removed from the board *shikkō yakuin,* and translated this term, fairly literally, as "corporate executive officer." The stated objective was to separate strategic oversight from implementation. The *shikkō yakuin* system spread rapidly among large Japanese companies. In a survey of 1,310 listed firms conducted by the Tokyo Stock Exchange in September 2000, 35.5 percent of the respondents had adopted the *shikkō yakuin* system, an increase of 32 percentage points from the previous survey, conducted in 1998 (Tokyo Stock Exchange 2000, p. 2).

According to Sony officials, the decision to change the status of twenty-eight directors to *shikkō yakuin* was a wrenching one. As mentioned earlier, the position of director, and therefore, board member, was the ultimate career aspiration of many a corporate employee, and a change in status to *shikkō yakuin* was inevitably seen as a demotion. The experience of being "demoted" to *shikkō yakuin* was apparently so traumatic for some directors that Sony's chairman wrote a letter to their wives, explaining that the decision was not really a demotion. He also made the transition to the new status easier by allowing *shikkō yakuin* to keep their cars and other perks of their former positions.

Sony and other observers touted the *shikkō yakuin* system (and the concurrent introduction of stock options) as evidence that corporate governance in Japan was converging with the U.S. system. A closer look at the actual functioning of the *shikkō yakuin* system, however, suggests that this was quite not the case. Sony argued that the *shikkō yakuin* system would improve corporate governance by separating the supervisory and operating functions of a firm. The board of directors would supervise the business and maintain a holistic outlook on business strategy, while the *shikkō yakuin* would pay attention to the operational aspects of business. In general, the rationale behind dividing supervisory and operational functions of a board is to install an objective body that monitors management, and represents the interests of a firm's stakeholders. However, Japan's *shikkō yakuin* system entailed naming one set of insiders (since the directors tended to remain insiders) as monitors, and another set as executive officers.

Reductions of board size through the *shikkō yakuin* system were also not accompanied changes in the status of the board vis-à-vis the CEO. The board of directors continued to serve at the discretion of the president. As my interview respondents reported, the president or the chairman (usually the retired president or retired executive of a parent company) still selected the president's successor.

The widespread enthusiasm of Japanese firms for the *shikkō yakuin* system also stood in stark contrast to their resistance to independent directors. While in the late 1990s, appointments of independent directors were much in the news, in reality they were still few and far between, and there was little desire among executives to place more outsiders on their boards. For example, the year 2000 survey of 1,310 listed firms by the Tokyo Stock Exchange suggested that only 19 percent of the firms had outside directors—no change from the 1990 survey noted earlier. Of firms with outside directors, only 57.5 percent reported that they had one or more "noninterested" directors (Tokyo Stock Exchange 2001). Even Sony, probably the most vocal advocate of corporate governance reform, had only three outsiders.[2]

To some extent, institutional constraints made it difficult to increase independent directors. Professor Iwao Nakatani of Hitotsubashi University was forced to resign his professorship in order to join Sony's board, as professors of national universities were forbidden by law from serving on corporate boards. My interviews with Japanese executives, however, suggested that resistance to independent directors was far more deep-rooted. In these interviews, the question of outside directors tended to generate the strongest opinions. "Japanese don't accept outsiders" was a response heard from a number of managers.

The spread of the *shikkō yakuin* system, combined with deep-seated resistance to independent directors and lack of change in the relationship between the board and the chairman, is further evidence of permeable insulation. Despite their rhetoric of board reform and corporate governance, corporate executives gave up little control to independent representatives of shareholders. My interview respondents suggested that the *shikkō yakuin* system had little to do with improving corporate governance. Rather, it was about solving problems of internal corporate politics. Several respondents said that the motive behind board size reduction was to shift power from factories and functional areas (such as R&D) and concentrate it more tightly in the hands of a smaller group of senior managers who could maintain broader perspective over the business as a whole.[3] By removing heads of once powerful factories and functional groups from the board, a firm sent a strong message about their reduced role in strategic decision making. Interview respondents also suggested that board reductions and the *shikkō yakuin* system symbolized changes in the long-standing policy of age-based promotion. A reduction in board size meant that a firm could no longer guarantee an eventual directorship to its most loyal employees, and signaled to employees that entrance to the highest ranks of management would henceforth be based on merit.[4]

The *Kansayaku* System and Commercial Code Reform

In the late 1990s and early years of the twenty-first century, another important focus of corporate governance reform concerned the system of *kansayaku*. The Commercial Code mandated that a firm appoint *kansayaku,* or corporate auditors, to monitor the board of directors on behalf of shareholders and to ensure that the board complied with the law. The role and relevance of the *kansayaku* was a central focus of a major reform of the Commercial Code that was passed in 2002. Prior to this reform of the Commercial Code, the *kansayaku* system was a topic of hot debate that exposed fault lines between the Ministry of Economy, Trade, and Industry (METI, formerly the Ministry of International Trade and Industry [MITI]) and Keidanren,[5] and which also revealed points of disagreement between globally oriented Japanese multinationals and more domestic firms.

The Japanese Commercial Code required a large firm to have at least three *kansayaku*, at least one of whom had to be an outsider. However, the definition of an "outsider" was not very restrictive, meaning someone who had not worked for the firm in the previous five years. Thus, "outside" *kansayaku* tended to be retired employees, or managers from closely related banks, subsidiaries, parent companies, or other affiliates.

In theory, the *kansayaku* monitored the board of directors for adherence to law, and evaluated the financial reports provided by a firm's outside auditors. A number of problems, however, made it difficult for *kansayaku* to be truly independent monitors. First, while the law stipulated that the shareholders' meeting must approve *kansayaku* appointments, shareholders in fact rarely rejected the recommendations of the company president. Staff limitations further reduced the scale and scope of *kansayaku* audits. A survey of 1,641 listed firms by the Japan Corporate Auditors Association (JCAA) found that in only 41 percent of listed firms did *kansayaku* have any staff at all, and in only slightly more than 50 percent of these cases was there more than one staff member (JCAA 1996, pp. 51, 52). Several interview respondents also noted that *kansayaku* staff were unlikely to be enthusiastic about seeking out their firm's dirty laundry. Staff members were usually career employees who rotated temporarily into the *kansayaku* office, and who had no desire to compromise their future with the firm. *Kansayaku* were also constrained by the lack of a vote in the board of directors' meeting. What is more, they suffered from low status and respect: The position of *kansayaku* was typically seen as a consolation appointment for someone who failed to be promoted to director.

The *kansayaku* system developed out of a number of revisions of the Commercial Code in the postwar era (Kanda 2001). Debate over the continuing role of the *kansayaku* became particularly heated in the 1990s. In September 1997, the LDP Law Section, Committee on the Commercial Code, proposed a bill that included several revisions to the Commercial Code. Several days later, Keidanren issued a set of virtually identical proposals. There were two important elements to the LDP/Keidanren proposals. The first was the limitation of director liability for shareholder derivative suits. The second concerned strengthening the function of the *kansayaku*. The LDP/Keidanren proposals suggested that with a few improvements, the *kansayaku* system could play the same role as independent directors.

In 2000, METI put out its own proposal for revision of the Commercial Code. As Elder (Chapter 7) notes, METI focused on the revision of the Commercial Code and its provisions related to corporate governance as a key to improvement in Japan's national competitiveness. METI officials argued that Japan had no choice but to adopt a more U.S.-style of governance in the face of increasing global competition, globalizing financial markets, and advancements in information technology.

METI's final proposal offered a choice: A firm could either appoint an auditing committee dominated by independent directors and be exempt from the *kansayaku* requirement, or maintain the existing *kansayaku* system (METI 2000). According to METI's logic, the market would eventually decide which form of governance was more effective. Interview respondents close to the preparation of this proposal indicated that METI's original position favored independent directors and the abolishment of the *kansayaku* system; the proposal to give firms a choice between two systems was a compromise under pressure from Keidanren. Insiders also noted that Keidanren was facing its own internal pressures, both from global firms that wanted to reshape their boards to reflect U.S. practices, and from domestic firms that resisted change.

The eventual fate of the *kansayaku* was determined in a revision of the Commercial Code passed by the Diet in 2002. While there had been partial amendments to the Commercial Code in the 1990s, the 2002 revision was the most extensive revision since 1950.[6] A Ministry of Justice-appointed Legislative Council for Company law (Hōsei Shingikai) with twenty members, mostly law professors, was entrusted with hearing opinions of interested parties, and drafting and revising the new law prior to submission to the Diet. According to the revised Commercial Code, firms could choose between the existing *kansayaku* system and a board structure similar to that of U.S. firms, consisting of outsider-dominated auditing, nomination, and compensation committees.

In their introduction to this book, Schaede and Grimes argue that insulation in post-developmental Japan is flexible: Firms have considerable leeway to make their own choices on how to respond to demands of a global economy (Chapter 1). In her chapter on trade associations, Schaede shows how this has resulted in widely varying degrees of insulation across industries (Chapter 8). The revised Commercial Code actually wrote a provision for permeable insulation into law, by allowing firms to choose whether to adopt a U.S.-style board or to maintain the existing *kansayaku* system (MOJ 2001). A likely outcome of this arrangement is a dual system of governance. Globally oriented firms would increase board independence and introduce auditing, nomination, and compensation committees, while more domestically focused firms would maintain the *kansayaku* system and continue to maintain managerial autonomy and insulation from demands of shareholders.

The Process of Change

Despite the rhetoric of a global standard of corporate governance, and the substantial publicity received by new practices such as stock options and the *shikkō yakuin* system, these changes had little real impact on corporate governance. Initial reforms did little to increase incentive alignment between managers and shareholders, and did little to promote board independence and management accountability. While firms adopted changes that were relatively small and painless, such as stock options, and enthusiastically adopted practices that were beneficial from a managerial perspective such as the *shikkō yakuin* system, reforms such as greater board independence that threatened managerial autonomy spread much less widely.

In interviews, managers often attributed this outcome to "culture"—an inherent Japanese suspicion of outsiders. A closer examination, however, suggests that changes in corporate governance could easily be explained by rational strategies of players in corporate governance reform, given the pressures they faced. The principal players in corporate governance reform in the 1990s and early 2000s were corporations themselves. For example, stock options were legalized after strong pressure from corporations. Similarly, the *shikkō yakuin* system and board size reductions were all carried out on the corporate level.

A fundamental premise of corporate governance is that the interests of managers and owners diverge, and that mechanisms must be put in place to prevent managers from taking actions that are not in the best interest of owners. Thus, it is natural that corporate executives would not be the most enthusiastic proponents of thorough corporate governance reform. Corporate governance reform led by managers is likely to lead to changes that are either innocuous, or in the best interests of managers.[7] A statement of an executive reported in a survey of corporate governance practices in Japan conducted in 2000 by the Tokyo Stock Exchange (2000, p. 24) reflected the management attitude towards change: "I will seek our own corporate governance style that matches our own corporate culture."

As might be expected, the most outspoken proponents of corporate governance reform were those firms that experienced the greatest pressures for change: firms with high levels of foreign ownership, such as Sony, Orix, and Omron. These firms not only felt acutely the pressures from foreign investors, but also prided themselves on their image as global companies—and corporate governance, as noted earlier, was closely associated with the theme of globalization. Yet, while the enthusiasm for corporate governance reform of such firms suggested influence of foreign investors, it is not clear just how foreigners exerted this influence. Senior managers whom I interviewed confirmed that they had very little direct contract with foreign investors until the late 1990s, after corporate governance reforms were well underway. Foreign investors also admitted that they applied little direct pressure on Japanese companies until the late 1990s, when they became more active in meeting directly with senior management teams. Almost every manager that I interviewed referred to CalPERS as an important influence in governance reform in Japan. However, at least among the firms that I interviewed, none had been contacted directly by CalPERS about their corporate governance.[8]

Japanese institutional investors were relatively quiet on issues of corporate governance. As a pension official told me: "Pension fund managers have many other things to do." In 1998, the Pension Fund Association issued guidelines that advised pension funds to start exercising voting rights (the usual pattern in the past had been for pensions to instruct the trust banks that held their investment shares to return blank proxy forms, signifying their agreement with management). Exercise of voting rights has become increasingly common, but as of 2001 had yet to be a strong check on corporate management. Furthermore, as of 2001, no particularly vocal advocates of corporate governance reform had emerged among Japanese institutional investors.

Another group absent from the debate on corporate governance was labor unions. In public statements and interviews, Japanese corporate executives made much of the importance of employees as stakeholders in the firm. Although some corporate governance systems, most notably the German system, mandated employee representation on corporate boards, it is interesting that not once in the course of my interviews did I hear a manager advocate German-style labor representation. Given the continued weakening of organized labor in Japan, and the delayed entry of labor into the corporate governance debate, it was unlikely that it would ultimately have much influence on corporate governance issues.

Managers interviewed noted that shareholder derivative suits were an additional, domestic impetus for governance reform. In the early 1990s, the filing fee for shareholder derivative suits was lowered from a percentage of damages asked to ¥8,200. As a consequence, shareholder suits rose dramatically. In 2000, a shareholder suit resulted in a ¥83 billion (approximately $664 million) decision against directors of Daiwa Bank for not stopping trading irregularities in the New York branch. In general, senior executives of Japanese firms claimed that the specter of shareholder suits made them more cognizant of satisfying shareholders. However, they also said that the threat of shareholder suits made it difficult to find outside directors willing to serve.[9] It is not clear, then, whether shareholder suits encouraged or discouraged movement toward greater board independence.

As of 2001, the dominant voice in corporate governance reform was that of corporate executives themselves. The distinct lack of strong pressure by domestic shareholders and relatively indirect influence of foreigners seemed to assure that the pattern of permeable insulation would continue. Without strong external pressures, firms could continue to pick and choose between practices related to corporate governance and adopt those that allowed them to appear more global, while giving up as little managerial autonomy as possible.

Discussion and Conclusion

This chapter has examined changes in executive compensation and board structure in 1990s Japan. The 1990s saw an upsurge in rhetoric about corporate governance reform as Japanese managers, bureaucrats, politicians, and the mass media all urged Japanese firms to adopt a global standard of governance to enable them to flourish in an increasingly global economy. This "global standard" of governance largely mirrored U.S. practice, and included alignment of incentives between top management and shareholders, and greater board independence to promote better monitoring and firmer discipline.

While adoptions of stock options, introduction of the *shikkō yakuin* system, board size reductions, and appointment of independent directors all received considerable publicity from early on, these practices appeared to have little real impact on corporate governance. Stock option grants were too small to really align incentives between investors and managers. The corporate executive officer system and board size reductions did little to increase the capacity of a board to monitor and discipline senior management. As of 2001, independent directors remained relatively rare. And, changes in board size and compensation were not accompanied by other fundamental changes in who appointed and dismissed the president, how managerial compensation was determined and disclosed, and how directors were selected and evaluated.

In several respects, corporate governance reform during this period reflected permeable insulation. A number of real changes occurred in response to pressures of increased globalization of financial and product markets. Stock options were legalized, many companies dramatically reduced the size of their boards, and a major revision of the Commercial Code was under way. But at the same time, corporations resisted changes that limited managerial autonomy and increased the influence of outsiders on corporate decision making. As a result, these changes had little effect in achieving the basic objectives of corporate governance—namely, aligning incentives of managers and shareholders, and increasing the monitoring of executives by shareholders or their representatives.

Further increasing the insulation of Japanese managers from their shareholders was the unraveling of institutions that had supported corporate governance in the past. With the decline of the main bank system, the apparent weakening of the *keiretsu*, and the end of administrative guidance, corporate executives arguably had more autonomy and were subject to less governance than ever before in the postwar period. Thus, insulation may have actually increased over time.

Corporate governance reform during this period also reflected the theme of permeability raised in other chapters. Firms with high levels of foreign ownership and a more global orientation were much more enthusiastic about adopting a global standard of governance, and about tailoring their boards and compensation systems to look more like the U.S. firms that represented this global standard. Sony and Orix, both firms with high levels of foreign ownership, pioneered board reforms and stood at the forefront of the corporate governance debate. Domestic firms, in general, kept a much lower profile. The revision of the Commercial Code acknowledged this divergence in interest between firms, and allowed firms to choose the governance structure more beneficial to them.

While global and domestic firms diverged in their interest in corporate governance reform, it is important not to exaggerate the extent of change, even among the more global firms. Sony, generally acknowledged to be the leader in corporate governance reform, maintained a board with only three outsiders out of ten directors—a level that, had Sony been a U.S. firm, would have exposed it to accusations of poor governance. While there was room for debate as to how many independent directors were desirable, the relative paucity of outside directors even among the most global Japanese firms suggested that there was a considerable gap between the rhetoric of a global standard and actual practice.

The future of corporate governance reform in Japan depends upon a number of factors that, as of 2001, were difficult to predict. A continuing increase in share purchases by foreigners could escalate pressure for change in corporate governance practices. Still, foreign influence in the markets should not be overstated. With Japan's high savings rate, aging population, and the low returns of traditional savings vehicles such as the postal savings system, it was likely that domestic investors would become more important and vocal players in the equity markets. The introduction of defined contribution pension plans (which give workers more responsibility for managing their own pension investments) and possible privatization of the postal savings system would potentially cause greater levels of domestic savings to flow into the stock market.

While the continued banking crisis meant that the main bank system would continue to collapse, the future of the *keiretsu* was not as clear. While the main banks that provided the lynchpin for *keiretsu* groups were retreating, and announcements of cross-*keiretsu* mergers and the severing of long-term business ties were very visible, other indicators of *keiretsu* relationships gave a different picture. Figure 9.1, for example, indicates that cross-shareholding between industrial firms decreased very little from the 1980s to the late 1990s, suggesting that a large portion of a firm's shares remained in the hands of trading partners and other close business associates. This potentially set the stage for increasing conflict between shareholders who held shares as investment, such as pension and other investment funds, and firms that held shares as a means to manage business relationships.

Revised accounting standards were another possible influence on corporate governance. In the late 1990s and early 2000s, a series of reforms in accounting standards brought Japanese accounting regulations up to international standards. Arguably, better disclosure would help shareholders to monitor managers better. Accounting standards, however, are only as good as their enforcement. Without independent boards to demand more thorough audits, and with a seriously underdeveloped auditing profession (Japan has only a fraction of the number of certified public accountants in the United States), compliance with new accounting standards was far from certain.

What did the relative lack of reform in corporate governance during this period imply for the future of the Japanese economy? It suggests that despite the rhetoric, Japan was not converging with global practices. If anything, with the decline of the main bank system and some unraveling of the *keiretsu*, corporate managers were more insulated from their shareholders than ever before. The answer to the question of whether or not this would adversely affect performance depends on one's faith that U.S.-style corporate governance actually improves the performance of firms and economies. However, while the empirical evidence linking corporate governance practices and the performance of individual firms is still slim, there is considerable agreement that developed economies are based upon effective and coherent systems of corporate governance that resolve the divergent interests between managers and owners (La Porta et al. 1998). Permeable insulation in the Japanese system of governance may, in the short run, enable Japanese firms and the Japanese government to appear to adopt a global standard, while maintaining management autonomy and insulating management from shareholder demands. Whether this system is sustainable, however, and what its long-term effects on the Japanese economy are likely to be, are yet to be seen.

Notes

1. A close look at this figure reveals some other interesting trends. Ownership of shares by domestic investment funds increased, as shown by increasing holdings by trust banks and investment and annuity trusts. Shareholdings by corporations decreased only slightly. I discuss some of the implications of these trends in the discussion section of this chapter.

2. If Sony were an American firm, it might be criticized for having "only" three outsiders. When Xerox ran into financial trouble in 2001, it was criticized for having five insiders on a board of fifteen (Bianco and Moore 2001).

3. See, for instance, Fruin (1992) on the central and powerful role that factories play in Japanese corporation.

4. Interview respondents reflected a theme also highlighted by a number of writers on the Japanese economic system, who observed that in the 1990s firms were moving increasingly to a merit-based promotion system for employees at all levels (Ariga et al. 2000; Inagami 2000).

5. Keidanren, or the Japanese Federation of Economic Organizations, represents 1,004 of Japan's major firms and 117 industry groups. As the peak business association, it coordinates the lobbying activities of big business.

6. Although greater participation of politicians through the direct submission of bills to the Diet (such as the stock option reform, and the LDP bill to strengthen *kansayaku* and reduce director liability) suggested that the process of law making was changing, this revision of the Commercial Code proceeded according to the usual procedures of legal reform.

7. Corporate governance reform in the United States in the 1980s, for example, was largely the result of pressure by institutional investors and the discipline of hostile takeovers, rather than activity to improve governance initiated by corporate executives themselves.

8. It may be that important global investors such as CalPERS only invest in firms with sound governance in the first place. Firms on the forefront of corporate governance reform, however, such as Sony, Orix, and Omron, had high levels of foreign investment before they began to revise their governance structures—suggesting that, at least in these cases, the causality was not in this direction.

9. While insurance was available (i.e., directors and officers insurance), it does not seem to have been widely used. A typical response among corporate directors interviewed was "What's that?" There is also much gray area concerning in what situations directors are liable, who pays for the insurance premium, and the role of the firm in providing information to support the directors in the lawsuit.

References

Ahmadjian, Christina L., and James R. Lincoln. 2001. "Keiretsu, Governance and Learning: Case Studies in Change from the Japanese Automotive Industry." *Organization Science* 12: 683–701.

Aoki, Masahiko. 1990. "Toward an Economic Model of the Japanese Firm." *Journal of Economic Literature* 28: 1–27.

———. 2000. *Information, Corporate Governance, and Institutional Diversity: Competitiveness in Japan, the USA, and the Transitional Economies.* New York: Oxford University Press.

Ariga, Kenn, Giorgio Brunello, and Yasushi Ohkusa. 2000. *Internal Labor Markets in Japan.* New York: Cambridge University Press.

Berle, Adolf A., and Gardiner C. Means. 1932. *The Modern Corporation and Private Property.* New York: Harcourt, Brace, and World.

Blair, Margaret M. 1995. *Ownership and Control: Rethinking Corporate Governance for the Twenty-First Century.* Washington, DC: Brookings Institution.

Bianco, Anthony, and Pamela L. Moore. 2001. "Xerox: The Downfall." *Business Week* (March 5).

Charkham, Jonathan. 1994. *Keeping Good Company: A Study of Corporate Governance in Five Countries.* New York: Oxford University Press.

CGFJ (Corporate Governance Forum of Japan). 1998. "Corporate Governance Principles." Tokyo: CGFJ.

Daiwa Securities. 2000. "Stock Options." Tokyo: Daiwa Securities. Online at www.dvl.daiwa.co.jp/KOKAI/Stock, Web site discontinued (accessed November 2, 2000).

Dore, Ronald. 2000. *Stock Market Capitalism, Welfare Capitalism: Japan and Germany Versus the Anglo-Saxons.* New York: Oxford University Press.

Economist. 2001. "Governing the Modern Corporation" (May 3).

Fama, Eugene F., and Michael Jensen. 1983. "Separation of Ownership and Control." *Journal of Law and Economics* 26: 301–25.

Fruin, W. Mark. 1992. *The Japanese Enterprise System: Competitive Strategies and Cooperative Structures.* New York: Oxford University Press.

Fukao, Mitsuhiro. 1995. *Financial Integration, Corporate Governance, and the Performance of Multinational Companies.* Washington, DC: Brookings Institution.

Gerlach, Michael L. 1992. *Alliance Capitalism: The Social Organization of Japanese Business.* Berkeley: University of California Press.

Gilson, Ronald, and Mark J. Roe. 1993. "Understanding Keiretsu Overlaps." *Yale Law Journal* 102: 871–906.

Hoshi, Takeo, Anil Kashyap, and David Scharfstein. 1990. "Bank Monitoring and Investment: Evidence from the Changing Structure of Japanese Corporate Banking Relationships." In Glenn Hubbard, ed., *Asymmetric Information, Corporate Finance and Investment*. Chicago: University of Chicago Press.

————. 1991. "Corporate Structure, Liquidity, and Investment: Evidence from Japanese Industrial Groups." *Quarterly Journal of Economics* 106: 33–60.

Inagami, Takeshi. 2000. *Gendai Nihon no kōporēto gabanansu* (Corporate Governance in Japan Today). Tokyo: Tōyō Keizai.

JCAA (Japan Corporate Auditors Association). 1996. "Chōsa kekka chāto" (Charts of Survey Results). *Kansayaku* 367: 31–115.

Jensen, Michael, and William Meckling. 1976. "Theory of the Firm: Managerial Behavior, Agency Costs, and Ownership Structure." *Journal of Financial Economics* 3: 305–60.

Jensen, Michael C., and Kevin J. Murphy. 1990. "Performance Pay and Top-Management Incentives." *Journal of Political Economy* 98: 225–64.

Jensen, Michael C., and R.S. Ruback. 1983. "The Market for Corporate Control." *Journal of Financial Economics* 11: 5–50.

Kanda, Hideki. 2001. "The Auditor System in Japan." *Kansayaku* 439: 46–48.

Katz, Richard. 1998. *Japan, the System That Soured*. Armonk, NY: M.E. Sharpe.

LaPorta, Rafael, Florencia Lopez-de-Silanes, Andrei Shleifer, and Robert W. Vishny. 1998. "Law and Finance." *Journal of Political Economy* 106: 1113–55.

METI (Ministry of Economy, Trade and Industry). 2000. "Nijū seiki no kigyō keiei no tame no kaisha hōsei no seibi" (Maintenance of Company Law for Corporate Management in the Twenty-First Century). Industrial Structure Council, Subcommittee on New Growth Policies, Corporate Law Group (December 8).

MOJ (Ministry of Justice). 2001. "Shōhō to no ichibu o kaisei suru hōritsuan yōkō chūkan shian" (Outline of a Partial Revision to the Commercial Code, Interim Proposal). Legislative Council for Company Law (April 18).

Porter, Michael E. 1992. "Capital Disadvantage: America's Failing Capital Investment System." *Harvard Business Review* (September/October): 65–83.

Roe, Mark J. 1994. *Strong Managers, Weak Owners: The Political Roots of American Corporate Finance*. Princeton: Princeton University Press.

Schaede, Ulrike. 1994. "Understanding Corporate Governance in Japan: Do Classical Concepts Apply?" *Industrial and Corporate Change* 3: 285–323.

Sheard, Paul. 1994. "Interlocking Shareholdings and Corporate Governance." In Masahiko Aoki, ed., *The Japanese Firm: Sources of Competitive Strength*. New York: Oxford University Press.

Shōji Hōmu. 1997. "Hirakareta shōhō kaisei tetsuzuki o motomeru shōhō gakusha shōmyō" (Commercial Code Scholars Ask for Open Process of Commercial Code Revision). *Shōji Hōmu* 1457: 76.

————. 1998. "Kōporēto gabanansu ni kansuru shōhō kaisei mondai no dōkō" (Trends in the Issue of Revision of the Commercial Code in Respect to Corporate Governance). *Shōji Hōmu* 1494: 54

Tokyo Stock Exchange. 2000. "Survey on Listed Companies' Corporate Governance. Tokyo: Tokyo Stock Exchange.
———. 2001. "2000 Share Ownership Survey." Tokyo: Tokyo Stock Exchange.
Useem, Michael. 1996. *Investor Capitalism: How Money Managers Are Changing the Face of Corporate America*. New York: Basic Books/HarperCollins.
Ward, Ralph D. 1997. *Twenty-first Century Corporate Board*. New York: Joseph Wiley.
Yamamura, Kozo. 1997. "The Japanese Political Economy After the 'Bubble': Plus Ça Change?" *Journal of Japanese Studies* 23: 291–331.

Part IV

Conclusion

——— 10 ———

Permeable Insulation and Japan's Managed Globalization

Ulrike Schaede and William W. Grimes

In the increasingly multilateral trade and policy environment of the twenty-first century, Japan faces several conflicting challenges. Internationally, Japan's trade prowess, increasing manufacturing presence around the world, and economic leadership in Asia have made the country an integral member of multilateral organizations such as the World Trade Organization (WTO). Japan is increasingly expected to uphold the norms of free trade and economic openness as articulated in a variety of international treaties, and to assume a geopolitical role commensurate with its global economic position.

Domestically, Japan has been challenged by the need to transform an industrial structure that has proven unfit to ensure growth across most sectors in the new economy of the twenty-first century, a situation reminiscent of the early 1970s. Having built their economic success on high quality manufacturing, many Japanese manufacturing firms are still among the world leaders, whether in cars, office machinery, or consumer electronics. Yet with the decline of some of the former flagship industries, no new sectors have stepped up to allow for a transfer of employment and technical skills into industries with high growth potential. Low mobility of labor and capital have made such adjustment even more difficult. As a result, many declining industries continue to receive protection, at a time when there has been an obvious need to support growth in both currently successful industries and the emerging new economy sectors.

Following the oil shock of 1973, Japan went through a period of industrial soul-searching and realized that its high dependence on energy-intensive industries (shipbuilding, for example) made the country too vulnerable to fluctuations in the price of oil. Industrial restructuring was supported by industrial policies promoting new, more capital-intensive sectors, while subsidizing the slow phase-out of maturing ones. A similarly fundamental reform was needed in 2001. However, in the meantime, the world had changed around Japan, and this change eventually also affected the Japanese state and its ability to administer such policies. Most importantly, as a result of economic growth and deregulation, the Japanese state had lost many of its former tools to entice companies to cooperate with its strategies. At the same time, as an upstanding member of the WTO, Japan could not return to an explicit program of export promotion and import protection.

The policies and approaches that Japan has adopted at this critical juncture are those of "permeable insulation": allowing entry and market competition in areas where that is the best approach for existing market players, while protecting (or allowing self-protection in) less competitive sectors. Sectors that can tolerate additional competition from new domestic or foreign entrants are clearly differentiated from those that cannot. While all this has never been explicitly spelled out as a policy program—in part reflecting the decline in state ability to launch such programs—the concept of permeable insulation best describes the mix of policies that can empirically be observed as Japan enters the twenty-first century. This approach is by no means singular to Japan; in fact, one could argue that many governments follow a similar dual approach to policy-making. Nevertheless, the approach needs to be clearly delineated lest we misunderstand the motives driving Japan's policy-making in the twenty-first century.

Why Permeable Insulation Matters

In some ways, Japan's shift toward permeable insulation makes the country look more like other industrialized democracies, where public stands on policy issues are often situational, driven by diverse domestic political interests. Yet, for long-time observers and Japan novices alike, understanding this shift and fully appreciating its implications are of utmost importance in order to capture fully the nature of Japan's policies and its evolving role in the international political economy of the twenty-first century. Even policies that promote openness as a primary goal often leave multiple opportunities for protection; conversely, protective policies hold within them loopholes or contradictions that allow for an increasing degree of permeability. Therefore, every policy measure should be evaluated not only for how it reads on paper, but for its supplementary, or in some cases original, motivation and policy consequences. For example, supporting Japanese firms' relocation of production abroad may trigger domestic fears about hollowing out; but it is also an elegant way to locate small, slow, or troubled firms elsewhere. Pushing more open financial markets certainly increases international influence, but may also serve to insulate Japanese producers and financial institutions from international currency volatility.

Foreign firms and governments, as well as Japan scholars, must therefore realize that while the twenty-first century brings new opportunities for doing business with Japan, these opportunities often have hidden limits. The extent of both opportunities and limits varies by sector, and the contours of permeable insulation are subject to change as economic and political conditions fluctuate. While permeable insulation is a generic phenomenon in Japanese political economy, it also calls for detailed, microlevel, sector-specific analysis. Whether one studies corporate governance, regulation, political processes, or Japan's role in the international political economy, more than ever before a firm-level or industry-level analysis is the most appropriate approach to understanding Japan.

Ubiquity of Permeable Insulation

The chapters in this book have provided seven examples of how permeable insulation has played out in practice in both public and private actions. The opto-electronics sector has long been one of Japan's darling industries. Supported in the 1950s through export associations and government sales promotions abroad, this industry grew from the production of copy-cat cameras into the world leader in a broad array of optical equipment. Firms' production networks in East and Southeast Asia from the 1960s onward were designed without government guidance, and re-imports of cameras and other products into Japan were welcomed. Importantly, however, the production networks of Japanese manufacturing firms in Asia often built on vast hierarchies of medium-size, small, and very small firms that followed the main assembler to the foreign location. This meant maintaining relatively closed manufacturing networks despite the increasingly multinational nature of production.

In many industries, such investment was generously supported by government programs providing subsidies for outbound foreign direct investment (FDI). The inherent irony in Japanese government support for outbound FDI cannot be overlooked: The world's undisputed leader in designing industrial policies for export-led economic growth has over time also become the world's largest supporter of relocating production abroad, thereby depriving the country of some of its export base. A closer look at government FDI financing reveals, however, that by the late 1990s many of the recipients were small firms that were either in declining industries or were suppliers to leading firms. Thus, FDI support represented not only the promotion type, but also the phasing-out type of industrial policy at the turn of the century. From a political point of view, considerable FDI support was a means of compensating troubled small firms, with the interesting twist that moving their manufacturing operations abroad would weaken their future claims to compensation.

The increased presence of Japanese firm networks in Asia further strengthened Asia's predominant position in Japan's trade. In conjunction with the exposure of Japanese financial institutions to Asian debt, this created a clear incentive for Japan to contribute to regional exchange rate stability. When policy makers sought to insulate the domestic economy from currency instability, they faced something of a "Catch-22," in that they could only do so by inviting ever greater foreign participation in the Japanese financial markets. The surprising juxtaposition of openness and insulation clearly captures the dynamics of permeable insulation.

A similar activist logic of concurrent international openness and insulation can be observed in Japan's attitude in, and employment of, the new multilateral trade organizations. The establishment of the WTO's dispute settlement system.led to a huge increase in Japan's role as a legal player. Whereas in the 1980s Japan had been involved in multilateral trade disputes largely as a defendant or third party—and more often than not on the losing side—beginning in the 1990s it adopted a more proactive stance. Not only did Japan begin to appear with greater

frequency as a plaintiff before the new WTO, it also was more successful in many of the cases in which it was a disputant. The underlying
reason was an astute strategic use of WTO rules, either as a sword to
prop open markets abroad, or as a shield to defend restrictive market
practices at home.

Such pragmatic adaptation to the new global rules and pressures is
by no means limited to international transactions. It is equally visible
domestically. The comprehensive reorganization and realignment of
Japan's ministries in 2001 was hailed by politicians as evidence of the
change in relations between bureaucrats and politicians, industry, and
society. An analysis of the actual structure of the new ministries and
their tasks, however, suggests that there is some old wine in the new
bottles. Ministry of Economy, Trade, and Industry (METI) is a prime
example: While officially claiming to be concerned with global warming, recycling, and other reactive policies, proactive attempts to shape
sectors were alive and well. Just what type of policies METI adopted
depended on the needs and requests of a given industry. While leaving
alone industries that had long since become independent from state
nurturing, METI continued to attend to those sectors that either preferred continued support, or were in the initial stages of development
and in need of a jump start. Whether METI was necessarily always
successful in these attempts is beside the point; more importantly, it
stayed involved in some industries while allowing others to charge
ahead without state fetters. The outcome of these policy attempts was
permeable insulation.

One way to implement this more permeable industrial policy was to
delegate a large portion of regulation to industry. Following years of
deregulation, the various ministries had lost many of their previous
tools to entice cooperation by their regulated firms. Industries were
happy to take over and structure their own rules of trade, as this allowed firms to decide among themselves whether they preferred to
self-promote by opening up markets to competition, or to self-protect
by upholding barriers previously established through official protection. This shift explains why the government's deregulation programs
often yielded less actual reform than expected. What is more, by giving choice to industry, the shift toward self-regulation also allowed for
sectoral differences in the outcome of deregulation and the degree of
insulation across industries.

As the phenomenon of self-regulation grew stronger, permeable insulation also became a private-sector phenomenon. The debates and processes of corporate governance reform beginning in the late 1990s offer a prime example, combining the "sword and shield" approach with that of allowing firms to follow their own preferences. Eventually, some competitive firms decided to adopt internationally accepted mechanisms of corporate governance, including increased disclosure, more transparent board processes, and shareholder value maximization as true management goals. This enabled firms to attract foreign financing and to pursue multinational strategies. However, not all firms were well served by such a switch, and those that were not worked hard to ensure that the new corporate governance rules also allowed for continued insulation.

The case studies in this series offer just seven stories of permeable insulation, but many more can be told. Examples of other areas of Japan's political economy characterized by this new approach include Japan's new venture capital market, a large portion of which consists of government funding for new and old industries; telecommunications, where a substantially open and competitive market in cellular phones coexists with a continuing land-line monopoly by the still partially government-owned NTT; and government-sponsored research consortia in information and biotechnologies that, even if partially opened to foreign participants, continue to be aimed at the advancement of Japanese firms.

Implications of Permeable Insulation

Permeable insulation both results from, and affects the very structure of, political processes and economic outcomes. While it may be too early to fully capture the long-term ramifications for Japan's political economy, as of 2001 several indications had already begun to emerge.

Politics

The approach of permeable insulation is both a reflection and a further reinforcement of the shift of power and emphasis within Japanese politics, away from bureaucrats and toward both politicians and industry. Formerly, when industrial interests were more strongly aligned around the objective of economic growth, bureaucrats could effect policies fairly easily by pushing growth-related measures and compensating those sectors or interests that were occasionally at odds. Two concurrent trends have undermined these processes: First, with continuing growth, industry interests have become more diversified. Some need more protection, while others demand price stabilization for raw material imports or more export promotion; still others are most interested in less government. Second, budget constraints in a stagnant economy and increasing demands for compensation have come to limit the government's largesse. At the same time, deregulation has reduced the number of administrative "carrots" the ministries can offer their regulated industries in return for cooperation with state policies.

As a result, the ministries remain important for those sectors that want government protection, but have become increasingly powerless vis-à-vis industries that want to pursue their own interests and agendas. Party politics is similarly divided. Compensation-based politics remains an important part of many politicians' electoral strategies, but the lack of government money and the economic crisis at the turn of the century have led to a hardening of divisions, even within the Liberal Democratic Party. This reinforces the trend toward limiting compensation to only the weakest or most politically potent sectors of the economy.

To deal with the shifting patterns of economic and political power, the government has adopted the dual-track policy approach of protecting some sectors, while allowing others to break through existing protective measures. As we have seen throughout this book, this has yielded some surprising policy outcomes across a large number of issue-areas. Domestically, dual-tracking may well contribute to a further reduction of government influence over business, because offering permeability policies as a type of compensation to certain sectors will eventually curtail the standing of the government by allowing for increasing plurality. Meanwhile, the inherent difficulties of insulation created contradictions even for policies dealing with a single sector. For example, in the Fujifilm-Kodak case cited by Pekkanen (Chapter 4) and Schaede (Chapter 8), Japan's Fair Trade Commission supported METI's arguments in the WTO dispute settlement process by publicly claiming that no antitrust violations were committed by Fujifilm in Japan—in spite of the fact that the same commission had, in the past, investigated and reprimanded the company for such violations.

Again, it is important to note that permeable insulation is not a unique Japanese policy approach. Most governments are sometimes forced by domestic interests to adopt self-contradictory public positions regarding trade disputes or global political issues. What is relevant to note here is the significant change within Japan—from a highly predictable, growth-promoting, and often surprisingly unified public appearance by the government, to a more situational approach to policy. The more diversified domestic interests have finally become visible in Japan's statements in the international arena.

Economics

Permeable insulation is fundamentally a reactive government approach to the changing business needs of the twenty-first century, and business naturally has sought to benefit from it. To be sure, band-aids are often less painful than shock therapy, and whether Japan's industries from the 1990s onward were most efficiently served by these policies is a question best addressed from hindsight. As of 2001, measures of insulation resulted in substantial protection of domestic industries, ranging from large firms such as in the cement or construction industries, to a host of small and medium-size firms across all industries. This helped maintain employment in many areas, thus easing the pains of economic recession for society, but it also was likely to retard adjustment. In some sectors, protection could have long-term benefits for the economy as a whole. This was particularly true for industries with real prospects for long-term growth and competitiveness, where preventing large-scale bankruptcies ensured a healthy rebound by multiple, competing firms once the economy recovered. In declining industries, however, protection created a long-term drag on the economy.

Thus, an important ramification of permeable insulation for industry structure lies in its tendency to reinforce the bifurcation of Japanese industry into progressive, internationally competitive sectors on the one hand, and slow-growing or declining, domestically oriented industries on the other. This bifurcation—which is also evident in patterns of political support—became increasingly apparent with the continuing recession of the 1990s. As of 2002, it was too early to tell whether this bifurcation was a structural and persistent problem, as Katz (1998) has argued, or rather a transitory phenomenon caused by economic stagnation. Regardless, the politics of permeable insulation means that, at least in the medium run, Japan's government is unlikely to adopt any policy measures to eliminate this bifurcation; rather, the division of industry is likely to be further reinforced.

Sustainability

Over the long term, one might question whether permeable insulation is politically sustainable. If insulation indeed keeps growth tepid, it may create increasing pressure for competitive firms to move operations overseas, as Nelson argues (Chapter 6). Nurturing uncompetitive sectors and losing competitive ones is an obvious formula for aggravating and prolonging economic stagnation. Only if permeable insulation is used in such a way as to promote adjustment to new economic realities will it create long-term benefits for the Japanese economy.

The danger of aggravating economic stagnation potentially has major political implications as well. As we have noted, compensation-based politics works best when the overall economy is growing rapidly. But when the economy is stagnant or declining, and resources are fixed or decreasing, the conflict over their allocation is accentuated. The fundamental question for Japanese politics is whether the established coalitions of organized interests can continue to thrive on those limited resources, without either underscoring (or accentuating) internal schisms or causing the untapped political dissatisfaction of consumers and taxpayers to come to the fore. If citizen discontent were to reach a critical threshold, serious breakdowns might occur in the effective conservative coalition that has supported Japan's postwar political order for so long. Such breakdowns would undoubtedly mean flux in political parties and support patterns of organized interest groups. While we can only speculate on the resulting scenarios, one possible outcome is an increase in permeable insulation as a result of political strife, in the sense that industries would find it even easier to push their own agendas.

In the event that the current politics prove to be unsustainable, Japan might become ever more subject to the global competitive and regulatory environment. In this scenario, one might expect that the feasibility of "insulation" will slowly be undermined and Japan will be forced onto the road of ever-increasing "permeability." In other words, permeable insulation might be understood as a harbinger, or a first step toward, convergence with global (or American) economic practices.

Such an argument might be supported by data on increased foreign direct investment into Japan, to suggest that domestic protection would either become impractical or irrelevant.

However, as of 2001 convergence was a distant possibility for Japan. The only truly global, large industries at the beginning of the twenty-first century were wholesale finance and automobiles. Analyzing FDI into Japan in the 1990s reveals that foreign investments in wholesale finance and automobiles dwarfed all other inbound FDI, leaving most other Japanese product markets untouched. While these two industries are certainly important in terms of their contribution to total world production, they alone are hardly enough to effect Japan's idiosyncratic distribution system, labor practices, or regulatory policies across the board. In industries other than these two global ones, significant reform would require Japan to revise its domestic laws and regulations. Permeable insulation, however, means that those industries most in need of reform from a global trade perspective are precisely the ones where change is least likely to occur—either because the industry resists deregulation, or because self-regulation is used for self-protection.

Even in those instances where foreign competitors have entered Japanese product markets, they have often realized the benefits of insulation and have reversed their stance on market opening (see Chapter 8). For example, after trade negotiations had allowed a few U.S. insurance companies into Japan in the mid-1990s, these companies quickly joined their Japanese competitors in warning that further market opening might "destabilize" the domestic market. Once accepted as insiders, foreign firms enjoyed the same protection that, as outsiders, they had tried so hard to break up. Thus, even in industries with foreign participation, more market openness was not necessarily bound to follow.

Finally, firm behavior depends on many factors other than the external competitive situation. Organizational change is always difficult, and even in industries where "best practices" are identifiable, the benefits of adopting those are often outweighed by the costs of change. Where organizational best practices are not apparent, change is even less likely; more importantly, disagreement on best practices means convergence toward a single style of organization or behavior is less likely still. Beyond finance, automobile production, and perhaps a small number of other industries, therefore, to expect convergence of most firms in most sectors in Japan (or any other country) would be unrealistic.

Japan in the World Economy

At the turn of the century, Japan's policies of permeable insulation were already having important effects on Japan's role in the world economy—and by extension, on the world economy itself. Permeable insulation implies that the government and firms of Japan seek to carve out niches of stability for themselves in an increasingly globalized economy, while obeying the rules of international organizations and the discipline of international markets. For example, Japan shows a careful legal adherence to the General Agreement on Tariffs and Trade (GATT), General Agreement on Trade in Services (GATS), and related rules while carrying out its own style of industrial policies and promotion of its firms' overseas activities. Policy makers are thus striving to make globalization an opportunity rather than a threat for Japanese firms.

These activities are likely to contribute to a certain amount of continuing friction with Japan's main trading and political partners, especially the United States and Europe. But at the same time, they may also be attractive as a model to other countries that are more cautious about embracing economic globalization. Political leaders in East and Southeast Asia, for instance, may see this approach as generally beneficial not only to Japan, but also for their own countries, which could affect the process of globalization in the entire region. Implicit strategies of permeable insulation could be seen as contributing to the stability of the global economic order, precisely because they help to put brakes on the actual speed and level of globalization.

More broadly, permeable insulation might be a means of buffering societies and political systems from the severe disruptions that globalization and marketization can cause. Karl Polanyi (1957) argued nearly half a century ago that organizing societies exclusively in order to facilitate the smooth operations of the market creates the potential for violent social upheaval and misery. The arguments of several Japanese writers in the debate over internationalization of the yen follow a similar logic. If they are mistaken in their view, permeable insulation might just be a means of slowing down global integration, and of missing opportunities for long-term growth. If they are right, however, then widespread use of permeable insulation may help to maintain the global economic system, even as it slows down the process of globalization.

Japanese policy makers and corporate leaders have embarked on the implicit strategies of permeable insulation in full knowledge of the challenges that face the Japanese economy in the era of globalization. The policies and practices of permeable insulation do not try to stand against the tide of global markets, but rather seek to shape the direction of the currents. The specific actions in any issue-area may partly reflect nervousness about rapid change that is common throughout the world, but they also follow a familiar trajectory of policies and processes practiced for decades in Japan. The ubiquity of government intervention, of industry associations as drivers of sectoral policy, and of corporate governance for the benefit of management rather than shareholders, mean that Japan's response to the generic pressures of globalization remains distinctive. Permeable insulation is Japan's way of managing globalization by simultaneously opening up to, and maintaining some of its core structural features of protection in, the twenty-first century.

References

Katz, Richard. 1998. *Japan: The System That Soured*. Armonk, NY: M.E. Sharpe.
Polanyi, Karl. 1957. *The Great Transformation: The Political and Economic Origins of Our Time*. Boston: Beacon Press.

About the Editors and Contributors

The Editors

William W. Grimes is an Assistant Professor of International Relations at Boston University. He is the author of *Unmaking the Japanese Miracle: Macroeconomic Politics, 1985-2000* (Cornell, 2001). He has also written monographs, articles, and book chapters on Japanese macroeconomic and financial policy, US-Japan relations, and other topics related to Japanese political economy. He has been a visiting researcher in Japan at the University of Tokyo, the Ministry of Finance, and the Bank of Japan.

Ulrike Schaede is an Associate Professor at the Graduate School of International Relations and Pacific Studies, at the University of California, San Diego. She is the author of *Cooperative Capitalism: Self-Regulation, Trade Associations, and the Antimonopoly Law in* Japan (Oxford UP, 2000). In addition to teaching in Germany, Japan, and the United States, she has conducted research in Tokyo at various times, for a total of five years, as a visiting scholar at Hitotsubashi University, the Bank of Japan, the Ministry of Finance and the Ministry of International Trade and Industry. She has written extensively on Japanese government-business relationships and regulation, trade associations and antitrust policy, as well as financial regulation, financial market reform and corporate governance in Japan.

The Contributors

Christina L. Ahmadjian is an Associate Professor at the Hitotsubashi University Graduate School of International Corporate Strategy. Her research interests include corporate governance, business groups, and the impact of globalization on Japanese business practices. She has published articles on the Japanese economy in journals including *American Sociological Review*, *California Management Review*, and *Organization Science*. In 2000-2001 she was an Abe Fellow and visiting researcher at the University of Tokyo.

Mark Elder is Assistant Professor of International Relations and Political Economy at James Madison College, Michigan State University. His areas of research interest include Japanese and East Asian political economy, comparative economic policy making, and business-government relations. He has been a visiting researcher at the both the Institute of Oriental Culture and the Institute of Social Science at the University of Tokyo.

Patricia A. Nelson is a Lecturer in International Business at the University of Edinburgh Management School. She has written on international political economy, foreign direct investment, U.S.-Japan relations and high–technology issues related to Japan. Recently, she held a postdoctoral fellowship at the Weatherhead Center for International Affairs at Harvard University and was a visiting scholar at the Research Institute of Economy, Trade and Industry (RIETI) in Tokyo.

Saadia Pekkanen received a Ph.D. in Government from Harvard, an M.I.A. from Columbia, and a B.A. (Hons.) from Richmond College, London. She was a Postdoctoral Fellow at the Harvard Academy for International and Area Studies, and is presently an Assistant Professor of Political Science at Middlebury College, Vermont. Her research lies at the intersection of international law and international relations, with a specific focus on the WTO, Japan, and Asia.

Mireya Solís is an Assistant Professor of Politics at Brandeis University. She is currently finishing a book on the politics of preferential finance for Japanese overseas investment. She has published several articles or book chapters on FDI, regionalism, and Japanese-Mexican relations. Dr. Solís has worked as a consultant for Mexico's Ministry of the Economy on free trade negotiations with Japan, taught at a Mexican University, and been affiliated with the research institute of the former Export-Import Bank of Japan, with the United Nations University in Tokyo, and the Center for U.S.-Mexican Studies at UCSD.

Index

Stagflation, 5
Stagnation of the 1990s, 3, 18, 28,
    34, 38, 40n7
  See also Recession
Stock options, 216, 217, 222–224,
    232
Structural change, 3, 9
Subsidization, 11, 108–109, 112,
    114, 115–118

T

Tax evasion, 64, 66–67
Tax reforms, and yen
    internationalization, 67
Three-Year Deregulation Program,
    192
Tokyo offshore market, 50, 52, 59
Toshiba, 200
Trade association, 12, 195, 197–198,
    200, 201–206, 209
Trade habits. *See Shō kankō*
Trade restrictions, 199
Trade-Related Investment Measures
    (TRIMs), 88–90
Trade-Related Aspects of Intellectual
    Property Rights (TRIPs), 80
Transaction costs, 55, 57–58, 72n4,
    72n6

U

U.S.-Japan relations, 5, 191, 196
Unfair trade practices, 198, 208, 211
Unilateralism, aggressive, 86
United States Trade Representative
    (USTR), 87, 88
Uruguay Round, 83, 84–85

W

Withholding tax, 58, 59, 63–64, 66–
    67, 73n16
World Trade Organization (WTO), 6,
    9, 11, 18, 19, 77, 243, 246, 249

Y

Yen loans, 59
Yen, 57–58, 59–61, 68–70
  See also Internationalization of the
    yen
Yen-Dollar talks, 49, 58

Z

Zero Interest-Rate Policy (ZIRP), 3,
    34, 40n13
Zoku, 21, 23, 39n1